225 Do-It Yourself Designs

GARDEN, LANDSCAPE and PROJECT PLANS

HOME PLANNERS, LLC
Wholly owned by Hanley-Wood, LLC

Garden, Landscape & Project Plans

Published by Home Planners, LLC
Wholly owned by Hanley Wood, LLC
3275 W. Ina Road, Suite 220
Tucson, Arizona 85741

Distribution Center:
29333 Lorie Lane
Wixom, Michigan 48393

Jayne Fenton, President
Jennifer Pearce, Vice President, Group Content
Jan Prideaux, Editor in Chief
Kristin Schneidler, Editor
Jill M. Hall, Plans Editor
Laura S. Moreno, Plans Editor
Jay C. Walsh, Graphic Designer
Sara Lisa, Production Directorr
Brenda McClary, Production Coordinator

Photo Credits
Front and back cover:
Digital Imagery ©2001 Photodisc, Inc.

Pages 2-3, 320: Photos courtesy of
The Netherlands Flower Bulb Information Center

©2001 by Home Planners, LLC

10 9 8 7 6 5 4 3

Printed in the United States of America

Library of Congress Catalog Card Number: 2001097987
ISBN softcover: 1-881955-96-6

Table of Contents

4   *Gardens & Landscapes:*
        A Layman's Guide
        Tips on do-it-yourself landscaping

8   *Deck and*
        Project Building Basics:
        Helpful information
        about the building process

10 *Stunning Gardens:*
        47 backyard and border designs

106 *Breathtaking*
        Landscapes:
        48 woodland and wildflower designs

204 *Imaginative*
        Projects:
        57 gliders, gazebos,
        garden sheds and more

250 *Distinguished Decks:*
        24 outstanding outdoor living plans

276 *Studios and*
        Storage Spaces:
        47 spacious garage
        and guest house designs

308 *When You're*
        Ready to Order
        Everything you need to know
        to order plans in this book

GARDEN AND LANDSCAPE PLANNING

Before you get started, you'll want to investigate your possibilities and learn all you can about do-it-yourself landscaping. Talk with friends, relatives and neighbors who have installed their own gardens; ask about their experiences and why they made their particular choices. Ask what they would have done differently and what they are most pleased with.

Then, use your own imagination—combine what you've seen, heard and read about gardening and outdoor plans to devise the landscape that best suits your home, your family and your lifestyle. Take into account how you will use your yard area. Do you entertain often? Formally or informally? Do you have small children whose needs must be accommodated in the yard area? Do you want a spa or a hot tub addition? Will you want to build a pool in the yard at some point in the future? Do you prefer a formal-looking yard or one that's more casual? What style of house do you have? Do you enjoy spending time on your garden, or would you rather have an easy-care, low-maintenance landscape? The answers to these questions will put you on the path to finding the landscape that is right for you.

BACKYARD LANDSCAPES

Backyards are more conspicuous than front yards, and consequently can be less dependent on the style of your home and those in the neighborhood. However, there are other considerations that must be taken into account. For instance, backyards are usually the main outdoor areas for recreation, hobbies, entertaining and fruit and vegetable gardening. Depending on your personal lifestyle and the needs of your family, there are elements you may want to incorporate.

Some of these include:
- Storage sheds, small barns or garages for storing gardening equipment
- Gazebos or arbors for privacy areas or entertaining
- Whirlpools or swimming pools
- Play areas such as sport courts and play structures
- Protected areas for food or flower gardening and compost bins
- Deck, patio or terrace areas for sunning, relaxing and entertaining

A useful backyard will include all of the items that make it a practical and inviting area for all members of the family, without it being a burden to maintain. Look in our Projects chapter, beginning on page 204, for some ideas.

Gardens & Landscapes: A Layman's Guide

FRONT-YARD LANDSCAPES

Landscapes, like any other home amenity, look best if they fit the home they surround. You'll want a front-yard landscape plan that complements and enhances the style of your home while fitting in well with the other homes in your neighborhood. For example: If you have a very traditional home, you'll want a plan that is stately and formal-looking. A low-slung ranch house might look best with an informal rustic landscape.

Other factors to think about:
- The climate in your area. You'll want to choose plants and trees that thrive in your climate.
- Topography of your lot. You'll need to work around slopes and other irregularities.
- Use of your front yard. Will your front yard be used as an outdoor gathering place, or is it mainly "for show?"
- Degree of maintenance. Do you love to work in the yard, or are you a reluctant gardener?

TOOL TIME

As a do-it-yourself gardener or landscaper, you'll want to invest in some gardening tools. Be cautious when shopping, however—garden centers and home improvement stores keep an impressive array of garden supplies on hand, and you may be tempted to say, "Just give me one of everything!" Find out which tools are essential for you and your garden, and choose accordingly.

Here are some more tips:
- Decide which tools you'll use the most, and which you'll use less frequently. Purchase only the tools that you need; you can always rent or borrow the ones you don't use as much.
- Choose the best-quality tools that you can afford; they'll last the longest and provide the best investment.
- If you're trying to decide between a manual tool and a power tool, keep in mind that manual tools are sometimes faster, more efficient and less noisy than power tools.

Our chapter on gardens begins on page 10—here, you'll find borders and beds that are both beautiful and useful. And, starting on page 106, you'll find some larger-scale landscapes—some designed to complement specific architectural styles, and some that work around pools, decks and arbors.

Remember—in addition to a do-it-yourself landscape or garden increasing the appeal and value of your home, you'll also gain a tranquil outdoor retreat. With the proper planning and equipment, your dream of a beautiful outdoor area can easily become a reality—and you'll have the satisfaction of knowing that your efforts made it possible.

Gardens and landscapes are an important part of your home, providing an extension of interior rooms and quiet pockets of nature that soothe irritated nerves and calm a troubled spirit. If that's not enough, consider the extra value that beautiful landscaping contributes to your home. From bodacious borders to tall trees, your landscape or garden can introduce you to a colorful piece of the outdoors that awaits the special magic created by your green thumb.

Deck Building Basics

Where you build your deck depends on several factors. Often, the orientation of your home and available outdoor space narrow your options and placement is obvious.

BUILDING PERMITS

There are a number of practical matters to keep in mind before and during construction. Before you purchase materials or begin building, be sure you have all building permits. If your deck includes any electrical work, such as lighting on stairways, or plumbing, such as a food-preparation sink, you'll need permits for each of these.

BUILDING CODES

Equally important is constructing the deck to meet local codes. Some of the items that are regulated (and often require permits) include the size of the deck, setback distances (the distance from the property line to the deck), railing and stair construction, footing depths, fastening methods, lumber grades for certain deck components and fence or screen height around the deck.

DECK LAYOUT

Creating a site plan is an exercise that works well with deck layout and placement. A site plan allows the homeowner to sketch out on paper existing features—property lines, utility lines, permanent mature plants, land contours, buildings, roads, views to preserve and views to conceal.

A DESIGN FOR COMFORT

Climate, and the many small climates in and around your lot called micro-climates, deserve special consideration. A poorly positioned deck, in terms of climate, could jeopardize your outdoor comfort, making the deck area unlivable many days of the year. Note the direction of prevailing breezes. Do you want exposure to cooling breezes, or shelter from the blustery winds?

Living with the sun is a similar love-hate relationship. In cold northern climates and during certain times of the year, a sun-bathed deck is a blessing; whereas in warm southern climates, afternoon shade is almost always required during summer months. To determine shading and sun requirements, note sunrise and sunset patterns and how shade from structures and trees falls on your proposed deck site. Be aware that sunshine and shade patterns are seasonal. The summer sun is high in the sky and shines for a longer period; thus shadow patterns are different than in winter, when the sun is lower in the sky and shines for a shorter time. Designing combination sun/shade locations for the deck for different seasons is ideal.

SELECTING LUMBER

Each plan on pages 252 to 275 has available a list of the lumber and other materials required to build the deck.

A number of wood species are used for decking. Some of the more common include: Redwood, Western Red Cedar, Douglas Fir, Spruce and several species of Pine, including Southern Yellow Pine, Northern Pine and Ponderosa Pine.

One of the primary considerations is preventing the deck support structure from decaying. For this reason, lumber that is in contact with or in close proximity to the ground must be decay-resistant.

GLOSSARY OF DECK-BUILDING TERMS

BEAMS—Lateral support lumber members that are attached to posts. Joists rest on top of the beams.

BLOCKING—Boards the same dimension as the joists, placed between the joists to supply additional support.

BRACING—Part of the substructure, required when decks are four feet or more above ground. Braces are attached to posts to prevent lateral movement.

DECKING—The actual deck surface. Deck boards are attached to the joists.

FLASHING—Metal material that angles over the ledger board to protect it and to prevent moisture from accumulating on the ledger and against the house wall.

FOOTINGS—Supports often made of concrete that are positioned on or in the ground. Footings must rest on firm soil so the deck support system will not shift or sink.

HEADER—Also termed facing board, a length of lumber that attaches to the outside of the deck.

JOISTS—Lateral support boards that are attached to (or lay on top of) beams. Decking boards are attached to the joists.

LEDGER BOARD or **LEDGER PLATE**—A board that is attached to the house, usually bolted to the floor joist. This allows the house to support one side of the deck.

PIERS—Attached to footings, and used to support the deck posts. Often made of concrete. Posts are often attached to piers.

POSTS—The upright support lumber members that are attached to piers and footings. Posts extending above the level of the deck can also serve as railing supports.

RISER—A term used with stair construction. The vertical distance the step rises from one step to the next. Also, the board that creates the rise.

SPLICING—When the length of deck span prevents beams or joists from reaching the complete distance, splicing involves placing two lengths of wood together to complete the distance. It is best to splice beams at the posts for strongest connection.

TOENAILING—Nailing two boards together with nails driven into boards at an angle. The fastest but least effective method of joining boards.

TREAD—A term used with stair construction. Refers to the surface or surface board that is walked on.

If you are interested in more detailed information about building decks, a complete Deck Construction Details package is available from Home Planners. Composed of five oversized sheets, the package contains all the necessary data to help you construct your own deck.

Project Building Basics

GLOSSARY OF PROJECT-BUILDING TERMS

ANCHOR BOLT—A device for connecting wood members to concrete or masonry.

BALUSTRADE—A complete handrail assembly. Includes rails, balusters, subrails and fillets.

BATTER BOARD—Simple wooden forms used early in construction to mark the corners of the structure and the height of the foundation walls.

BEAM—A horizontal framing member of wood or steel, no less than five inches thick and at least two inches wider than it is thick.

BOARD—Any piece of lumber more than one inch wide, but less than two inches wide in thickness.

BLOCKING—Used for added support for floor joists and to prevent twisting.

COMMON RAFTER—Any of several identical structural members of a roof that run at right angles to walls and end at right angles to main roof framing members.

CONCRETE—A mixture of cement, sand, gravel and water.

CROSS-BRIDGING—Diagonal wood braces that form an "X" between floor joists.

DRIP EDGE—A strip of metal used to protect the edges of a roof structure from water damage.

DRYWALL—A method of covering wall and ceiling surfaces with dry materials, rather than wet materials such as plaster. Refers primarily to the application of gypsum wallboard, also called drywall.

EDGE JOIST—The outer joist of a floor or ceiling system that runs parallel to other joists.

FOUNDATION—The part of a building that rests on a footing and supports all of the structure above it.

FRAME—The wood skeleton of a building. Also called framing.

HEADER—Any structural wood member used across the ends of an opening to support the cut ends of shortened framing members in a floor, wall or roof.

HEADER JOIST—The outer joist of a floor or ceiling system that runs across other joists. See edge joist.

JOIST—A horizontal structural member that, together with other similar members, supports a floor or ceiling system.

O.C.—Abbreviation for On Centers, a measurement from one center line to the next, usually of structural members.

RIDGEBOARD—The horizontal board at the ridge to which the top ends of rafters are attached. Also called a "ridge beam" or "ridge pole."

It is important to conceptualize how your new project addition will blend in with property lines, utilities, other structures, permanent mature plants, land contours, drainage and roads. Consider the following:

Location: If you decide to build a gazebo, it will likely become the focal point of your property. If you are constructing a playset, select an area that is visible from the house so you can watch the children.

Drainage: If your property has moist areas, avoid them if you can. Don't place a playset or garden swing in an area that remains damp for two or three days after a rain.

Utilities: Plan ahead for any utilities your project may require, electricity or water for sheds, gazebos and playhouses, or gas for heat or a grill. Call your local utilities providers for locations of underground cable and water lines, if necessary.

BUILDING PERMITS

When your advance planning and site selection are complete, it's time to obtain the required building permits. Separate building permits are usually needed for each construction discipline: one for the structure, one for the electrical work, one for the plumbing, one for the heating and so on. Check with your local building officials before you begin your project to determine which permits you need. If your project is small, permits may not be required.

BUILDING CODES

Along with building permits come the codes that must be met. Codes ensure that your project meets all standards for safety and construction methods.

Some of the regulated items local inspectors will check include: distance of project from property lines, handrail heights, stair construction, connection methods, footing sizes and depths, material being used, plumbing, electrical and mechanical requirements and neighborhood regulations.

SELECTING LUMBER

Each project in this book has a list of lumber and other building materials required. You will need to determine and select the type of wood you want to use. Many wood species are used for outdoor structures. Among the most common are: Redwood, Western Red Cedar, Douglas Fir, Spruce, Southern Yellow Pine, Northern Pine and Ponderosa Pine.

One of the primary considerations in selecting the correct lumber for your project is to prevent the base structure from decaying. For this reason, lumber that is in contact with, or even in close proximity to, the ground must be decay-resistant. Select a resistant species and treat your lumber with a preservative before using it in your building or project.

Photo courtesy of the Netherlands Flower Bulb Information Center

Stunning Gardens:
47 backyard & border designs

Sometimes, a garden is designed for a specific purpose—attracting hummingbirds, songbirds or butterflies, for example. Other gardens are created for specific climates and regions, and still more are made for easy maintenance. All these types of gardens and more are found in the 47 garden plans on the following pages—peruse this comprehensive collection to find the one you prefer.

Formal Rose Garden

The grandeur of a European palace or estate garden comes alive in the formality and scale of this landscape design, which features a formal rose garden. In creating this mood, the designer makes the landscape completely symmetrical. Both sides of the garden are exact mirror images of each other, with extensive lawn areas on each side that can be used for relaxing or entertaining.

In the tradition of the formal rose garden, neat crisp evergreen hedges outline the rose plantings, providing interest and structure even during the off-season when the roses have been cut back to near the ground. The straight lines of the stepping-stone paths form a strong cross shape in the center of the garden. Each arm of the cross begins with a formal red rose and ends at the edge of the garden in a strong focal point. The sight line looking up the horizontal arms, which is emphasized by the overhead trellises and pergolas, terminates in groups of oval-shaped trees backed by lattice panels. Flowering vines adorn the trellises.

From the bluestone paving at the house, a sight line leads across the paving stones and culminates with a reflecting pool situated in a paved area at the far end. Note that, although the same paving material was used in the front and back areas, the pattern is formal near the house and more informal at the back. Within the strong geometrical space of the rose garden, an early-spring flowering perennial provides a blanket of color until the roses burst into their summer-long show.

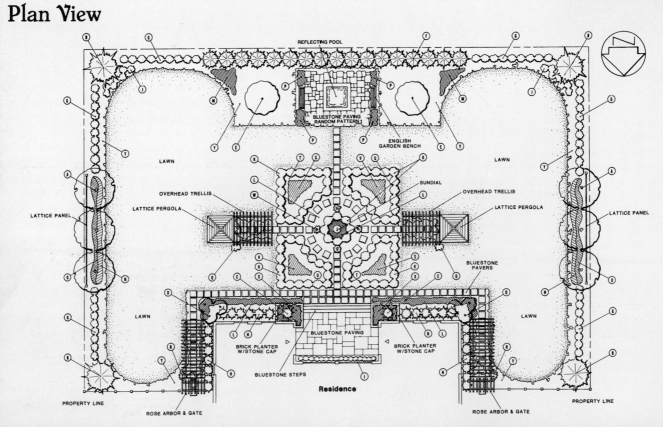

Plan View

REFLECTING POOL

BLUESTONE PAVING RANDOM PATTERN

ENGLISH GARDEN BENCH

LAWN

SUNDIAL

LAWN

OVERHEAD TRELLIS

OVERHEAD TRELLIS

LATTICE PERGOLA

LATTICE PERGOLA

LATTICE PANEL

LATTICE PANEL

BLUESTONE PAVERS

LAWN

LAWN

BLUESTONE PAVING

BRICK PLANTER W/STONE CAP

BRICK PLANTER W/STONE CAP

BLUESTONE STEPS

Residence

PROPERTY LINE

PROPERTY LINE

ROSE ARBOR & GATE

ROSE ARBOR & GATE

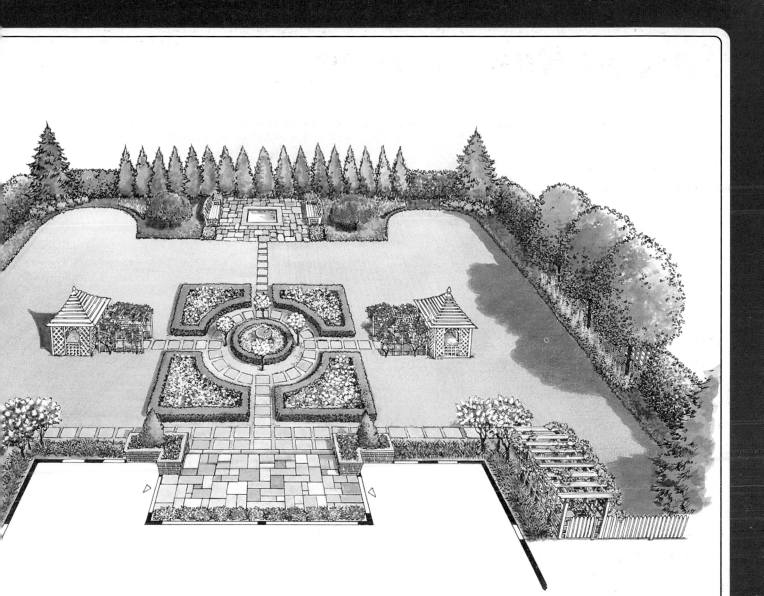

The rose arbor and gate at each side of the house feature climbing roses, echoing the main theme of the garden.

GARDEN PLAN
HPT110001
Shown in Summer
Design by
Jim Morgan

Cut-Flower Garden

You can have your garden flowers and cut them too with this charming backyard plan. The designer skillfully created a landscape that features a garden planted just to produce flowers to cut for indoor arrangements, yet still looks as pretty as a picture. Here you'll find a serious gardening plot attractively integrated into a landscape of flowering trees, shrubs and groundcovers with plenty of patio and lawn for the family.

Because you'll be removing most of the flowers as they begin to open, a cut-flower garden has more in common with a vegetable garden than a flower garden, so it's best to camouflage the plants from direct view. The designer chose a white picket fence to surround the structure. Two gated arbors, draped with flowering vines, provide easy access to the garden. The flowers planted in front of the fence aren't meant for cutting but for you to enjoy while relaxing on the patio.

Within the gated cut-flower garden itself, stepping-stone paths provide easy access for tending the flower beds. The designer devoted one section to perennial flowers, which return to grace the garden year after year. Another section contains annuals, which need replanting each year. The perennials include an assortment of spring-, summer- and fall-blooming plants so you'll have months of different blossoms to cut, while the long-blooming annuals keep on producing more flowers after they're cut. All the flowers specified for this design make long-lasting arrangements.

Plan View

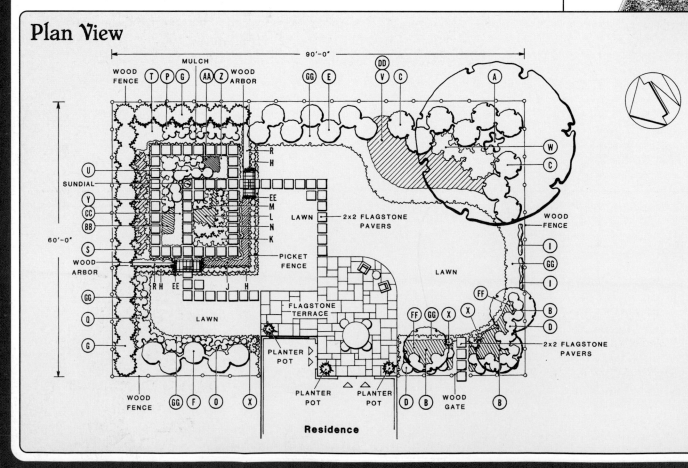

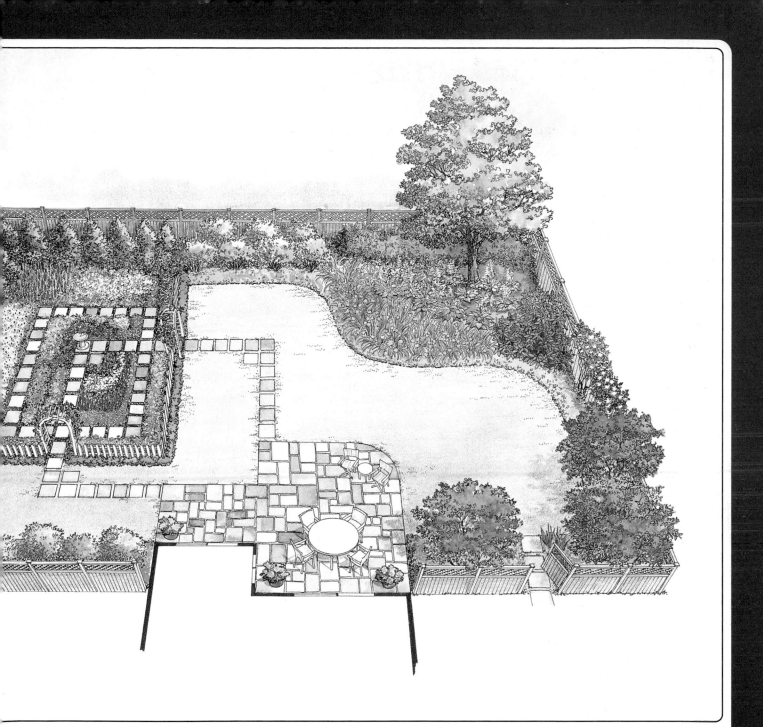

Here's a backyard brimming with flowers to enjoy both indoors and outdoors. You can harvest armloads of flowers from the gated cut-flower garden to display in your home.

GARDEN PLAN
HPT110002
Shown in Summer
Design by
Damon Scott

Dooryard Herb Garden

Designed in the style of old-fashioned dooryard gardens, this modern adaptation brings useful, edible plants within easy reach of your house. Site these beds and borders near the kitchen door so you'll have easy access to their bounty when cooking. Or move the entire garden to the center of a sunny lawn.

A herringbone-patterned brick walkway along one side of the garden guides you to one of the two entry gates. Mulched paths and irregular flagstones, interplanted with a scented, mat-forming groundcover, define the beds and borders. A picturesque wooden fence enclosing the entire garden provides a sense of structure, while its rectilinear form is echoed and softened by hedge plantings. If your space is limited, you might eliminate one or both of the hedges, the fence, or all of the hard- and softscape elements outside the garden beds.

The only maintenance tasks required involve harvesting, occasional cleanup and replacing the annual herbs each year. You'll also need to refresh the mulch each year to prevent weeds from sprouting and to keep the beds neat.

Plan View

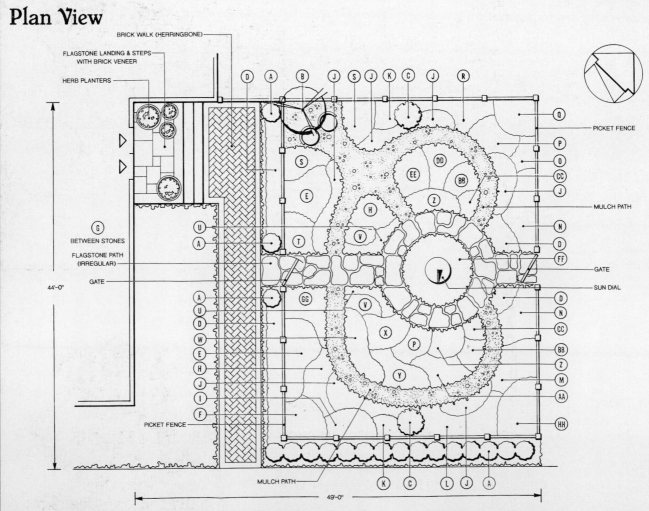

An herb garden fenced in cottage-garden style and located just off the back door is both attractive and practical.

GARDEN PLAN
HPT110003
Shown in Summer
Design by
Salvatore A. Masullo

Evening Patio Garden

This patio garden is designed to be used during summer evenings when people are most likely to sit or entertain guests outdoors. The designer chooses flowers in mostly white and pastel colors that pop out of the shadows and glow in the moonlight. Lamps are strategically placed to provide nighttime lighting; some lamps are used to cast reflections on the formal pool or are directed upward to illuminate the beautifully sculpted tree trunks. A waterfall cascading as a sheet into the pool creates soothing sound effects.

The waterfall flows from a free-standing stone wall that creates a backdrop for the pool. (The mechanism is available as a kit from water garden suppliers.) A stepping-stone island near one edge of the pool allows you to move closer to the waterfall and be immersed in its sound. This patio garden is designed to be sited in a lawn away from the house, but it can be easily modified to link directly with the house. You can do this by keeping the shape of the patio and extending the plantings and stepping-stones to the house's foundation.

Plan View

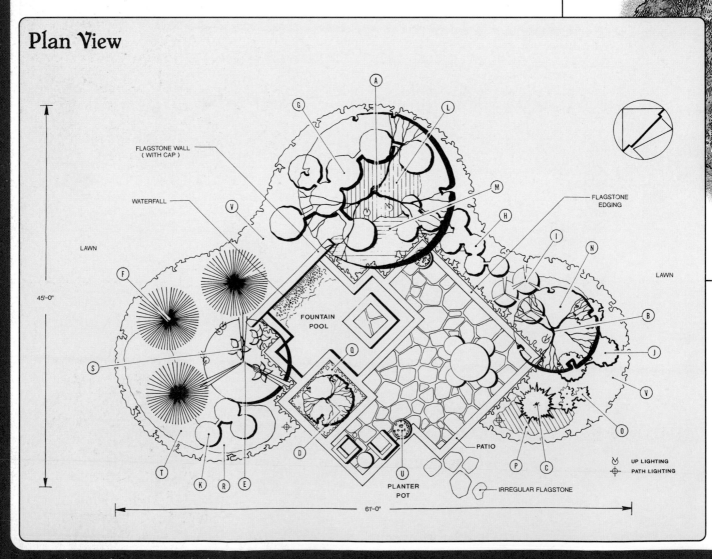

You'll love entertaining outdoors if you install this design, which offers great garden views, musical sound effects and dramatic nighttime lighting.

GARDEN PLAN
HPT110004
Shown in Summer
Design by
Michael J. Opisso

Bubbling Fountain

Imagine being engulfed in delicately scented air as you relax on your patio. You can enjoy such sensory pleasures everyday by installing this intricate design filled with fragrant plants. Be sure to provide plenty of seating around the patio so you'll have places to sit and enjoy the perfumed air.

This plan is as adaptable as it is beautiful. The designer includes a patio and combination fountain/planter, but you could plant the border around any existing patio. You might decide to add only a central planter or fountain, or both. You could locate the design right up against your house so that sliding glass or French doors open directly onto the patio—this allows you to enjoy the flowers' perfume from indoors as well. If you choose this option, site the planting so the lattice is directly opposite the wall of the house to capture and hold fragrance.

The central planter and pots scattered about the patio are filled with fragrant annuals and tender perennials. During the cold winter months, try moving the pots to a sunny location inside the house, where they will continue to bloom and perfume the air.

Plan View

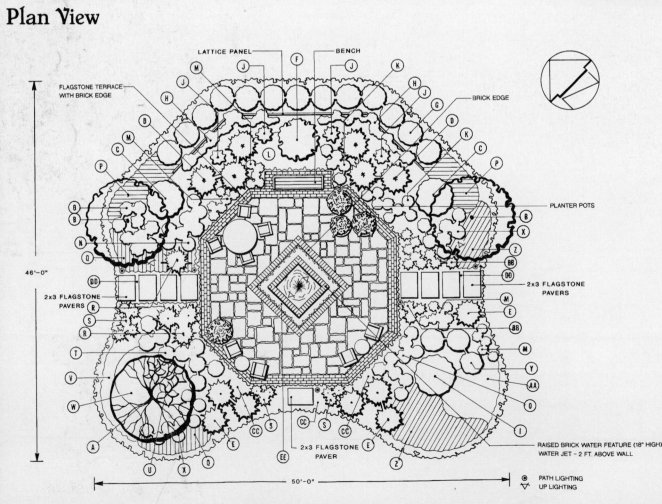

Relaxing on this patio becomes a delightful sensory experience filled with sweet, flowery fragrances and the music of a bubbling fountain.

GARDEN PLAN
HPT110005
Shown in Summer
Design by
Jeffery Diefenbach

Effortless Informality

Your cares melt away when you enter this very private and tranquil garden through the vine-covered arbor. The designer sites an informal flagstone terrace with two seating areas in a sea of evergreen groundcover, entirely eliminating a lawn and making the garden about as carefree as it can be. Evergreens on the property border create privacy, while airy trees—selected because they cast light shade and are easy to clean up after—create a lacy overhead canopy. The overall effect is serene.

A half-circle rock wall, built of small moss-covered boulders, sets off the larger of the two seating areas and gives dimension to the area. (Five moss rocks on the opposite side of the patio echo and balance the wall.) Several types of perennials spill over the top and sprout from the crevices of the wall, decorating the area with their dainty flowers and foliage and creating a soft, natural look. Large drifts of spring bulbs and other perennials make lovely splashes of color where they grow through the groundcover. Flowering shrubs—many of which also display evergreen leaves—give the garden year-round structure and interest, while offering easy-care floral beauty.

The lack of a lawn makes this garden especially easy to care for. The groundcover absorbs most of the leaves that drop from the deciduous trees in autumn, and the terrace can be quickly swept or blown free of leaves and debris as needed. All you'll need to do is cut off the dead tops of the perennials once a year in late winter.

Plan View

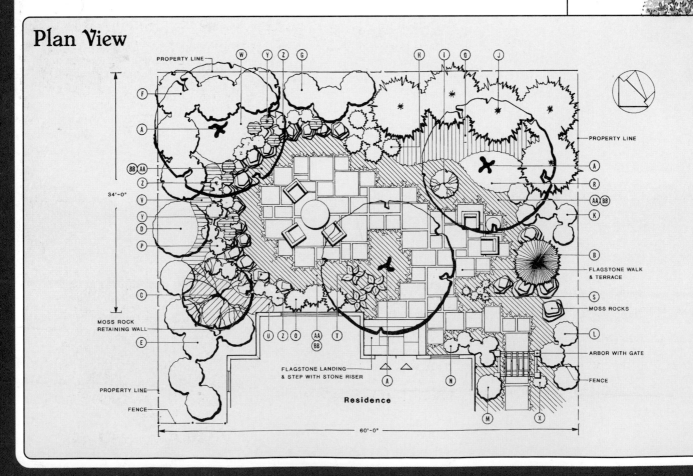

You'll spend many more hours just relaxing in this backyard retreat than you will taking care of it. Since there's no lawn, you'll escape weekly lawn mowing, and will even be able to leave the garden untended during extended vacations.

GARDEN PLAN

HPT 110006
Shown in Summer
Design by
Michael J. Opisso

Naturalistic Getaway

Mimicking the way water flows in nature, the waterfall in this double garden pond cascades in a sheet from a small high pool to a lower larger one. To increase the natural appearance of the ponds, the designer arranged several rocks to peak above water level in the lower pool. The rocks also act as natural perches for the birds, frogs and turtles that are attracted to the water.

Echoing the cascading waterfall, many of the plants used in the design have flowing weeping forms. Three tall flowering trees anchor the design with their drapery of branches. A small shrubby tree near the edge of the pond arches its branches over the rocky edge to soften the rocks with foliage. Beneath the trees, an assortment of shrubs, perennials and groundcovers provides a changing color display from spring through autumn.

The bed is designed on a small berm, which provides the height needed for the waterfall. Stone steps climb the back of the berm and lead into the path and sitting area, which are made from naturalistic irregular flagstones. The ponds are easily constructed with a flexible liner that is concealed by rocks and stones.

Plan View

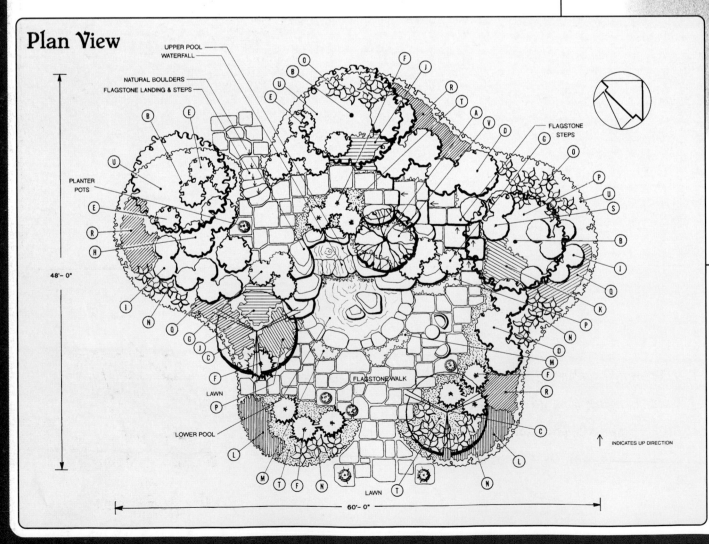

Bring the feeling of the great outdoors to your backyard
with this garden pond and waterfall. The scenery is filled
with rugged stones and soft flowers and foliage—
a perfect naturalistic getaway.

GARDEN PLAN
HPT110007
Shown in Spring
Design by
Frank Esposito

Quiet Pocket Garden

Locate this circular bed in a large open area of your front- or backyard, where it will create a beautiful island of flowers and foliage. The garden becomes a focal point of the yard, and because it contains evergreens and small flowering trees and shrubs, it also provides privacy by blocking views into and out of the yard. Best of all, the planting is designed so you can stroll along a curving stepping-stone path into its center to discover a secluded sitting area within.

This private sitting area is formed from an open pocket in the center of the bed that features paving stones, two curved benches and an overhead structure. These elements furnish and define the pocket, creating the atmosphere of a garden room—a secluded outdoor retreat. There you can sit in quiet solitude, if you wish, but there's also room enough for the whole family.

The garden's year-round structure comes from its trees, shrubs, stones and pergola. During the growing season, an assortment of colorful flowering perennials and foliage plants fleshes out the scene, creating a changing show.

Plan View

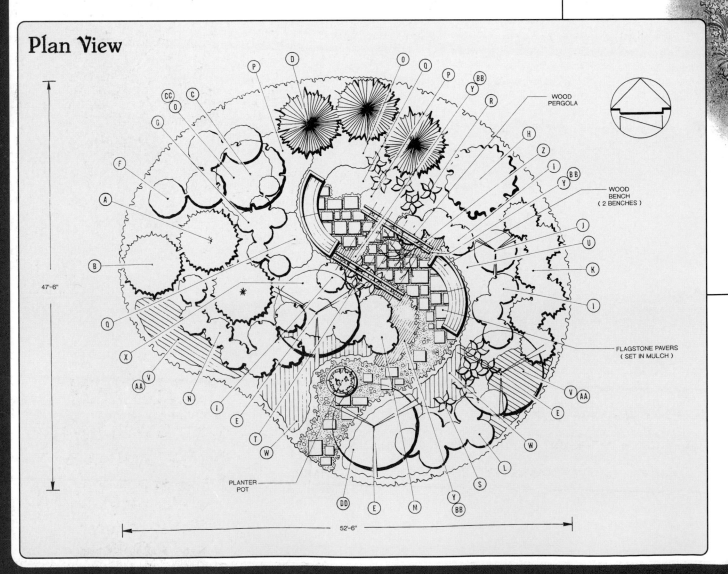

47'-6"

52'-6"

WOOD PERGOLA

WOOD BENCH (2 BENCHES)

FLAGSTONE PAVERS (SET IN MULCH)

PLANTER POT

The surprise in this design is an open area situated within the center of the bed, where two dramatically curving benches and an overhead structure create an outdoor sitting room.

GARDEN PLAN
HPT110008
Shown in Spring
Design by
**Timothy Barry
and Paul Rodel**

Pergola Planting

Sitting in the open shade cast by the pergola evokes the secure feeling of being in an outdoor room where you can fully enjoy the flowers in the surrounding garden. This plan's designer enhances the feeling of an outdoor room by adding lattice panels to the ends of the pergola, enclosing it further and providing the perfect place for a colorful cover of climbing vines.

Meant to be situated in an open area of the yard, this pergola planting creates a decorative centerpiece in the lawn—you can site it in either the front- or backyard. To prevent the pergola from looking too massive and dominant, the designer adds several tall trees to the bed, off-setting and balancing its size and shape and anchoring it to the surrounding landscape.

The flagstone patio under the pergola has two entrance paths from the lawn—one on each long side—so that you can walk through the garden. That way, the large island planting becomes a lovely destination rather than an obstacle in the middle of the lawn.

Plan View

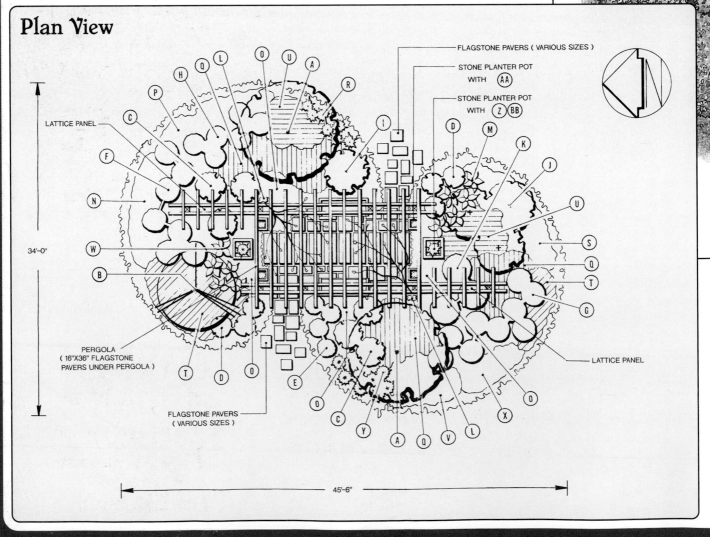

Site this beautiful pergola and its surrounding garden bed at a distance from the house, where it creates a dramatic focal point that draws visitors to come and explore.

GARDEN PLAN
HPT110009
Shown in Summer
Design by
Frank Esposito

Special Retreat

This roomy gazebo (not included in plans*) forms the centerpiece of a beautiful garden setting, evoking the romance of a bygone era. Fragrant vines climb up the back of the structure and spread out over the roof, creating even more privacy and filling the air with their delightful perfume. Here's a special garden where you can eat by candlelight on a summer evening, or simply hide out from the world on a hot afternoon.

Three different trees give the design height, which offsets the size of the gazebo, while also offering overhead color at various times of the year. Carpeting the ground under the trees is a compatible combination of easy-care shrubs, perennials and groundcovers. A stepping-stone path leads through the garden, with two entrances from the lawn, and circles the gazebo to make tending the garden easy.

Groups of boulders anchor the design, giving it a naturalistic feel and echoing the stones in the paths. One cluster of boulders is designed as a bubbling fountain, creating a pleasant sound that can be enjoyed by visitors to the gazebo or anyone resting on the nearby bench.

*To view a wide variety of gazebo plans, turn to the Projects section on p. 204.

Plan View

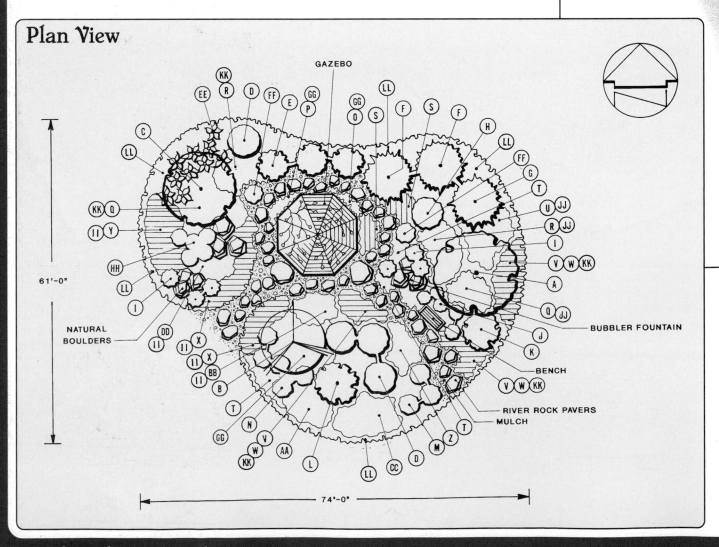

Capture the romance of a bygone era with this romantic gazebo garden. The flower-filled setting creates a very special retreat that would work as the centerpiece of almost any backyard.

GARDEN PLAN
HPT110010
Shown in Summer
Design by
Janis Leonti

Splash in the Birdbath

Your yard will be home to jewel-toned, quicksilver hummingbirds once you install this colorful bed. A rich display of bright annuals and perennials, specially selected to attract hummingbirds, creates a delightful setting. All birds need water, and hummingbirds are particularly attracted to flowing water, so the birdbath in this design features a small bubbler device.

Informal flagstone pavers lead through the garden to a semicircular mulched area set with flagstones that surround the birdbath. The path to the wooden pergola (not included in plans), which creates a lovely sitting area, leads through the pretty flowers. Climbing vines and hanging planters attached to the pergola provide additional nectar and create a pleasant shady area where you can watch the hummers dart by. Hang the pots so you can watch the birds at eye level from the sitting area. Neutral-colored plastic pots look best and cut down on evaporation, minimizing watering chores.

Site this design in a sunny location close to your house so you can observe the birds from indoors as well. Or, if you prefer, locate the bed in a quiet corner of your yard to enhance the tranquil atmosphere.

Plan View

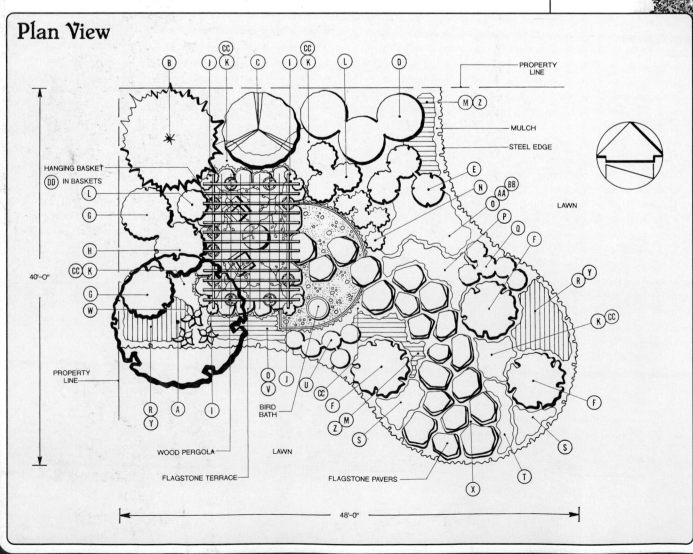

Sit beneath the flower-draped pergola and enjoy glimpses of hummingbirds as they pause in midflight to drink nectar and splash in the birdbath.

GARDEN PLAN
HPT110011
Shown in Summer
Design by
Patrick J. Duffe

Shady Pond Garden

Designed to be an oasis in the shade, these garden beds surround a dramatic, yet naturalistic focal point—a small pond. The three lobes of the centrally located pond dictate the rhythm and design concept of the surrounding beds. Visitors enter via one of three entrances that divide the garden into three distinct beds: a large semicircular bed to the northwest, a roughly S-shaped bed to the southwest and an island bed in the center, nearest the pond. Stepping-stones, set on a slightly sunken ridge, cut across the pond and allow visitors a panoramic view of the garden from the central stone.

Mid-sized evergreens ring the entire garden, giving it a sense of privacy and seclusion. A diverse mix of shade-loving flowering shrubs and trees, ferns and perennials provide varying texture and color throughout the year.

Site this garden under existing, high-canopied trees. To prevent fallen tree leaves from clogging the pond and fouling the water, cover the pond surface with bird netting in autumn. The black netting is almost invisible and allows you to easily catch and scoop out the leaves.

Plan View

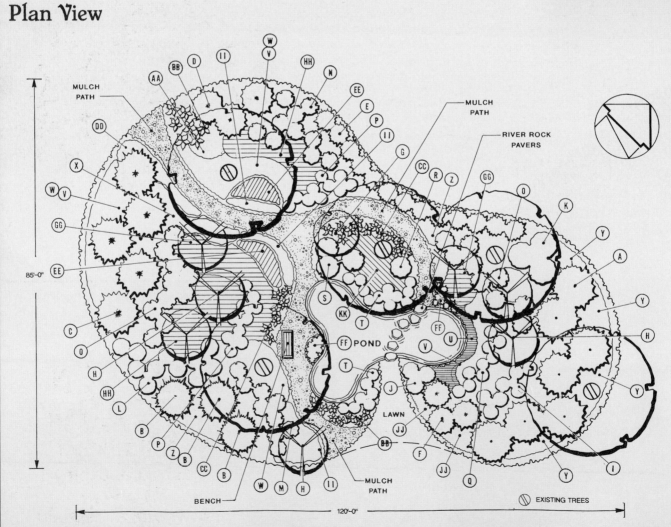

Plant this lovely pond garden where its shade-loving plants will flourish. You'll enjoy the beauty of this design all year long.

GARDEN PLAN
HPT110012
Shown in Spring
Design by
Salvatore A. Masullo

Fern & Flower Glen

This naturalistic garden bed is meant to beautify an area where mature, tall trees cast light shade. The designer plants several small, spring-flowering trees under these existing taller trees—singly and in clusters—to create the realistic feel of a woodland, where low understory trees readily grow beneath towering deep-rooted trees. The designer places clusters of shade-loving flowering shrubs under the trees and carpets the ground with feathery ferns, flowering perennials and colorful foliage plants.

Two mulched paths lead through the garden, allowing you to stroll beneath the branches and sit in the shade to enjoy the scene. Several tall, narrow evergreens create a privacy screen behind the bench and direct your view inward.

This design is easily adapted to sites where existing trees don't conform exactly to the pattern shown here. Simply space the flowering trees a reasonable distance from mature trees, adapt the placement of other plants accordingly and give the paths a different course, if need be. The secret to the gardener's success is in choosing adaptable shade-loving plants and arranging them in pretty drifts.

Plan View

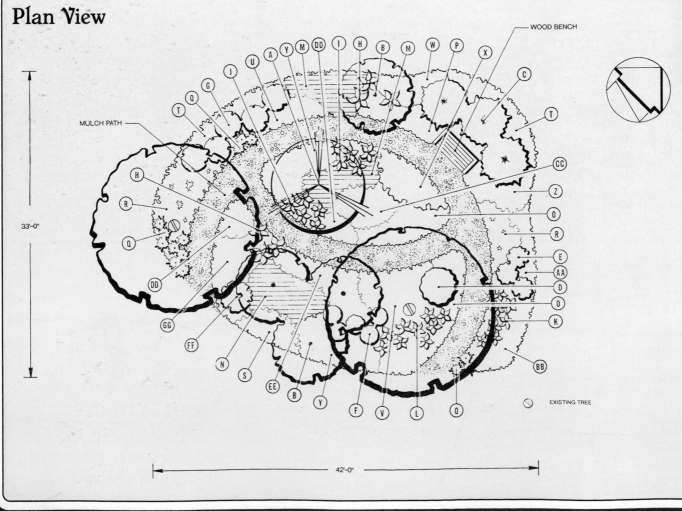

Instead of struggling to grow a lawn in a shady site, try planting this charming flower- and fern-filled bed to dress up the area. The plants used here will flourish under deep-rooted, high-branched trees.

GARDEN PLAN
HPT110013
Shown in Spring
Design by
Jim Morgan

Shade-Loving Shrub Garden

The roughly C-shaped design of this shady bed creates an eye-pleasing curve. The garden's undulating interior edge forms all kinds of interesting nooks and crannies, which invite visitors to explore. Site this bed under the spread of high-canopied trees, which offer filtered shade—the kind that allows many types of shade-loving plants to flourish.

Shade-loving shrubs dominate the bed, with drifts of spring-flowering bulbs, colonies of ferns and groups of perennials interspersed throughout to add more color. Bulbs dot the mulched areas between the shrubs in spring. Once the bulbs finish their display and go dormant, the mulch serves as pathways into the rest of the bed.

Many of the shrubs have lovely flowers during spring and summer, followed by showy berries that appear in fall and persist through winter. The designer adds a birdbath to accommodate the birds attracted by the berry-producing shrubs. Structural elements include a garden sculpture and a stepping-stone path that leads to a rustic bench, where visitors can sit and enjoy the naturalistic setting.

Plan View

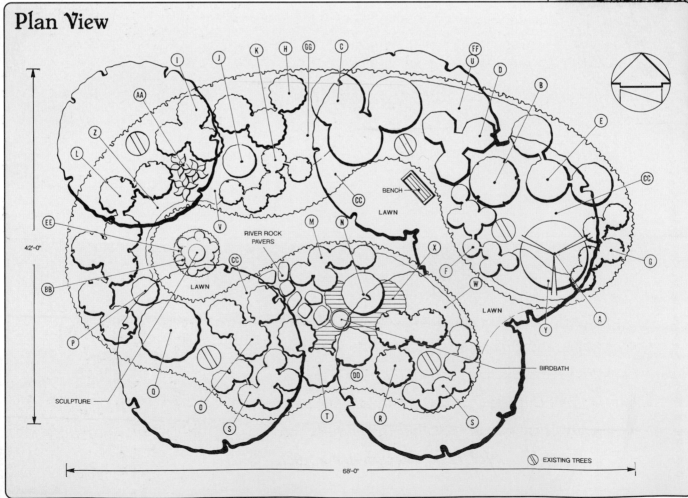

42'-0"

68'-0"

BENCH

LAWN

RIVER ROCK PAVERS

LAWN

LAWN

SCULPTURE

BIRDBATH

EXISTING TREES

A shady front- or backyard can be transformed into a lovely garden setting by planting this undulating border beneath the existing trees. Modify the plan to suit the locations of your existing trees and dig planting holes for shrubs only where you will not sever tree roots that are thicker than one inch in diameter.

GARDEN PLAN
HPT110014
Shown in Spring
Design by
Maria Morrison

Naturalistic Grass Garden

Many cultures seem to have an identifiable garden style—there are formal Italian fountain gardens, French parterres, English perennial borders and Japanese contemplation gardens. For many years, we didn't have an American-style garden. Now, a new trend has arisen, which the originators have dubbed the "New American Garden." This style of landscaping is naturalistic and relies on sweeps of ornamental grasses to create the feel of the prairies that once dominated much of the American landscape.

The backyard garden presented here follows that theme. The grasses used vary from low-growing plants hugging the borders to tall plants reaching six feet or more. Some of the grasses are bold and upright; others arching and graceful. When the grasses flower, they produce plumes that dance in the wind and sparkle in the sun. Foliage colors include bright green, blue-green, variegated and even blood-red. During autumn, foliage and flowers dry in place, forming a stunning scene of naturalistic hues in varying shades of straw, almond, brown and rust. Most of the grasses remain interesting to look at all winter, unless heavy snow flattens them to the ground. In early spring, the dried foliage must be cut off and removed to make way for the new growth—but this is the only maintenance chore required by an established garden of ornamental grasses!

The design includes a large realistic-looking pond, which can be made from a vinyl-liner or concrete. At the end of the path leading from the bridge, a small seating area provides retreat.

Plan View

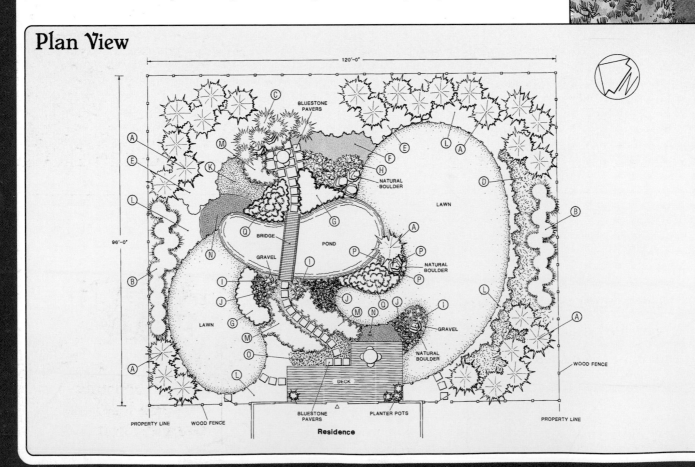

Low in maintenance requirements and high in natural appeal, this garden of ornamental grasses delights the senses all year with subdued foliage colors, sparkling flower plumes and rustling leaves.

GARDEN PLAN
HPT110015
Shown in Summer
Design by
Damon Scott

Garden to Attract Birds

There is no better way to wake up in the morning than to the sound of songbirds in the garden. Wherever you live, you will be surprised at the number and variety of birds you can attract by offering them a few basic necessities—water, shelter, nesting spots and food. Birds need water for drinking and bathing. They need shrubs and trees, especially evergreens, for shelter and nesting. Edge spaces—open areas with trees nearby for quick protection—provide ground feeders with foraging places, while plants with berries and nuts offer other natural sources of food.

The garden presented here contains all the necessary elements to attract birds to the garden. The shrubs and trees are chosen especially to provide a mix of evergreen and deciduous species. All of these, together with the masses of flowering perennials, bear seeds, nuts or berries that are known to appeal to birds. The berry show looks quite pretty, too, until the birds gobble them up! Planted densely enough for necessary shelter, the bird-attracting plants create a lovely private backyard that's enjoyable throughout the seasons.

The birdbath is located in the lawn so it will be in the sun. A naturalistic pond provides water in a more protected setting. The birdhouses and feeders aren't really necessary—though they may be the icing on the cake when it comes to luring the largest number of birds—because the landscape provides abundant natural food and shelter. Outside one of the main windows of the house, a birdfeeder hangs from a small flowering tree, providing an up-close view of your feathered friends.

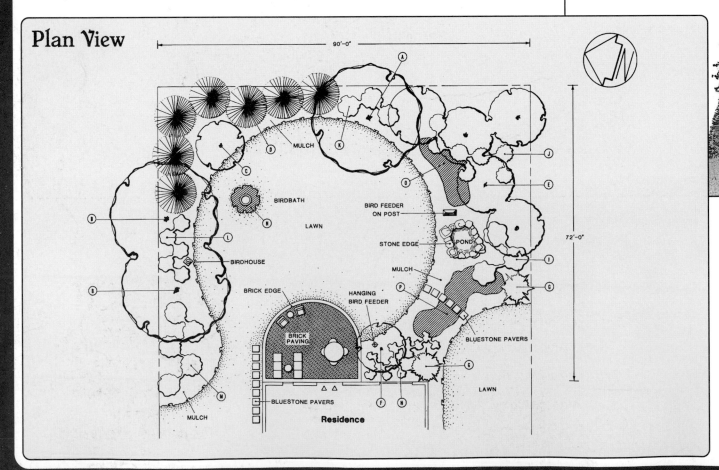

Plan View

90'-0"

72'-0"

MULCH

BIRDBATH

LAWN

BIRD FEEDER ON POST

STONE EDGE

POND

MULCH

BIRDHOUSE

BRICK EDGE

HANGING BIRD FEEDER

BLUESTONE PAVERS

BRICK PAVING

BLUESTONE PAVERS

LAWN

MULCH

Residence

Nature lovers will delight in the abundant
number of birds that will flock to this beautiful garden.
An attractive collection of berried plants and
evergreens offers food and shelter for the wildlife,
while creating a handsome, pastoral setting.

GARDEN PLAN

HPT110016
Shown in Autumn
Design by
Michael J. Opisso

Formal Herb and Vegetable Gardens

The formal herb garden evolved as it has because the design is both functional and lovely to look at. Exuberantly spreading herbs find themselves restrained by the brick-edged beds. At the same time, the paths show off the herbs' charms and provide an attractive structure during the off-seasons. The designer chose a collection of the most useful fragrant and culinary herbs and arranged them in a pattern that enhances their colorful flowers and foliage. A central sundial, a cocoa-shell mulch emitting a delicious chocolate aroma and a bench under the trees for relaxed viewing further accent the herb garden.

The raised-bed vegetable garden, built from attractive on-end timbers, not only creates a structure to contain the crops but also reduces the need to bend over, facilitating planting and harvesting. The area between the beds is mulched with wood chips to eliminate muddy feet and weeds. You'll appreciate the handy storage shed and efficient three-bin composter, positioned on the right.

The designer repeated the gracefully arching semicircles of the herb garden in the brick terrace and the lawn, visually linking the elements of the garden and creating a sense of unity. Likewise, the arc of flowering trees around the herb garden repeats and reinforces the same curve. The trees help enclose the garden and create privacy, while a wide variety of easy-care perennials, bulbs and shrubs provides a long season's worth of flowering interest.

Plan View

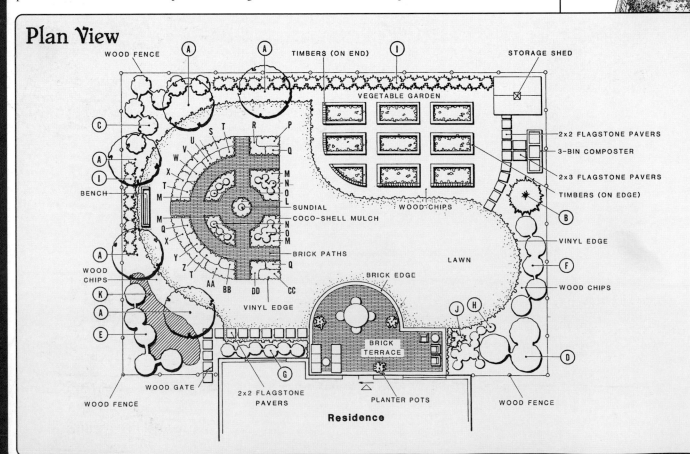

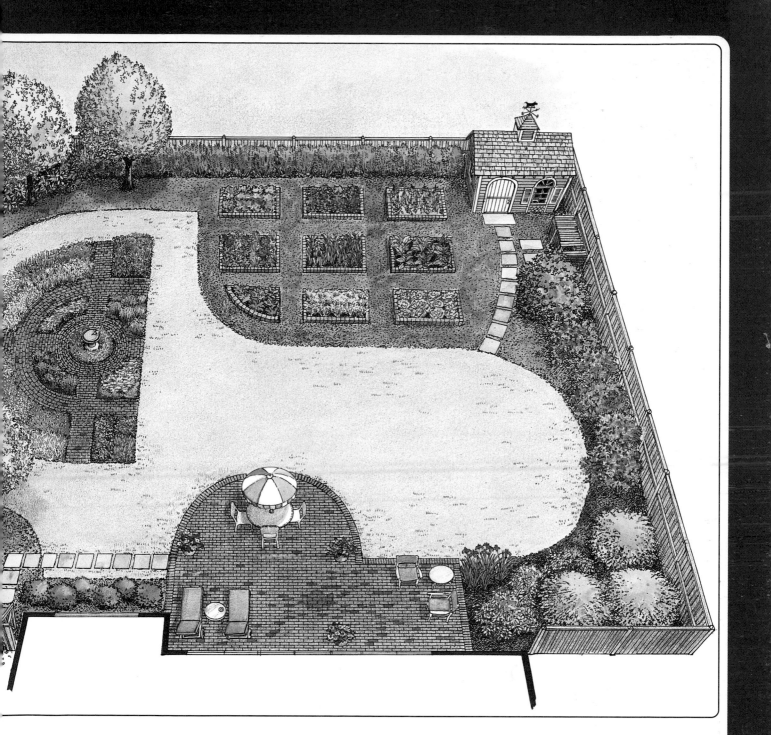

Casual elegance defines the character of this garden plan, featuring a brick terrace, formal herb garden and raised-bed vegetable garden. The repeating shapes and lines of the landscape create a unified feeling.

GARDEN PLAN
HPT 110017
Shown in Summer
Design by
Michael J. Opisso

Water Garden

There are few places more tranquil, more relaxing or more cooling on a hot summer day than a garden with a view of the water—even if the water is no more than a garden pool. In the garden pictured here, two ponds filled with water lilies are used to create a tranquil setting. The first pond is situated near the house, where it is visible from the indoors. The deck is cantilevered over the pond to enhance the closeness of the water, and is covered with an overhead trellis, which ties the two areas together. The trellising also frames the view of the pond from the deck, and of the deck from the garden areas.

A second, smaller pond is set into the corner of the garden and has a backdrop of early-spring flowering trees, ferns and shade-loving perennials. This intimate retreat is made complete by setting a bench and planter pots beside the pond.

Throughout the property, river-rock paving enhances the natural feeling of the water and provides a sitting area nearby for quiet contemplation. Moss rocks, placed in strategic places in the garden, further carry out the naturalistic theme, as do most of the landscape plants. The shrubs and perennials bordering the undulating lawn provide the needed soft-textured, informal look that makes both ponds seem natural and right at home.

Plan View

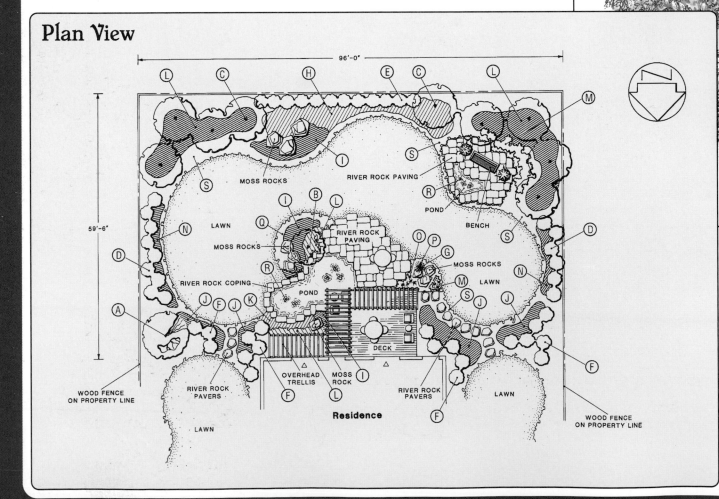

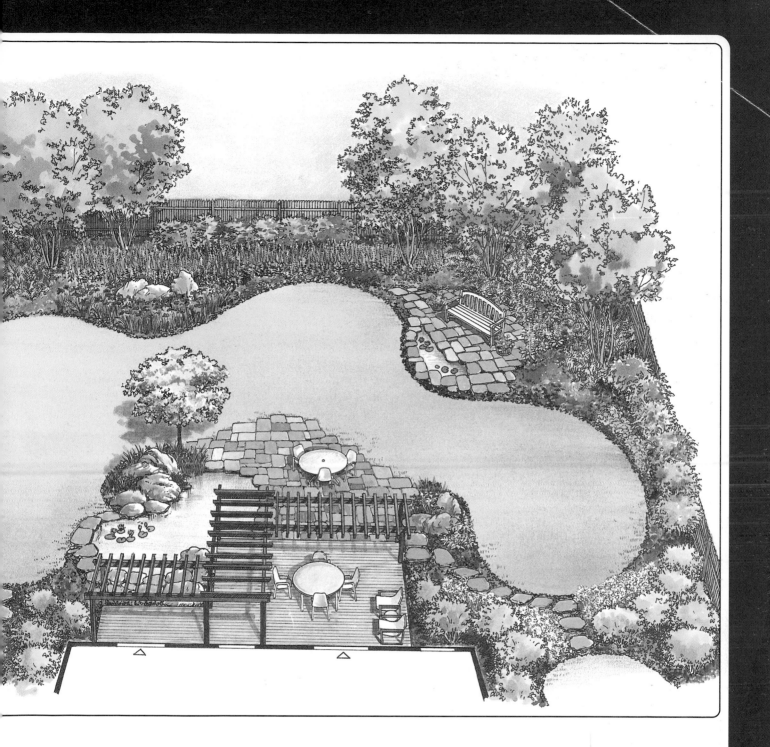

This backyard features not one, but two ponds in which to dip your toes during summer's heat. If you choose to keep your shoes on, sit on the patio near the large pond or on the bench by the small one to cool off in the reflection of the colorful surroundings.

GARDEN PLAN
HPT 110018
Shown in Summer
Design by
Michael J. Opisso
and Damon Scott

Rugged and Rocky

Take your cue from Mother Nature: if you love the rocky outcroppings of the mountains or deserts, that may be the way to go in your garden. Boulders—single and sturdy, combined into groupings, or stacked for low walls—bring to a garden a solidity and substance that are impossible to create any other way. And rocky sites create an environment for a variety of special plants.

The designer raises the soil level of the yard slightly to create a curving contour at the back of the yard. The soil is retained by a wall of large boulders on one side and rough-chiseled natural stones forming a simple, low curvilinear dry wall on the other side. Underneath the trees and between the rocks and boulders, various creeping plants spread and spill their way toward the lawn. A combination of drought-tolerant deciduous and evergreen shrubs and trees provides softening foliage and flowers.

Flagstone pavers allow for circulation from the garden gates to the stone-paved terrace, which features two levels that have only a stair-step difference in height. Several types of creeping, fragrant paving plants mingle between the stones, releasing their scent when walked on. Rock garden plants mix in a chaos of color among the scattered boulders in the gravel-surfaced planting bed near the patio. The permanent structure provided by the plants, large boulders and paving stones creates a garden of year-round beauty.

Plan View

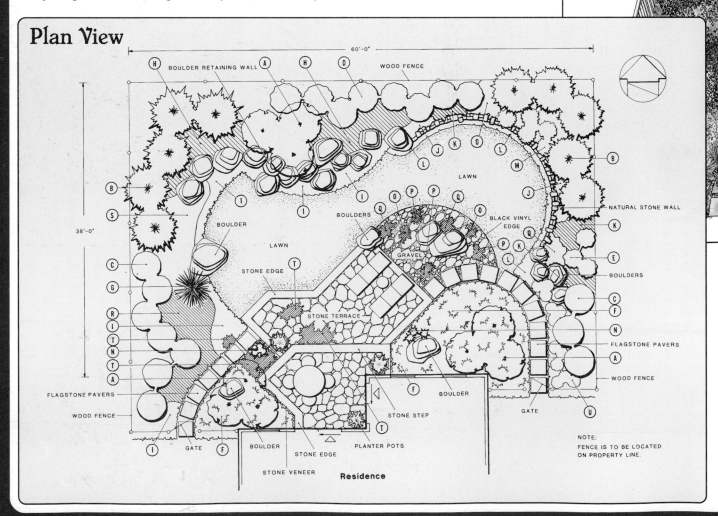

For much of its visual excitement, this dynamic design relies on the contrast between the overlapping curves of the pathway, gravel bed and low rock wall on the right and the angles of the split-level stone terrace on the left. In arid areas, you may wish to substitute crushed granite or pea gravel for the lawn.

GARDEN PLAN
HPT110019
Shown in Summer
Design by
Michael J. Opisso

Cozy Spaces

The English cottage garden, beloved for its romantic, old-fashioned and homey appeal, is the kind of country garden to have again these days—whether or not you actually live in a cottage. The backyard design pictured here includes a cottage garden of easy-care, mixed perennials enclosed by a quaint picket fence. Suitable for many types of homes, from cottage to Colonial, this garden offers intimate scale and small spaces to create a comfortable backyard in which family and friends can feel at home. And there are plenty of flowers to cut all summer long for making indoor arrangements.

Paving stones lead from the front of the house to the backyard, where an arbor beckons visitors into the cozy patio and garden. Straight ahead, in the midst of the flower garden, a sundial acts as a focal point, drawing the eye right across the patio and into the garden beyond. A picket fence encloses the informal patio and flower garden, while defining the patchwork quilt of flowers inside it. Walk through the garden gate and down the path, and you will discover a garden swing nestled in the shade—a perfect spot for a romantic interlude or for whiling away the hours on a lazy afternoon.

Not to be outdone by the garden itself, the shrub borders edging the property offers an ever-changing arrangement of flowering shrubs backed by a privacy screen of tall evergreens. The trees located at each corner of the house balance and unify the patio and flower garden, while framing the garden when viewed from a distance.

Plan View

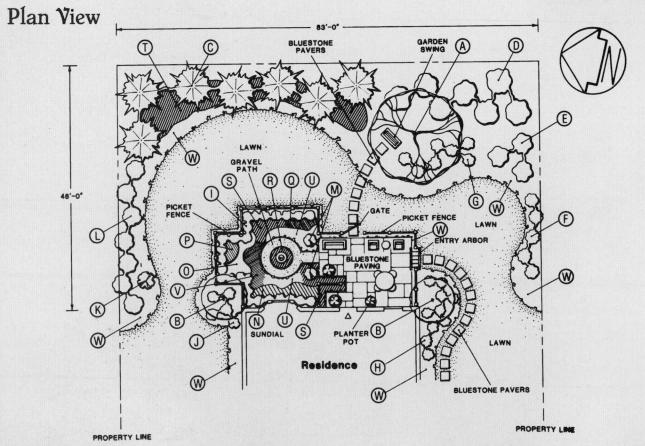

It isn't necessary to live in a cottage to have a cottage garden. Almost any informal home would be enhanced by this charming backyard with its effervescent color, secluded retreats and cozy spaces—all wrapped up in a white picket fence.

GARDEN PLAN
HPT110020
Shown in Summer
Design by
Michael J. Opisso

Second-Story Deck

A second-story deck can be the answer to many difficult landscaping problems. Sometimes this deck type is built with a mother-daughter house to provide a private deck for a second-story apartment. If a house is built on sloping property and cannot accommodate a ground-level deck, a raised deck is the answer. With split-level or raised-ranch houses, where the kitchen is often on the second level, a second-story deck right off the kitchen eliminates the need to carry food and dishes up and down stairs.

Even a high deck can have two levels and therefore two separate use areas, as the designer accomplishes with this deck. The upper area features a built-in barbecue, service cabinet and space for dining. The lower area invites family and guests to lounge and relax in the sun. Because the deck is high enough off the ground that an accidental fall could be dangerous, a railing and planters ensure safety. Filled with masses of annuals, the planters bring living color above ground.

Without screening, the underside of the deck would be an eyesore when viewed from the yard. The designer solved this problem by enclosing the void beneath the deck with latticework and using a hedge to soften the effect. If the area beneath the deck is to be used as storage, a door can be added to the latticework. The triangular shape of the deck is far more pleasing than a square or rectangular design. Three flowering trees at the corners of the deck anchor this shape and further serve to bring color and greenery up high. Tall evergreens help to screen the deck from the neighbors.

Plan View

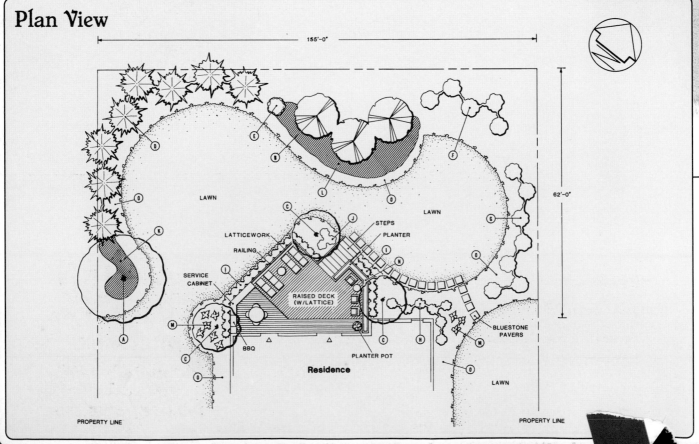

High above the rest of the garden, this second-story deck affords a beautiful view of the grounds. And the deck looks beautiful too, because latticework and soft plantings integrate it into the landscape.

GARDEN PLAN
HPT110021
Shown in Summer
Design by
Michael J. Opisso

Kid's Vegetable Garden

Young gardeners will thrive in this backyard, which is specially designed to entice a child into horticulture with a circular vegetable garden and a barn-and-silo playhouse or toolshed. The stepping-stones in the garden make a perfect spot for hopscotch, and the swing set, sandbox and lawn provide other places to romp.

Vegetables grow just as well in beds as in rows, and the circular bed used here better suits a child's sense of necessary disorder. Surrounded by a gravel path and crisscrossed by pathways, the garden presents four individual easy-care beds that can be planted with several types of vegetables. Begin with your child's favorites in order to create enthusiasm for gardening. Then add a few new ones to encourage investigation. Eating a vine-ripened tomato grown personally by the child may be enough to convert a typical play-obsessed ten-year-old into a lifelong gardener.

Parents will like this backyard design, too. It combines a permanent structure of easy-care trees, shrubs and perennials, which produce a beautiful color display spring through fall, and a handsome brick patio for relaxing and entertaining. The circular shape of the vegetable bed, which can be turned into a pretty herb or flower bed if the kids lose interest, echoes the curves of the lawn, making it an attractive, yet functional, design element. For safety's sake, the entire backyard is open and visible from the patio and has only one gate.

Plan View

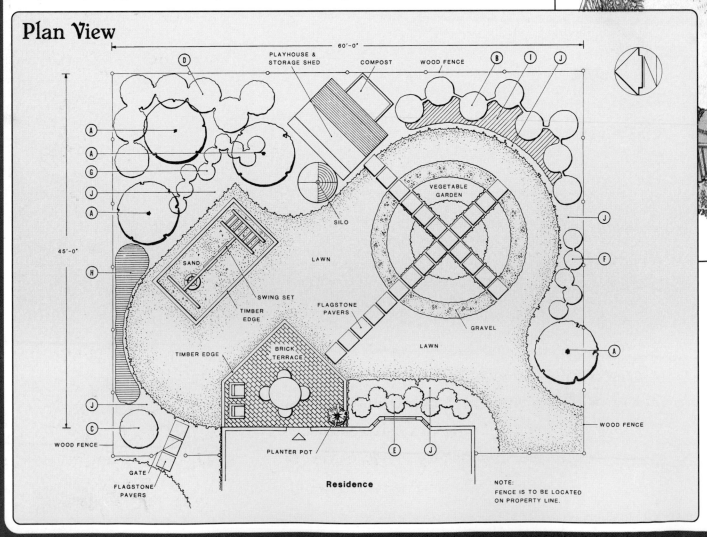

A child can skip right along the stepping stones to tend a personal vegetable garden in this cleverly designed backyard. With a barn-and-silo playhouse and compost bin adjacent to the garden, your child can exercise imagination in creative play while helping with the chores and learning about recycling.

GARDEN PLAN
HPT110022
Shown in Summer
Design by
Michael J. Opisso

Children's Play Yard

*I*f there's one thing that can be said about children's play areas, it's that their function usually far outweighs their attractiveness. However, this backyard design presents an excellent solution to a functional children's play yard that is still pleasing to look at. The backyard includes all the fun elements a child would love. On one side of the yard are grouped a play structure for climbing and swinging, a playhouse, and a sandbox enclosed in a low boardwalk. A play mound—a perfect place for running, leaping and holding fort—rises from the lawn on the other side of the yard.

These play areas are integrated into the landscape by their circular form, which is repeated in the sandbox, play mound, boardwalk, and the sand areas under the playhouse and play structure. The curved brick patio and planting border carry through the circular theme. The stepping stones leading to the play areas also follow a circular path—a playful pattern that invites a child to "follow the yellow brick road."

From the house and patio, the views of both the garden and the play areas are unobstructed, affording constant adult supervision from both indoors and out. The border surrounding the yard creates a private setting that offers a changing show of flowers from the masses of shrubs and perennials. Beyond the play structure, a large tree shades the area, providing landscape interest, and perhaps even a place for adventurous young feet to climb.

When the children are grown, this design can be adapted as a playground for older folk by removing the playhouse and play structure and planting lawn, or a flower or vegetable garden.

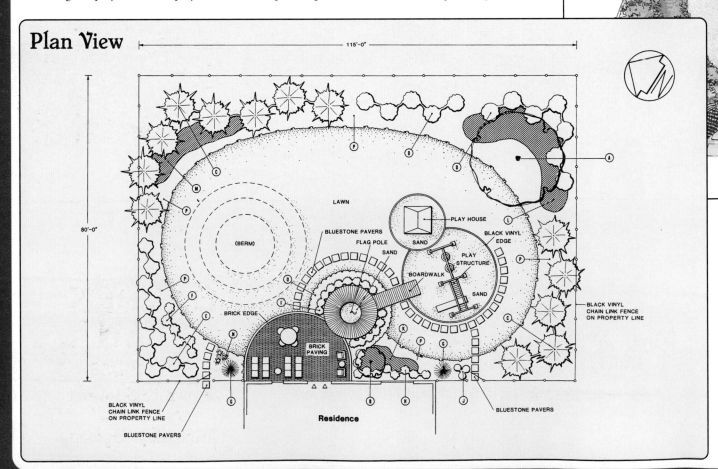

Plan View

115'-0"

80'-0"

LAWN

(BERM)

BLUESTONE PAVERS

FLAG POLE

SAND

PLAY HOUSE

SAND

BLACK VINYL EDGE

PLAY STRUCTURE

BOARDWALK

SAND

BRICK EDGE

BRICK PAVING

BLACK VINYL CHAIN LINK FENCE ON PROPERTY LINE

BLACK VINYL CHAIN LINK FENCE ON PROPERTY LINE

BLUESTONE PAVERS

BLUESTONE PAVERS

Residence

Here is a special backyard designed for both children and adults. The yard offers youngsters their own place to escape into a world of imagination and discovery without compromising the attractiveness of a garden setting.

GARDEN PLAN
HPT110023
Shown in Summer
Design by
Michael J. Opisso

Vegetable Gardener's Outdoor Kitchen

Here's a wonderful plan for the serious backyard gardener and outdoor chef: a yard featuring a raised-bed vegetable garden and a spacious deck with an outdoor kitchen for serving and enjoying the homegrown bounty. And the plan doesn't neglect floral beauty for the sake of produce: large patches of easy-care, long-blooming perennials catch the eye, while flowering shrubs and evergreens provide privacy and beauty.

Vegetable gardens are difficult to live with in many suburban backyards because they look barren during the off-seasons. Once the spinach, lettuce and cabbages are harvested, it's back to bare dirt again. But this plan is designed with raised beds to provide visual structure and, at the same time, improve growing conditions by creating warmer, better-drained and more fertile soil. The size of the beds in this garden permits easy tending because all the plants are within an arm's reach and grow closely together to discourage weeds. Wood chips cover the permanent pathways to reduce mud and improve the garden's appearance. The storage shed and compost area for recycling garden and kitchen waste are located conveniently close to the vegetable beds, but they're attractively screened by evergreens.

Plan View

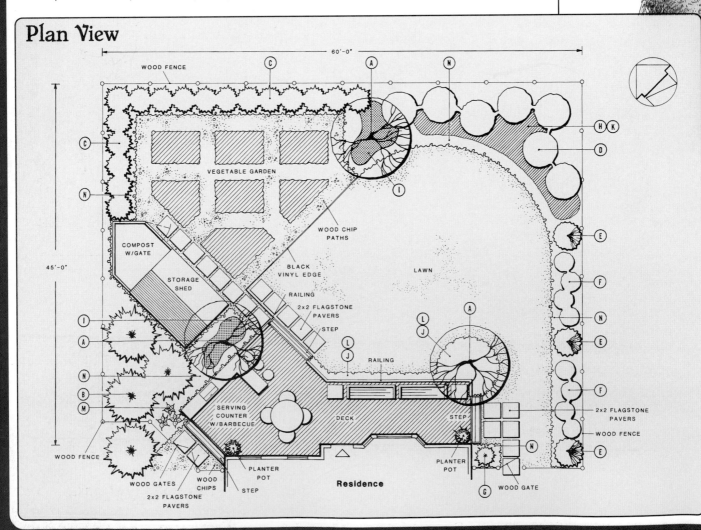

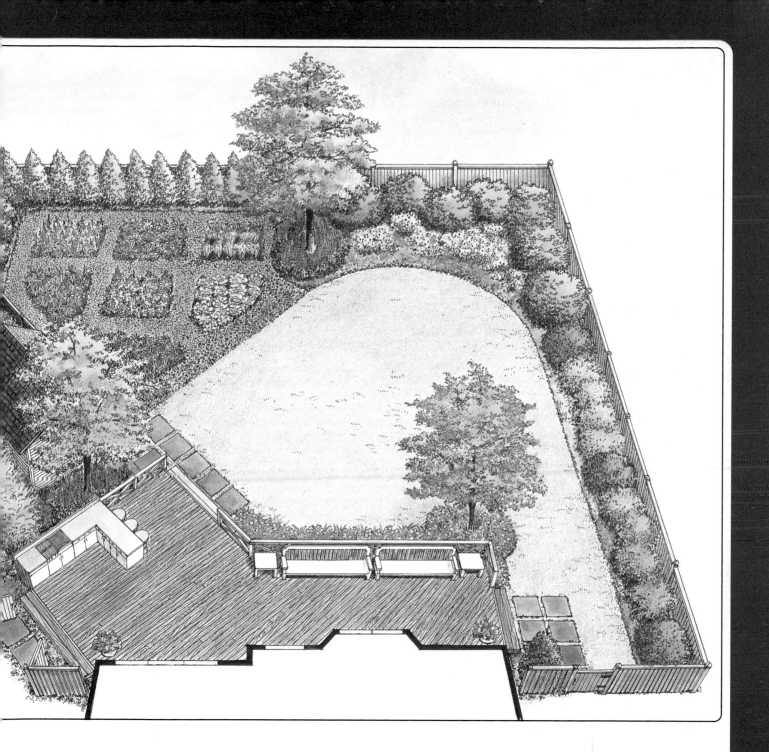

A spacious deck with an outdoor kitchen is effectively
incorporated into this design for a medium-sized backyard.
The large area devoted to vegetable gardening can produce
more than enough vegetables for a family of four.

GARDEN PLAN

HPT110024
Shown in Summer
Design by
Michael J. Opisso

Sunlight Is Insufficient

A shade garden need not depend on flowers—which usually need some sun to perform well—for color. You can enliven a shady area with a border that relies on a rainbow of foliage color to provide subtle, yet engaging beauty. An assortment of plants with variegated or unusually tinted foliage, such as burgundy, blue-green, golden yellow and chartreuse, thrives in shady conditions. This design contains an artful mix of foliage plants with colors and textures that range from understated to bold.

In this gently curving border, the designer combines a variety of deciduous and evergreen shrubs and trees with perennials to provide year-round foliage color. Many of the plants also add floral accents to the design. The simple green of some of the evergreen plants acts as a foil for variegated and colored leaves in the border and helps to create a harmonious scene. A semi-circular flagstone path leads to a bench, enticing visitors to sit in the cool shade and enjoy the splendor of the leafy display.

Plan View

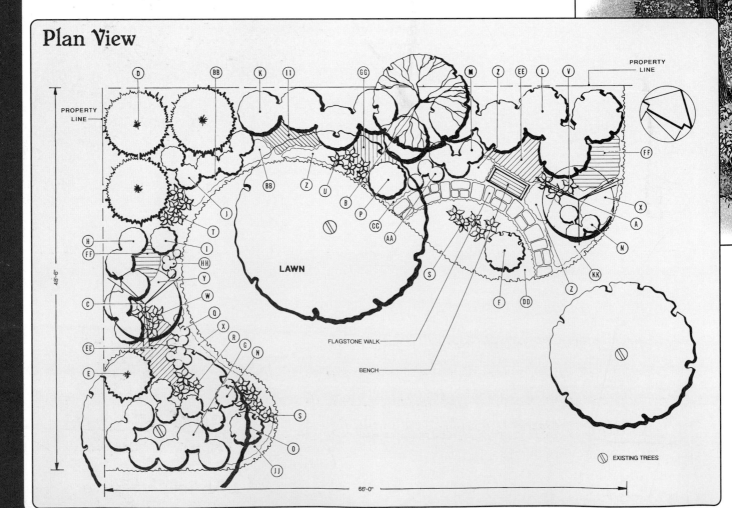

PROPERTY LINE

PROPERTY LINE

LAWN

FLAGSTONE WALK

BENCH

EXISTING TREES

48'-6"

66'-0"

Designed for a location where sunlight is insufficient to support most free-flowering plants, this showy border derives its color from an array of shade-loving shrubs and perennials featuring variegated, golden or purplish-red leaves.

GARDEN PLAN
HPT110025
Shown in Summer
Design by
Michael J. Opisso and Anne Rode

With Loving Care

The single intention of the backyard design shown here is to provide plenty of beautiful, fragrant flowers, spring through fall, for you to gaze upon, bury your nose in and tend with loving care. This is a gardener's garden—a garden for plant lovers.

The island bed of fragrant flowers situated off-center in the lawn balances the visual weight of the shade tree. Here, where the plants will be easily accessible from all sides, grow old-fashioned perennial bloomers whose sweet perfume has pleased generations. A weeping evergreen shrub anchors this bed, giving it year-round structure so that it looks attractive even in winter.

More fragrant perennials, planted in masses in the borders to intensify their scent, thrive in the light shade cast by the trees. Spring- and fall-blooming vines drape over the fence, softening its facade with colorful blooms. Even in early spring, fragrant-flowered bulbs push their way through the low groundcover, making perfect candidates for indoor arrangements.

The hardscape, consisting primarily of a brick patio coupled with a flagstone path leading from the gate to the patio, offers simple, yet attractive, lines. The very straightforwardness of these construction features places more importance on the garden's lovely flowers and plants. The dominant tree of the garden, a large deciduous shade tree, draws the eye to the spacious corner bed. The other trees specified are medium-sized flowering trees and evergreens for year-round greenery, while charming shrubs provide additional seasonal color.

Plan View

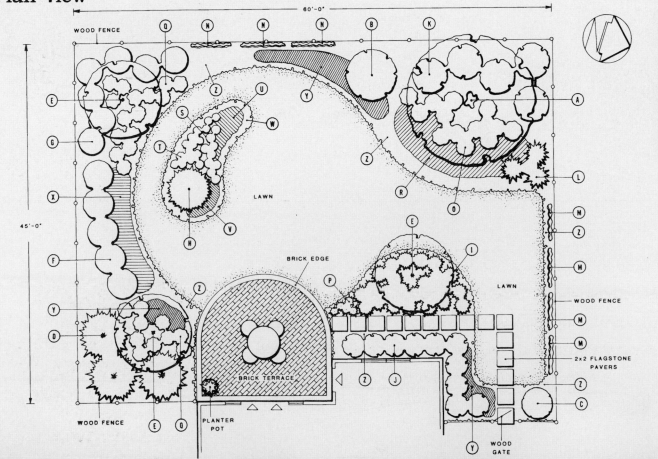

If you are a flower lover, this backyard plan filled with fragrant flowers is for you. The tear-drop-shaped island bed, planted with a collection of scented perennials, is designed so you can enjoy the plants close up and tend them from all sides. The elegant brick patio, shaped to mirror the planting bed to its right, provides ample space for the family to dine and relax.

GARDEN PLAN
HPT110026
Shown in Summer
Design by
Damon Scott

Enticing and Romantic

There's something enticing and romantic about a garden gazebo. It creates an intimate spot to sit and talk, perhaps making the difference between having a few friends over and having a party. If you enjoy entertaining, this backyard design featuring both a roomy deck and a lovely gazebo may be the one for your family.

The gazebo (not included in the plan) acts as the main focal point of the design, drawing the eye by its shape, size and location and enticing visitors by the stepping-stone path leading to its cozy confines. The lush plantings surrounding the gazebo anchor it to the design, creating a flowery setting that helps keep the structure cool and inviting.

The other primary feature of this garden is a large deck. The deck features octagonal lines to echo and complement the shape of the gazebo and has enough room to accommodate two separate dining tables. On the practical side, a built-in barbecue and a storage cabinet turn the deck into an outdoor extension of your home's living space.

The informal style of the design incorporates sunny and shady areas, as well as a mix of evergreen and deciduous trees and shrubs, to create a variety of textures and patterns. Background plantings of tall evergreens assure privacy, and a wide variety of flowering shrubs and perennials add seasonal color and interest. Three deciduous shade trees frame the skyline, provide necessary summer shade and let in warming winter sun. Deck Plan HPT110170 is shown on page 271.

Plan View

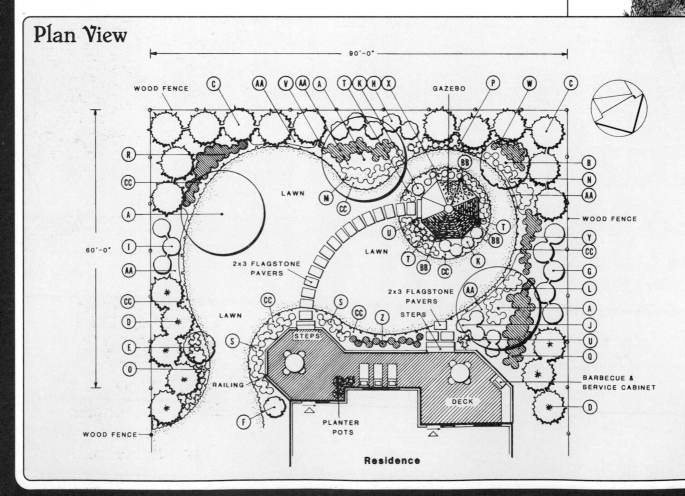

The visual interest and action revolve around the gazebo, which is balanced by a spacious deck, three deciduous shade trees and deep planting borders of colorful flowering shrubs and perennials.

GARDEN PLAN
HPT110027
Shown in Summer
Design by
David Poplawski

Hummingbird Garden

Quick as lightning and jealous of "their" garden, hummingbirds provide exciting backyard entertainment and are easy to attract with the right plantings. Although many people supply them with a sugar-and-water feeder, hummingbirds need vitamin-rich flower nectar for complete nourishment. Hummingbirds love red. They busily investigate all red flowers—and even red objects bearing little resemblance to flowers—preferring trumpet-shaped types accommodating their long beaks. To thrive in a garden, hummingbirds also need a source of water.

The designer created this backyard plan as a charming informal setting to attract hummingbirds from spring through fall, while arranging colors and plant textures to make a visual picture that will please you and your family throughout the year. The birdbath, surrounded by some of the hummers' favorite annual flowers, punctuates the circular lawn area. Just beyond, a wood swing suspended from a cozy arbor provides the perfect spot for watching. Evergreen shrubs and tall shade trees provide nesting sites and, at the same time, enclose the yard with overhead foliage. The spacious terrace echoes the curving lines of the lawn contours and makes a fine place for an outdoor party.

Besides feeding on the plentiful red, orange and pink tubular-shaped flowers used in this design, the hummingbirds will make your yard practically insect-free; they feed on tiny insects, snatching them from midair and collecting them from the flowers they visit. Avoid using pesticides, which will reduce the number of these insects and perhaps directly harm the hummers.

Plan View

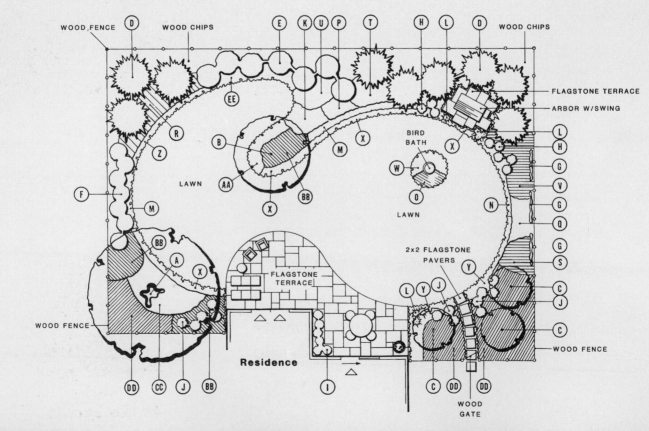

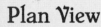

*This pretty backyard plan provides the basics to attract
hummingbirds—water and a spring-to-fall display of
nectar-rich flowers. This plan also includes the amenities
necessary for comfort—a patio, a swing, an attractive privacy
screen and privacy plantings.*

**GARDEN
PLAN**
HPT110028
Shown in Spring
Design by
Damon Scott

Everything Birds Need

This border includes everything birds need—food, water and nesting sites—and encourages them to become permanent residents of your yard. The design curves inward, creating a sense of enclosure and a sanctuary that appeals to even the shiest types of birds. The border's attractive design includes a pond, birdhouse and birdbath, which act as focal points and make the garden irresistible to people as well.

The large variety of pretty fruiting shrubs offers birds natural nourishment throughout much of the year, but you can supplement the food supply with store-bought bird food if you wish. Deciduous and evergreen trees provide shelter and nesting places, while the mulched areas give birds a place to take dust baths and to poke around for insects and worms.

Because water is so important to birds, the garden includes two water features: a small naturalistic pond and a birdbath set in a circular bed. Both offer spots for perching, bathing and drinking. In cold-weather climates, consider adding a special heater to the birdbath to keep the water from freezing; water attracts birds in winter even more than birdseed.

Plan View

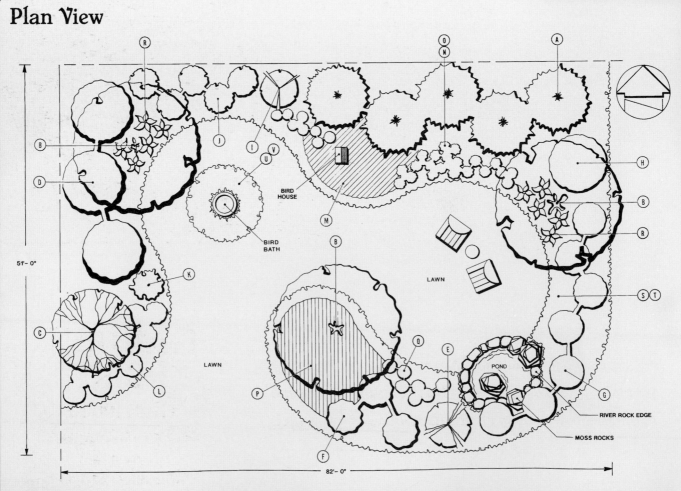

BIRD HOUSE

BIRD BATH

LAWN

LAWN

POND

RIVER ROCK EDGE

MOSS ROCKS

51'- 0"

82'- 0"

Birds flock to this border, which provides them with ample supplies of food and water and locations for nesting and bathing. There's plenty of room for bird-watchers as well.

GARDEN PLAN
HPT110029
Shown in Summer
Design by
Michael J. Opisso

Songbird Garden

This naturalistic garden plan relies upon several different features to attract as many different species of birds as possible. A songbird's basic needs include food, water and shelter, but this backyard plan offers luxury accommodations not found in every yard, and also provides the maximum opportunity for birds and bird-watchers to observe each other. Special features provide for specific birds; for example, the rotting log attracts woodpeckers and the dusting area will be used gratefully by birds to free themselves of parasites. In addition to plants that produce plentiful berries and seeds, the designer includes a ground feeder to lure morning doves, cardinals and other birds that prefer to eat off the ground. The birdhouse located in the shade of the specimen tree to the rear of the garden suits a wide variety of songbirds.

The angular deck nestles attractively into the restful circular shapes of the garden. The designer encloses the deck amidst the bird-attracting plantings to maximize close-up observation opportunities and create an intimate setting. Two other sitting areas welcome bird-watchers into the garden. A bench positioned on a small patio under the shade of a graceful flowering tree provides a relaxing spot to sit and contemplate the small garden pool and the melody of a low waterfall. Another bench—this one situated in the sun—may be reached by strolling along a path of wood-rounds on the opposite side of the yard. Both wildlife and people will find this backyard a very special retreat. Deck Plan HPT110166 is shown on page 267.

Plan View

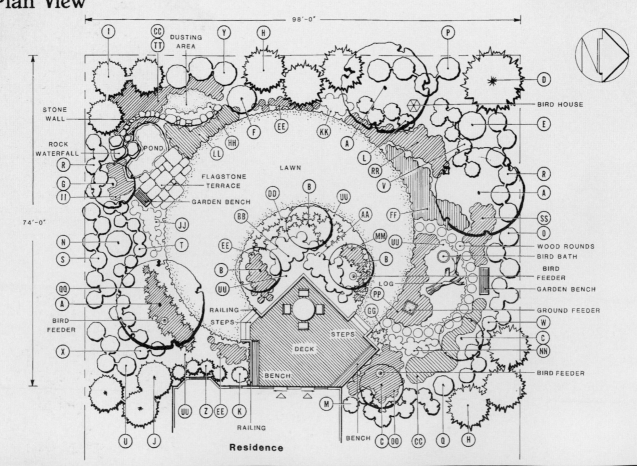

This large, naturalistic backyard design creates a wonderful environment for attracting a wide range of bird species, because it offers a plentiful supply of natural food, water and shelter. The deck and garden benches invite people to observe and listen to the songbirds in comfort.

GARDEN PLAN
HPT110030
Shown in Spring
Design by
David Poplawski

Inviting Spaces

*I*t's true that a lawn acts as an important design feature by creating a plain that carries the eye through the garden, establishing connections between the various garden elements and providing an open feeling while attractively covering the ground. However, it requires time and money to maintain. Other materials or plants that require less care can provide a similar effect. Japanese gardens often feature carefully raked gravel to mimic ocean waves; in the Southwest, prettily colored crushed granite covers many yards; in other areas, low evergreen groundcovers substitute for lawn grass. In this low-maintenance backyard, the designer incorporated a large deck and patio flanked by a lakelike expanse of dark gravel where a lawn might be. A water-permeable landscape fabric underpins the layer of gravel to help halt weeds.

Tall evergreen trees along the rear boundary guarantee privacy, while three large deciduous trees provide plenty of summer shade for the deck and patio. The angular deck features an interesting cut-out space for a small viewing garden. The deck steps down to a grade-level brick patio with a circular shape that complements the gravel expanse and the planting beds. From the brick terrace, a flagstone pathway leads to a bench positioned in the midst of a bed of flowering perennials. From there, you can reflect upon your garden, your house and your free time.

Plan View

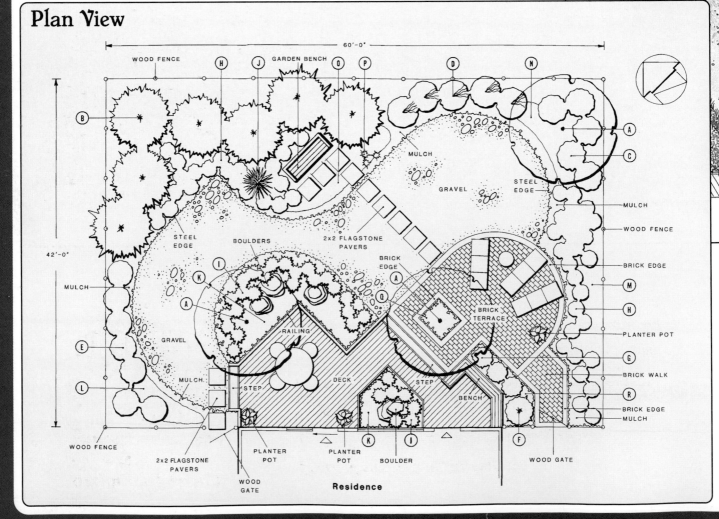

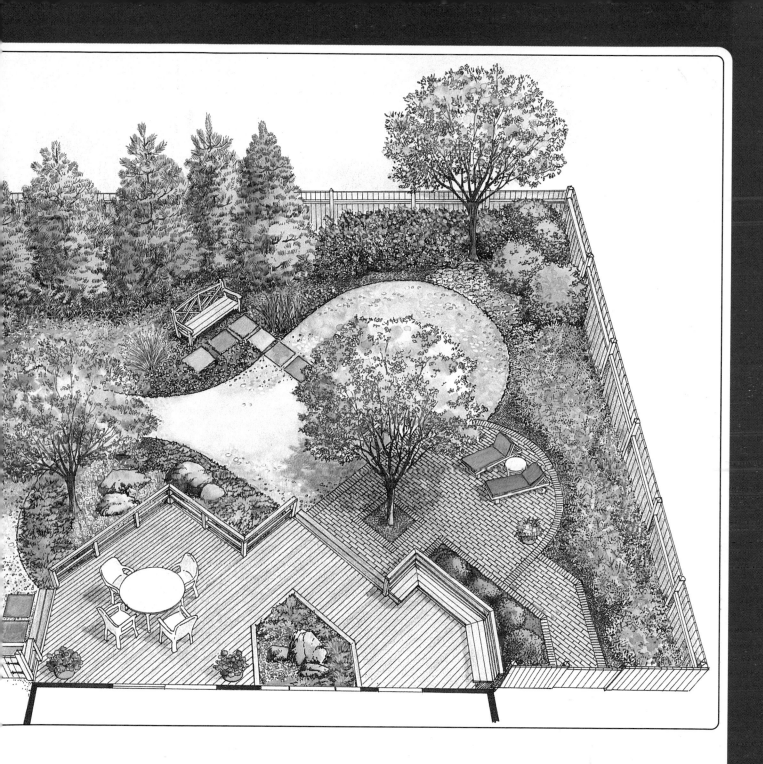

Eliminate the lawn, and the most time-consuming task of a gardener's maintenance routine is eliminated as well. Easy-care hard surfaces—a gravel bed, wood deck and brick patio—take the place of the lawn, providing inviting spaces for relaxing and enjoying the surrounding flowers and greenery.

GARDEN PLAN
HPT110031
Shown in Summer
Design by
Michael J. Opisso

Fragrant Shrub Garden

If you're the kind of gardener whose nose is always buried in the nearest blossom and feels disappointed to find a gorgeous rose as scentless as it is beautiful, this landscape plan might be just the one for you. The designer makes every effort to choose the most fragrant plants available to fill this low-maintenance garden with sweet and spicy aromas from spring through fall.

Curving paths and romantic, secluded sitting areas invite you to stroll and rest among the scented plants. Sit under the arbor and enjoy the intensely fragrant flowering shrubs directly behind you in spring and the heady scent of climbing roses overhead in summer. In fall, the delicate perfume of the late bloomers will delight you. Even if you don't move from the patio, the sweet, pervasive perfume from the inconspicuous flowers of the surrounding shrubs will enhance warm July evenings for years to come.

You'll find the garden is as easy to care for as it is fragrant because the designer selects low-maintenance shrubs (including many dwarf types), trees and groundcovers, instead of labor-intensive annuals and perennials, to provide color and fragrance. The carefully arranged shrubs have plenty of room to grow without crowding each other or outgrowing their spaces, so you won't have to worry about extensive pruning chores. Much of the area that would be lawn in most yards is devoted here to the brick patio and shrub borders, allowing more kinds of plants to be included and minimizing lawn-care chores.

Plan View

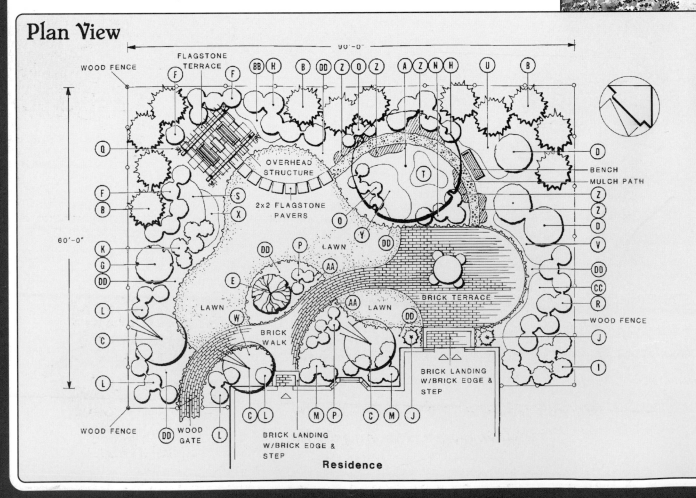

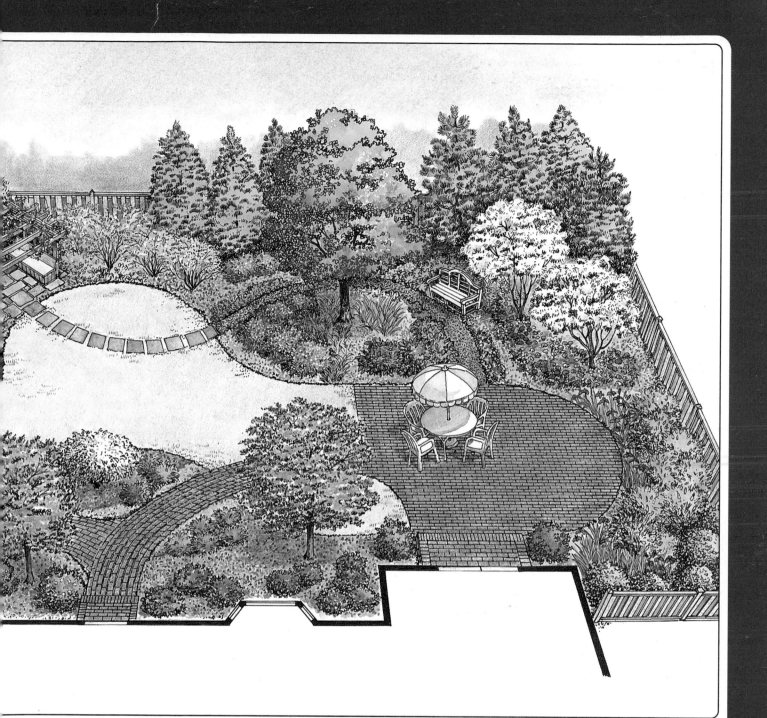

In this romantic garden devoted to especially sweet-smelling shrubs, you'll find special corners—an arbor, a patio and a wooden bench—pleasantly secluded. The repeated curves of the lawn, patio and paths to create a harmonious and restful space, where family and friends can enjoy the delightful sights and scents permeating the air.

GARDEN PLAN
HPT110032
Shown in Spring
Design by
Tom Nordloh

Romantic Outdoor Parties

Want to play a role from The Great Gatsby? Then close your eyes and imagine being a guest at a large party in this magnificent garden designed for formal entertaining. Imagine standing in the house at the French doors, just at the entrance to the paved area, and looking out at this perfectly symmetrical scene. The left mirrors the right; a major sight line runs straight down the center past the fountain to the statue that serves as a focal point at the rear of the garden. Three perfectly oval flowering trees on each side of the patio frame the sight line, as well as help to delineate the pavement from the planted areas of the garden.

The flagstone patio along the house rises several steps above the brick patio, giving it prominence and presenting a good view of the rest of the property. The change in paving materials provides a separate identity to each area, yet by edging the brick with bluestone to match the upper patio, the two are tied together.

Pink and purple flowering shrubs and perennials provide an elegant color scheme throughout the growing season. A vine-covered lattice panel, featuring royal purple flowers that bloom all summer long, creates a secluded area accessible by paving stones at the rear of the property. What a perfect spot for a romantic rendezvous!

Plan View

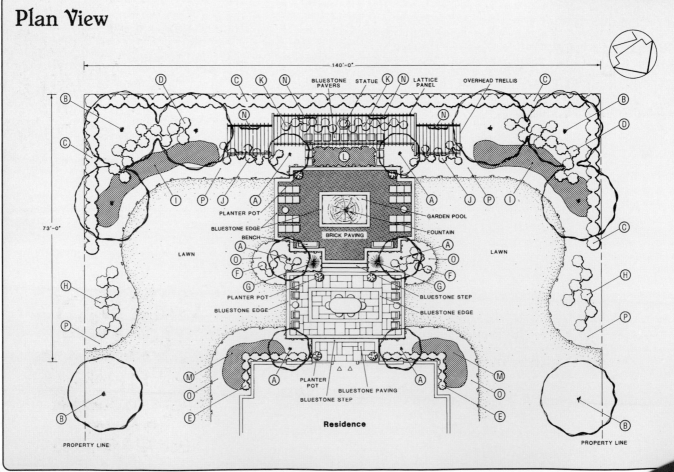

This formal garden provides a perfect setting for romantic outdoor parties or for simply relaxing in the sun on a Saturday afternoon.

GARDEN PLAN
HPT110033
Shown in Summer
Design by
Michael J. Opisso

Shady Backyard

Woe to the gardener who has to deal with established tall trees that cast a great deal of shade—a beautiful, colorful backyard is out of the question, right? Wrong! Nothing could be further from the truth, as demonstrated by this artfully designed shade garden.

The key to working with large existing trees is in using the shade as an asset, not as a liability, and in choosing shade-loving plants to grow beneath them. If the trees have a very dense canopy, branches can be selectively removed to thin the trees and create filtered shade below.

In this plan, the designer shapes the lawn and beds to respond to the locations of the trees. Note that all but one of the trees are situated in planting beds, not in open lawn. Placing a single tree in the lawn helps to integrate the lawn and planting beds, creating a cohesive design. At the right, the deep planting area is enhanced by pavers, a bench and a birdbath, creating an inviting, shady retreat. Near the house, a small patio provides a lounging spot; its curving shape echoes the curving form of the planting beds.

Throughout the garden, perennials, woody plants and groundcovers are arranged in drifts to create a comfortable and serene space. The garden is in constant but ever-changing bloom from early spring through fall, as its special plants—chosen because they thrive in just such a shady setting in their native habitats—go in and out of bloom. Fall brings big splashes of foliage color to complete the year-long show. To provide the finishing carpet to this beautiful and cool shade garden, choose a grass-seed variety selected to tolerate shade.

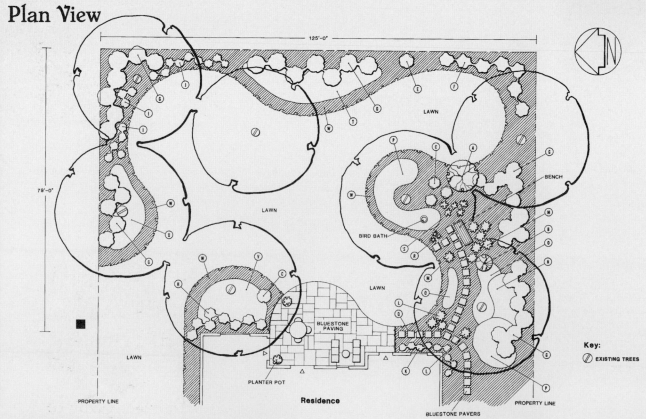

Plan View

LAWN

BENCH

BIRD BATH

LAWN

LAWN

BLUESTONE PAVING

PLANTER POT

LAWN

Residence

BLUESTONE PAVERS

PROPERTY LINE

PROPERTY LINE

Key:
⊘ EXISTING TREES

Shaded yards need not be dark and dull, as this backyard design demonstrates. Here, beneath the shadows of seven mature trees, a colorful collection of shade-loving shrubs, perennials and groundcovers flourishes.

GARDEN PLAN
HPT110034
Shown in Spring
Design by
Michael J. Opisso

Japanese-Style Garden

When a busy couple wants a landscape that is distinctive and requires little maintenance, the Japanese-style garden and backyard pictured here are a perfect solution. The essence of a Japanese garden lies in emulating nature through simple, clean lines that do not look contrived. The low, tight hedges underscore the plantings behind them, while providing a contrast in form. Looking straight out from the deck, the perimeter planting is a harmony of shades of green, with interest provided from contrasting textures.

Paving stones border the deck because, in the Japanese garden, every element has both an aesthetic and a functional purpose. The stones alleviate the wear that would result from stepping directly onto the lawn from the deck, and provide a visual transition between the man-made deck and the natural grass. The pavers act as more than a path; they also provide a sight line to the stone lantern on the left side of the garden.

The deck, like the rest of the landscape, has clean, simple lines and provides the transition from the home's interior to the garden. It surrounds a viewing garden, one step down. In the Japanese tradition, this miniature landscape mimics a natural scene. The one large moss rock plays an important role—it is situated at the intersection of the stepping-stone paths that lead through the garden. Here a decision must be made as to which way to turn. The stone water basin, a symbolic part of the Japanese tea ceremony, is located near the door to the house, signaling the entrance to a very special place.

Plan View

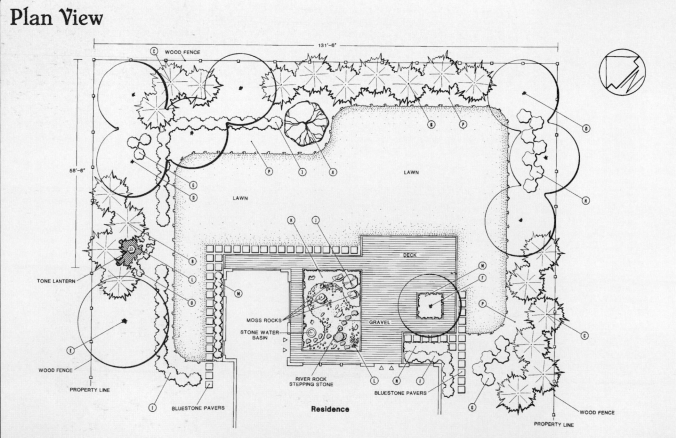

This beautiful Japanese-style garden provides space for outdoor living and entertaining in a tranquil setting. Featuring straight, simple lines, a small lawn, a large deck and extensive plantings of groundcovers and evergreens, the garden practically cares for itself.

GARDEN PLAN
HPT110035
Shown in Spring
Design by
Michael J. Opisso

Shady Flower Border

*I*f you're constantly complaining that nothing will grow in the shade of the trees in your backyard, consider planting this beautiful shady flower border. Lawn grass needs full sun and struggles to grow under trees, so why not plant something that flourishes in the shade and looks much prettier! This charming flower border features shade-loving perennials and ferns, fits under existing trees, and blooms from spring through fall. In this design, flowering perennials grow through a low evergreen groundcover, which keeps the garden pretty even in winter, when the perennials are dormant.

Also providing year-round interest are rocks and boulders, as well as a bench that invites you to sit and enjoy the pretty scene. The designer shows this garden against a fence along the property border, but you could plant it in front of a hedge or other shrubbery and place it anywhere in your yard. If your property is smaller, you can easily eliminate the corner containing the bench and end the border with the group of three rocks to the left of the bench.

Plan View

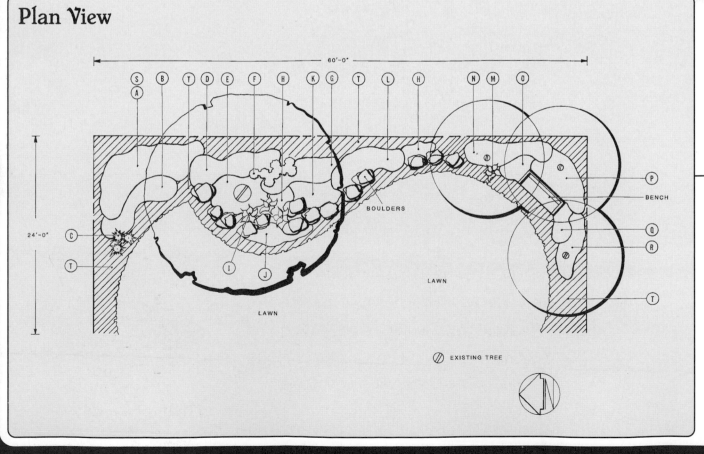

This garden of shade-loving plants flourishes under trees where grass struggles to survive. Be sure to keep the plants healthy by providing plenty of water and fertilizer, especially if the garden plants compete for moisture and nutrients with thirsty tree roots.

GARDEN PLAN
HPT110036
Shown in Summer
Design by
Michael J. Opisso

Street-Side Cottage Garden

Bursting with exuberant old-fashioned blossoms, this friendly cottage garden is designed to be enjoyed from both sides of the fence. The garden invites passersby to pause and enjoy the show from the street or sidewalk, thus creating a friendly neighborhood feeling. However, where space is very limited, you might prefer to plant only the inside of the fence and to plant the street side with a mowing strip of grass or a low-maintenance groundcover. You could even reverse the plan and install the hedge on the street side. Whether you have a side-walk or not, leave a buffer between the edge of the border and the street so that if you live in a cold-winter climate, there'll be room to pile snow.

Flowering perennial and annual climbing vines cover the wooden arbor, creating a romantic entrance. Roses, bulbs, perennials, annuals and a compact evergreen hedge are arranged in a classic cottage-garden style that is casual but not haphazard. The designer achieves a pleasant sense of unity by repeating plants and colors throughout the design without repeating a sym-metrical planting pattern. This helps create the casual feeling essential to a cottage garden.

Plan View

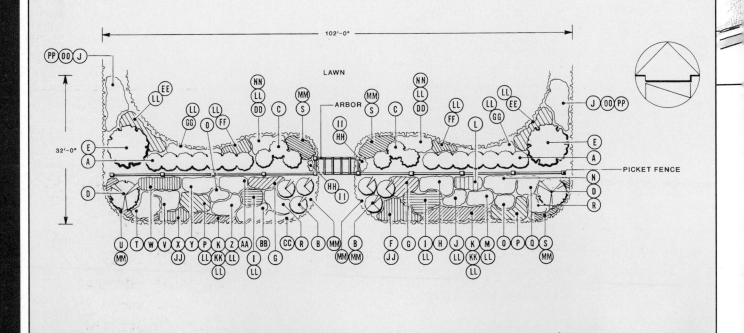

Create a friendly neighborhood feeling by planting this flower-filled cottage garden along the front of your property.

GARDEN PLAN
HPT110037
Shown in Summer
Design by
Maria Morrison

English Perennial Border

The British, being renowned gardeners, boast the prettiest flower gardens in the world. Their success in growing perennials to such perfection lies partly in the amenable British climate—cool summers, mild winters, plenty of moisture throughout the year and very long summer days. Even without such a perfect climate, North American gardeners can achieve a respectable show of perennials by using plants better adapted to their climate. Arrange them into the flowing drifts made popular early in this century by British landscape designers, and you'll have the epitome of a perennial garden in your own backyard.

The perennial border shown here fits nicely into a corner of almost any sunny backyard. Pictured with a traditional evergreen hedge as a backdrop for the flowers, the garden looks equally lovely planted in front of a fence or house wall, as long as the area receives at least six hours of full sun a day.

The designer carefully selected an array of spring-, summer- and fall-blooming perennials, arranging them in artful drifts for an ever-changing display. Spring and summer blooms paint a delightful pink, magenta and pale yellow color scheme sparked here and there with splashes of white and blue, while autumn brings deeper colors—gold, dark pink and purple. Patches of burgundy- and silver-hued foliage plants in the foreground help tie the elements of the garden together and play up the flowers.

Plan View

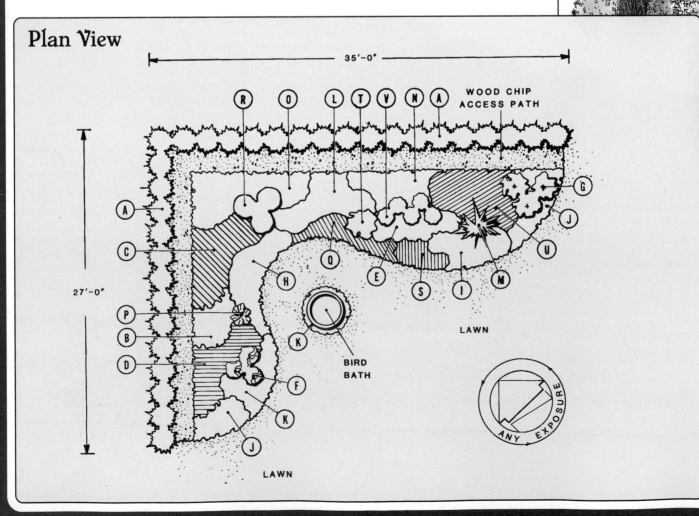

The English perennial border, with its graceful masses of ever-changing flowers, represents the epitome of fine perennial gardening. Planted in a corner of your property, this garden will provide enjoyment for years to come.

GARDEN PLAN
HPT110038
Shown in Summer
Design by
Michael J. Opisso

Low-Maintenance Island Bed

One of the great joys of a lovely low-maintenance garden is having the time to really enjoy it. If you'd like a garden bed that is eye-catching as well as easy-care, this design is for you. This bow-tie-shaped bed contains a delightful variety of low-maintenance perennials, evergreens, deciduous trees and shrubs, and spring bulbs. Such a diverse blend of easy-care plants guarantees you'll have both year-round color and the time to take pleasure in every season's display.

The berms at each end of the bed create a small valley that is traversed by a natural stone path. Trees screen the peak of the higher berm, adding a bit of mystery, and encouraging visitors to explore. Two pathways—one of mulch, the other of stepping stones—make it easy to enjoy the plantings up close and to perform maintenance tasks, such as occasional deadheading and weeding. Moss rocks in three areas of the garden and a birdhouse near the stepping-stone path provide pleasing structure and interest.

Plan View

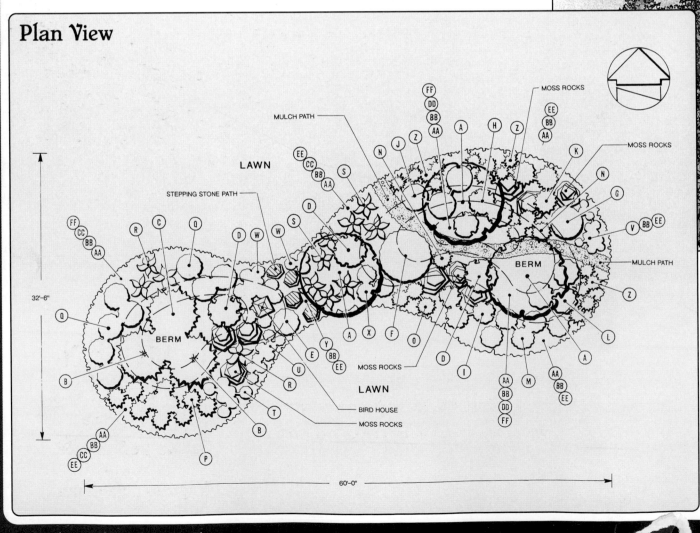

Locate this easy-care bed in an open area of lawn in the front- or backyard to create a pretty view that can be enjoyed from indoors and out.

GARDEN PLAN
HPT110039
Shown in Summer
Design by
Jeffery Diefenbach

Easy-Care English Border

A flower-filled garden created in the romantic style of an English border need not demand much care, as this lovely design illustrates. The designer carefully selects unfussy bulbs and perennials, and a few flowering shrubs, all of which are disease- and insect-resistant and noninvasive, and don't need staking or other maintenance. A balance of spring-, summer- and fall-blooming plants keeps the border exciting throughout the growing season. Because English gardens are famous for their gorgeous roses, the designer includes several rose-bushes, but chooses ones unharmed by bugs and mildew.

Hedges form a backdrop for most English flower gardens; the designer plants an informal one here to reduce pruning. A generous mulched path runs between the flowers and the hedge, so it's easy to tend them, while the edging keeps grass from invading and creating a nuisance. Plant this border along any sunny side of your property. Imagine it along the back of the yard, where you can view it from a kitchen window or from a patio or deck, along one side of the front yard, or planted with the hedge bordering the front lawn and providing privacy from the street.

Plan View

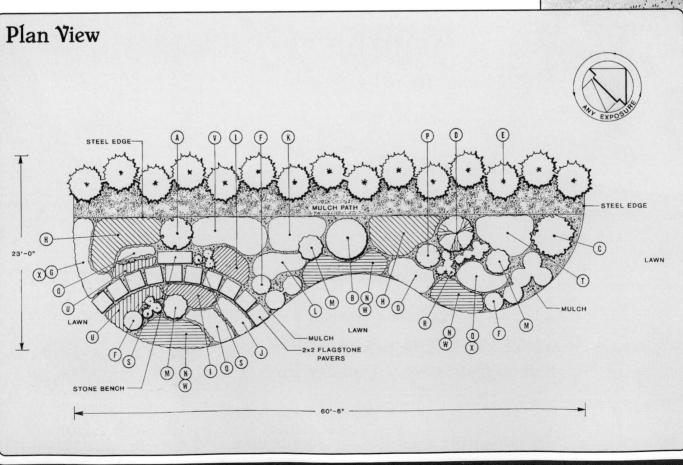

*Brimming with easy-care flowers from spring through fall,
this low-maintenance flower border evokes the spirit of an
English garden, but doesn't require a staff to take care of it.*

GARDEN PLAN
HPT110040
Shown in Summer
Design by
Maria Morrison

Blue-and-Yellow Island Bed

Blue and yellow flowers planted together reward the gardener with a naturally complementary color scheme that's as bright and pretty as any garden can be. It's hard to err when using these colors, because the pure blues and the lavender blues—whether dark or pastel—look just as pretty with the pale lemon yellows as with the bright sulfur yellows and the golden yellows. Each combination makes a different statement, some subtle and sweet as with the pastels, and others bold and demanding as with the deep vivid hues. But no combination fails to please.

The designer of this beautiful bed, which can be situated in any sunny spot, effectively orchestrated a sequence of blue-and-yellow-flowering perennials so the garden blooms from spring through fall. The designer not only combined the floral colors beautifully together, but also incorporated various flower shapes and textures so they make a happy opposition. Fluffy, rounded heads of blossoms set off elegant spires, and mounded shapes mask the lanky stems of taller plants. Large, funnel-shaped flowers stand out against masses of tiny, feathery flowers like jewels displayed against a silk dress.

Although the unmistakable color scheme for this garden is blue and yellow, the designer sprinkled in an occasional spot of orange to provide a lovely jolt of brightly contrasting color. A few masses of creamy white flowers frost the garden, easing the stronger colors into a compatible union.

Plan View

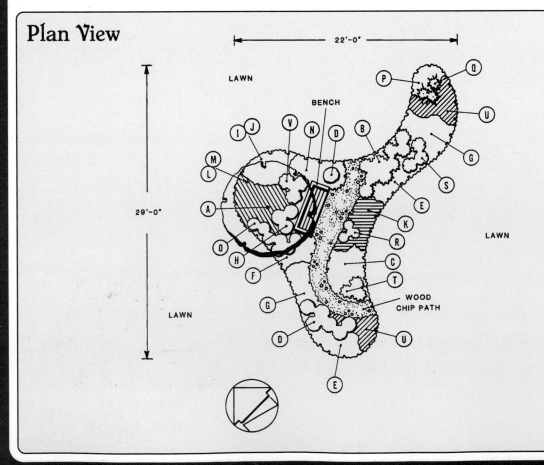

Natural color companions, blue and yellow flowers create a pleasing garden scene that looks great anywhere it's planted. This island bed works perfectly in an open sunny yard, but it could be modified to fit along the side of a house or to the back up against a fence or hedge along a property border.

GARDEN PLAN

HPT110041

Shown in Summer

Design by

Damon Scott

Sunny Location

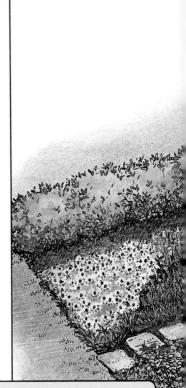

If you'd like to have an easy-care garden that offers more than a single burst of brilliant color, this season-spanning border packed with perennials is perfect for you. The designer selects a wide array of perennials that begin flowering in the spring, provide plenty of color throughout the summer and continue blooming into the fall. All you'll need to do is remove spent blossoms from time to time and divide plants every few years.

A deciduous hedge curves around the back of the border, providing a pleasant foil for the perennials throughout the growing season. Before dropping its leaves in autumn, the hedge puts on its own show of dazzling color just as the perennials are beginning to slow down. Once the perennials have finished blooming, you can leave the dried flower heads on the plants to add subtle beauty to the winter landscape.

The classic curved shape of this border will fit easily into a corner of your front- or backyard. If you have a large yard, you may want to install this border on one side with its mirror image on the other and with a path set between them.

Plan View

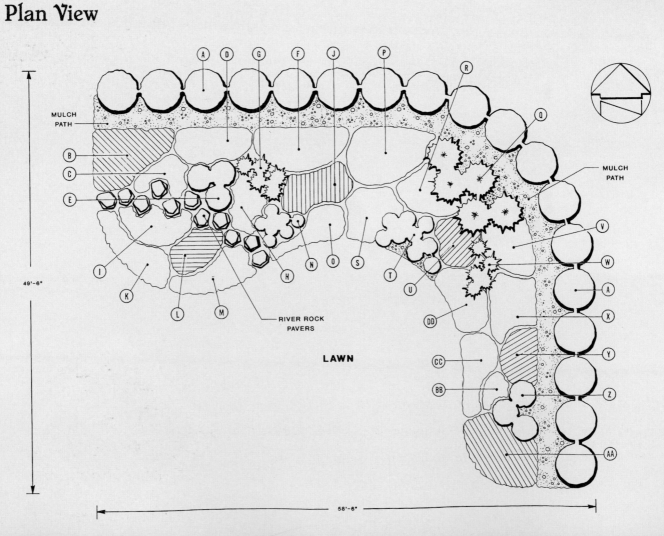

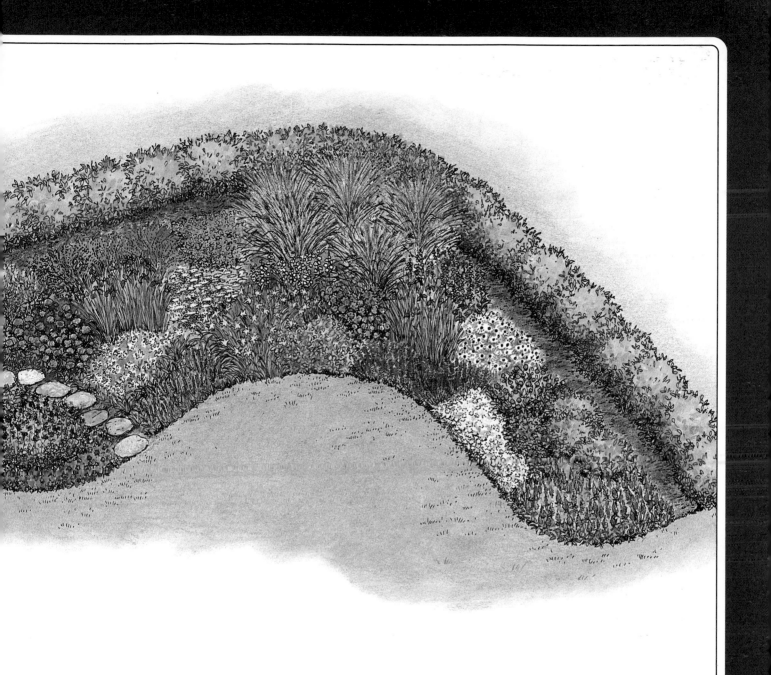

This bed brims with flower color from spring through fall, so be sure to site it in a sunny location where you can enjoy the scene from both indoors and out.

GARDEN PLAN
HPT110042
Shown in Summer
Design by
Maria Morrison

Raised Flower Bed

A colorful, easy-care flower bed like this paisley-shaped raised bed can be located almost anywhere on your property—it is perfectly suitable as an entry garden or as a transition between different levels in a backyard. The bed's curving, organic shape echoes the sinuous stone wall that divides its upper and lower sections. Flagstone steps further divide the bed and lead visitors from the lower, more symmetrical area to the upper, more asymmetrical section of the garden.

The designer incorporates lovely low-growing flowering perennials to spill over the wall, creating a curtain of flowers. Twin flowering shrubs flank the entry steps, while a single specimen of the same type marks the exit. The rest of the bed is planted with a profusion of easy-care perennials, bulbs, ornamental grasses and flowering shrubs.

This garden bed requires only a little of your precious time for routine maintenance. You'll need to remove spent blossoms, do a bit of cleanup in spring and fall, and divide the perennials every few years.

Plan View

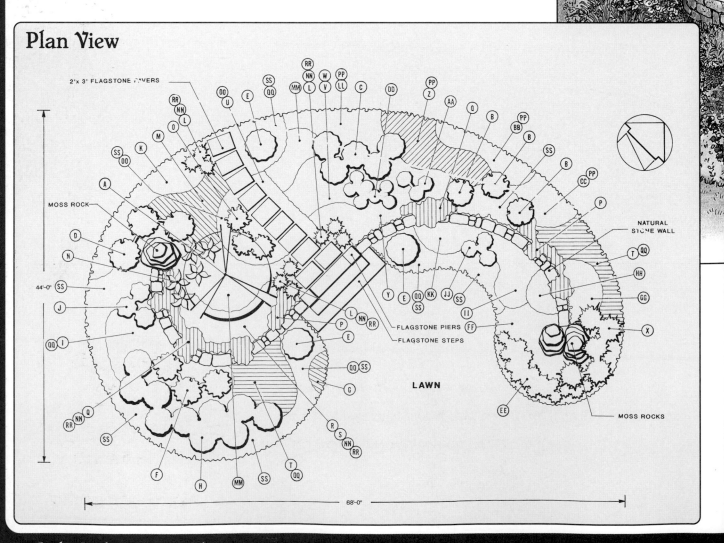

A curving stone retaining wall and small flowering tree give this flower garden dimension and form, which keep it attractive throughout the year.

GARDEN PLAN
HPT110043
Shown in Summer
Design by
Salvatore A. Masullo

Old-Fashioned Roses and Perennials

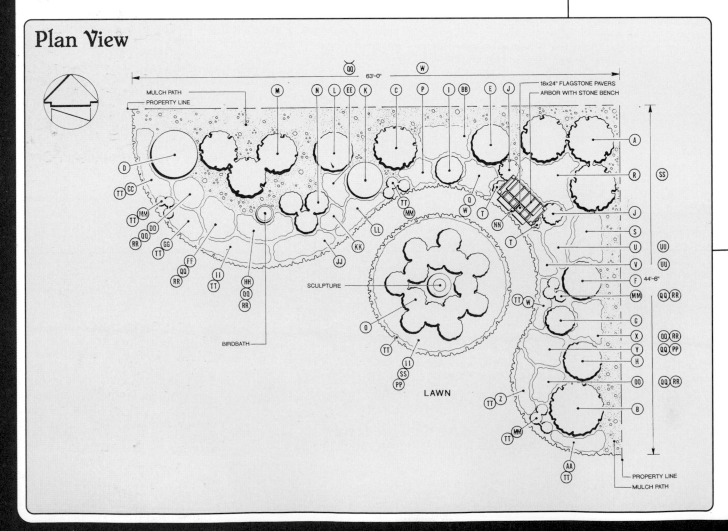

A romantic old-fashioned rose border is always in style. The voluptuous fragrance and heavy-petaled blossoms of roses bring charm to any sunny garden. Here, the designer chooses old garden roses, which offer scent as well as ease of care, unlike modern hybrid tea roses. Although many of these cherished plants bloom only once during the season, their other charms far outweigh the repeat-blossoms of their modern cousins. Many have excellent summer and fall foliage and a heavy crop of glossy rose hips in autumn.

In this border design, these belles of the garden are mixed with classic perennial partners and bulbs to create months of color and interest. A circular bed is tucked into this pleasingly curved border and is separated by a ribbon-like strip of lawn. A rose-covered pergola in the border frames a classically inspired sculpture in the bed's center, creating two balanced focal points. A stone bench placed under the arbor provides a lovely spot to contemplate the wonders of this flower-filled haven. Mulched pathways at the back of the border allow easy access for maintenance and for cutting flowers for the house.

Plan View

MULCH PATH
PROPERTY LINE

63'-0"

18x24" FLAGSTONE PAVERS
ARBOR WITH STONE BENCH

44'-6"

SCULPTURE

BIRDBATH

LAWN

PROPERTY LINE
MULCH PATH

Designed to beautify the corner of a backyard, this rose-filled border can be easily turned into a free-standing bed and placed in the center of a lawn by rounding off the straight sides into a more free-flowing shape.

GARDEN PLAN
HPT110044
Shown in Summer
Design by
Maria Morrison

Water-Wise Perennials

Although dry, sunny sites can be challenging, it's possible to enjoy a lush, colorful garden even in areas of your yard with fast-draining, sandy soil and full-sun exposure. Place this three-pronged bed anywhere in your landscape that gets the full force of the sun. The garden will be sure to thrive, since the designer takes special care to select water-thrifty plants.

Once these water-wise perennials become established, you'll expend very little effort keeping them watered. Keep in mind, however, that even drought-tolerant perennials need to be well watered during the first year after planting. And during periods of extreme heat or prolonged drought, you'll probably need to water a bit more than usual.

This colorful garden is divided into three planting areas by two shredded-mulch paths. A wooden arbor over one path adds structure, provides a visual anchor, and creates interesting shadows as the sun passes overhead. Moss rocks create a second, stronger visual anchor and furnish a backdrop for the surrounding plants. The ornamental grasses and yuccas add height and a sense of balance to the composition.

Plan View

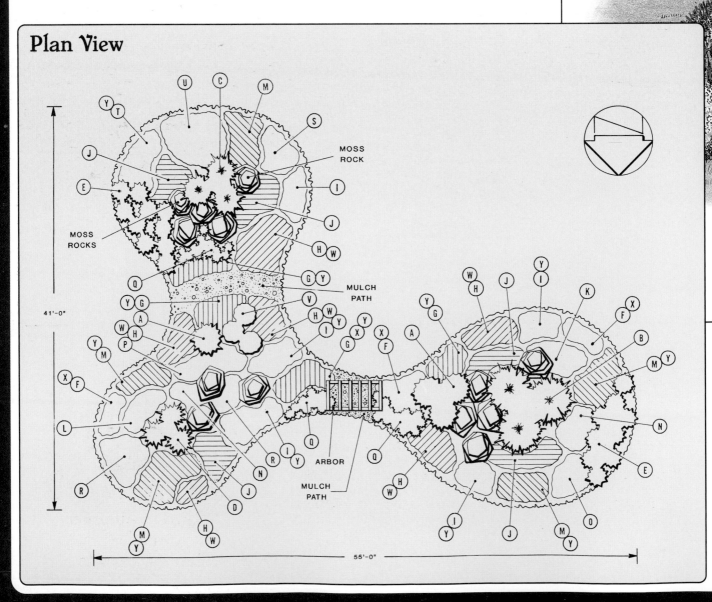

Not all flowers need even moisture and rich soil to perform well. This design features a beautiful array of perennials that bloom prolifically in poor soil and drought conditions.

GARDEN PLAN
HPT110045
Shown in Summer
Design by
Patrick J. Duffe

Easy-Care Shrub Border

Nothing beats flowering shrubs and trees for an easy-care show of flowers and foliage throughout the seasons. This lovely garden includes shrubs that bloom at various times of the year—from late winter right into autumn—so that blossoms will always be decorating this garden. In autumn, the leaves of the deciduous shrubs turn flaming shades of yellow, gold, orange and red. (These colors appear even more brilliant when juxtaposed against the deep greens of the evergreen shrubs.) During the coldest months, when the flowers and fall foliage are finally finished, many of the plants feature glossy red berries or evergreen leaves that take on deep burgundy hues.

The designer balances the border with a tall evergreen and two flowering trees, which serve as anchors at the border's widest points. Most shrubs are grouped in all-of-a-kind drifts to create the most impact—low, spreading types in the front and taller ones in the back—but several specimens appear alone as eye-catching focal points. A few large drifts of easy-care, long-blooming perennials, interplanted with spring-flowering bulbs, break up the shrubbery to give a variety of textures and forms.

Designed for the back of an average-sized lot, this easy-care border can be located in any sunny area of your property. It makes a perfect addition to any existing property with only a high-maintenance lawn and little other landscaping. The design adds year-round interest, creates privacy and reduces maintenance.

Plan View

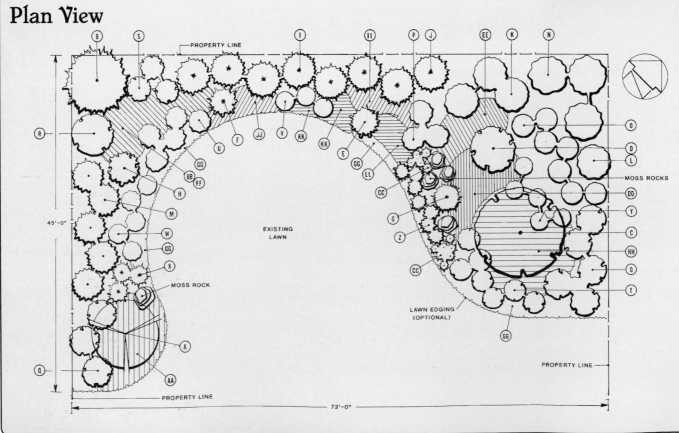

When easy-care, disease- and insect-resistant shrubs are used to create a border, and allowed to grow naturally without excessive pruning, the result is a beautiful, practically maintenance-free garden.

GARDEN PLAN
HPT110046
Shown in Spring
Design by
Salvatore A. Masullo

Red, White and Blue Flower Garden

Let the colors of Old Glory shine in your yard with this red, white and blue flower garden. Designed as a dramatic island bed to be planted in any open, sunny location in your yard, this versatile garden features combinations of flowering perennials and annuals carefully selected so the bed blooms from spring through fall in an ever-changing display of the colors of the flag. The long-blooming annuals, which should be planted in the spots where bulbs flower in spring, provide a constant mass of color against which the perennials bloom in an exciting sequence.

Red can be a difficult color in the garden, since scarlet tones, with their hints of orange, clash terribly with crimson shades, with their hints of blue or purple. Likewise, blue comes in many tints, not all of which combine well with the various reds. White flowers separate and calm the strong blues and reds of this bold color scheme, giving the garden brightness and sparkle. The designer selected the flowers for their pure, bright colors, choosing ones that blossom in the red and blue tints that look great together and that will assuredly look superb when planted as the centerpiece of your backyard.

The designer planned the garden in a somewhat formal fashion, with blocks of plants laid out around a wood-chip path and central flagpole. The path affords you access to the flowers for easy planting and tending, while bringing you right into the garden where you can enjoy the flowers at close range.

Plan View

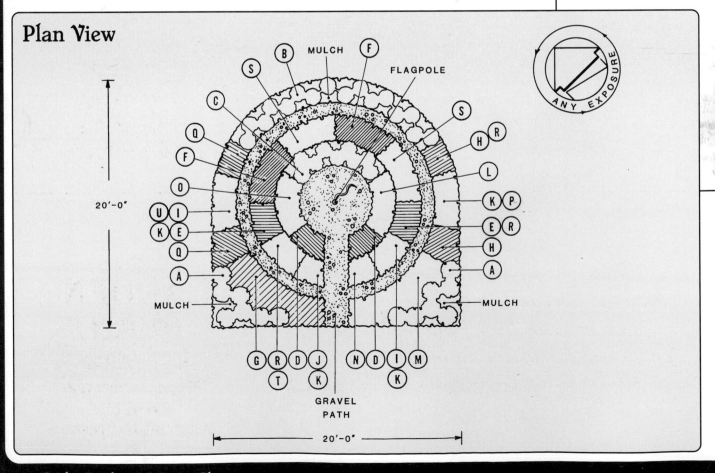

The bold and dramatic color scheme of this island flower bed is further emphasized by the formal nature of the garden plan. Geometrically laid out in changing bands of flowers, the garden forms a dynamic centerpiece for any summer yard.

GARDEN PLAN
HPT110047
Shown in Summer
Design by
Michael J. Opisso

Photo courtesy of the Netherlands Flower Bulb Information Center

Breathtaking Landscapes:

48 woodland & wildflower designs

A carefully planned and lovingly maintained landscape adds appeal to any home, particularly if the landscape and home complement each other. The following pages present 48 landscape designs which work with a variety of homes and lots. Some of these landscapes are designed to surround specific home styles, while others are intended to work around swimming pools, corner lots and play structures. Browse through these professionally designed landscapes to find the one that's right for your home and yard.

Easy-Care Plants

The landscape around this rustic stone-fronted house is truly charming. The designer organizes the space into separate, easily maintained units that blend into a pleasing whole. The planting pockets—in front of the large window and the two areas bisected by pavers to the right of the drive—contain well-behaved plants that require little care to maintain their good looks. The small island of lawn can be quickly mowed, and maintenance is further reduced if lawn edging is installed, eliminating the need to edge by hand. A ribbon of small and moderate-sized shrubs, underplanted with a weed-smothering groundcover and spring bulbs, surrounds the lawn.

A single deciduous tree, set in a circle of bulbs and easy-care perennials that juts into the lawn, screens the entryway from street view and balances a triad of slow-growing, narrow conifers to the far left of the house. Shrubs in front of the windows were chosen for their low, unobtrusive growth habit. A dwarf conifer with pendulous branches forms the focus of the shrub grouping in front of the larger window.

Paving is a strong unifying force in this design. The stone in the house facade is echoed in the walk that curves from the driveway up the steps to the landing and front door. Flagstone pavers border the other side of the drive and lead around the house. The cobblestone inlay at the foot of the drive not only breaks up the monotony of the asphalt, but also visually carries the lawn border across the entire width of the property. Also shown here is home plan HPB854 by Home Planners. For information about ordering blueprints for this home, call 1-800-521-6797.

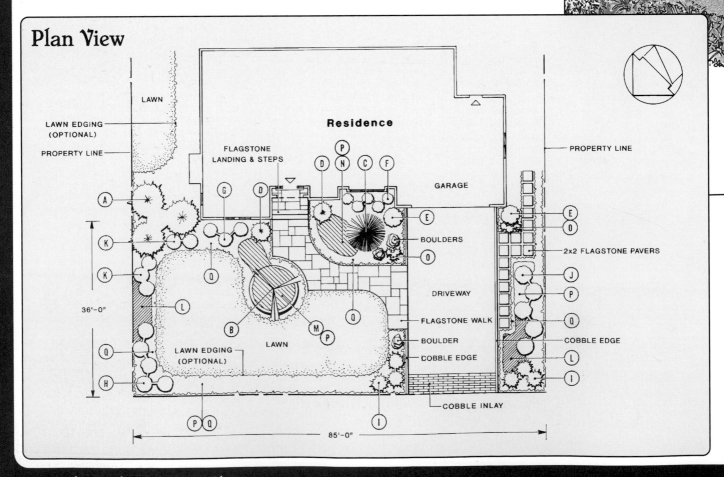

Plan View

Although packed with interesting plants, this landscape is quite manageable for the easy-care gardener. Mowing the little island of lawn is a snap, and caring for the rest of the yard is just as easy, considering the shrubs don't need pruning and fall cleanup is minimal.

LANDSCAPE PLAN
HPT110048
Shown in Spring
Design by
Salvatore A. Masullo

Graceful Grasses

Graceful, curving foundation plantings really make this landscape! Set against a carpet of green grass, the mixed plantings contain shrubs, perennials, bulbs and groundcovers chosen for compactness as well as for attractive foliage and flowers. One of a trio of handsome multi-trunked deciduous trees with attractive peeling bark anchors the largest planting. Set near the porch, the tree contributes cool shade during the summer.

The tree to the far left softens the driveway, as do the cobblestones bordering the asphalt. Like the cobbles, the other paving materials—brick and flagstone—are selected for their compatibility with the house style. A brick walk leads to an arching entry landing set at the base of the stairs. The curved landing and planting beds echo the curves in the porch detail and some of the windows. Both the walk and terrace are edged with flagstone, a material repeated in the pavers leading from the opposite side of the driveway to the back of the house.

The third tree in the triangle is planted at the front of the lawn, where its picturesque bark can be admired close up by passersby. At the same time that the tree attracts attention, it also provides some screening and privacy. It is set in a ring of mulch for easy mowing. Also shown here is home plan HPB974 by Home Planners. For information about ordering blueprints for this home, call 1-800-521-6797.

Plan View

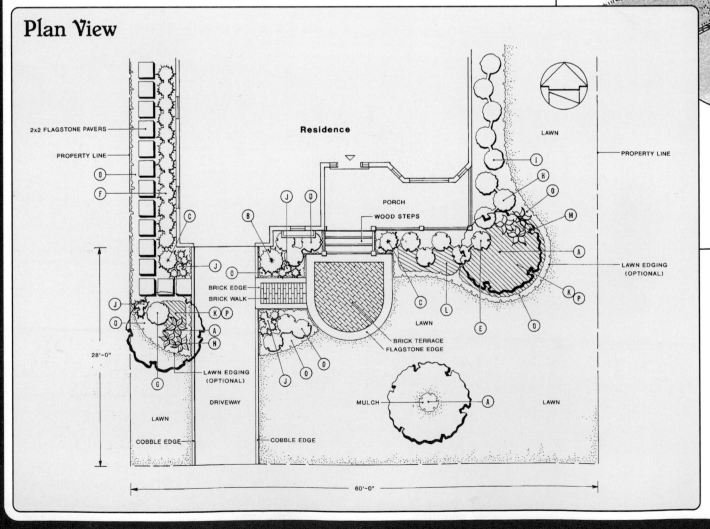

The foundation border curving around the house provides the main source of interest in this landscape. However, maintaining it won't tax the easy-care gardener because the plants are compact and disease-resistant.

LANDSCAPE PLAN
HPT110049
Shown in Summer
Design by
Damon Scott

Split-Level Landscape

The first step the landscape designer of this traditional split-level took was to make the rolling grade of the property an asset rather than a liability. The designer created a strong sense of entry with brick paving that angles from the driveway to the front door. These angles do more than add interest to the squareness of the house—they also present a pleasing sequence of entry, transition and arrival. This sequence is not only more visually appealing than a flat walkway coupled with a set of steps leading directly to the door, but also makes maneuvering from the driveway to the front door easier. The brick-and-timber combination for the walks and retaining walls offers a pleasing, informal quality that echoes the brick on the house.

Creating an entrance with various levels also allowed the designer to extend one of the steps into a retaining wall, which defines a key planting area. The small ornamental tree in this bed acts as a focal point and enhances the entry by providing privacy and enclosure. The sweeping bed lines, together with the three large shade trees, serve to unify the changes in height of both the house and the landscape. Also shown here is home plan HPA981 by Home Planners. For information about ordering blueprints for this home, call 1-800-521-6797.

Plan View

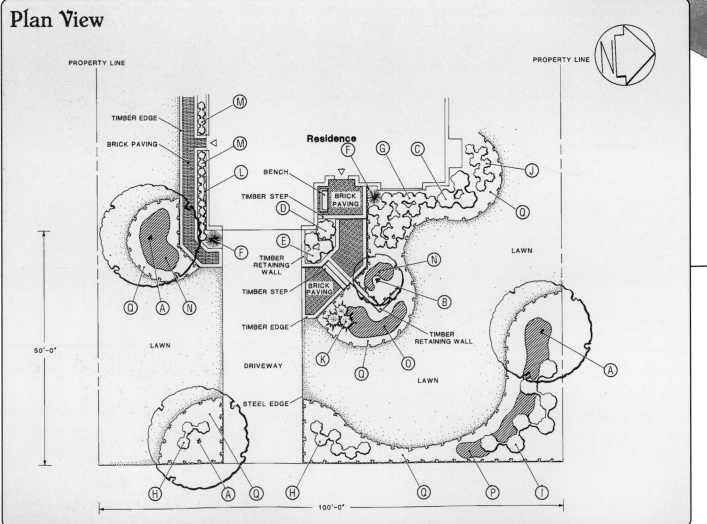

PROPERTY LINE

PROPERTY LINE

TIMBER EDGE

BRICK PAVING

Residence

BENCH

TIMBER STEP

BRICK PAVING

TIMBER RETAINING WALL

TIMBER STEP

BRICK PAVING

TIMBER EDGE

TIMBER RETAINING WALL

LAWN

LAWN

LAWN

DRIVEWAY

STEEL EDGE

50'-0"

100'-0"

A unique landscaping treatment can transform an ordinary split-level home into a showplace that stands out from its neighbors. Here, a multi-level entrance and a beautiful combination of plants create a year-round garden-like setting around the walkway.

LANDSCAPE PLAN
HPT110050
Shown in Spring
Design by
Michael J. Opisso

Sweet Symmetry

This extended Cape poses several challenges to the designer. Situated on a corner lot, the house needs access to both streets, but the noise from cars stopping at the intersection needs to be muffled. The two doors located in the front of the house should be distinguished and the long lines of the house played down. The landscape design provides walks leading to both entries while clearly defining the dominant main entrance with a formal brick entry court. Partially hidden by an upright shrub, the entrance to the breezeway remains out of view but is still easily accessible by family members. The semicircular planting bed in front of the walkway leading to the breezeway breaks up the long lines of the brick walk and lawn while balancing the large planting beds beside the house.

The landscape on either side of the front door features symmetrically placed trees and shrubs to reflect the formality of the brick entryway. Tall, uniformly oval trees complement the formal design while softening the long lines of the house.

Because the house is located on a corner, access to the street with a front walkway is desirable. For unity and harmony, the same brick used in the walkway across the front of the house is used in the front walk. An extensive shrub border screens the view of the house from the intersection and stifles traffic noise. A variety of shrubs and perennials makes up this border to provide interest throughout the year.

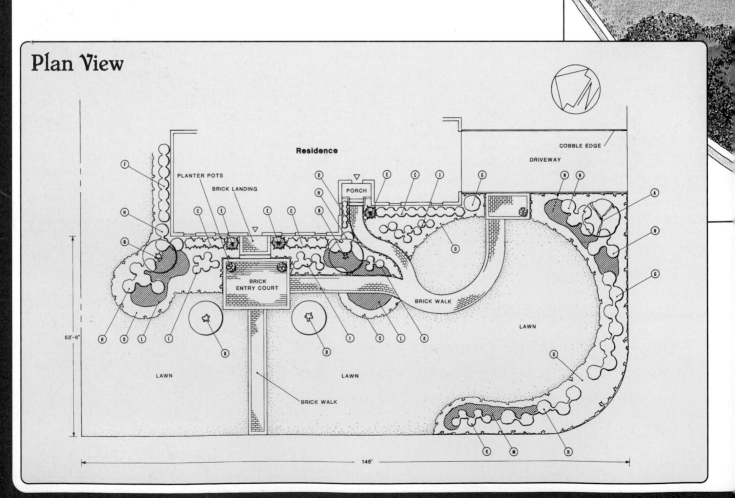

Plan View

Corner properties pose special landscaping challenges.
Here the landscape designer screens the street with a colorful
shrub border. A formal walkway leads from the main street,
where guests might park, to the front door. A more informal
walk provides access from the driveway to both entrances.

LANDSCAPE PLAN
HPT 110051
Shown in Autumn
Design by
Michael J. Opisso

Cape Cod Character

The quaint character of this traditional Cape Cod home calls for an intimate, comfortable landscape that reflects the formality of the house without being stiff or unfriendly. Notice how the repetition of curves throughout the landscape works to unite the design into a cohesive whole. The clean curving line of the large shrub border, which sweeps directly from the foundation planting toward the street, is repeated in the smaller curves of the planting borders along the street and in the shapes of the lawn areas. The stone walk and the driveway feature flowing curves. The front walk attractively leads to both the driveway and the street, where guests will probably park their cars.

Loose, informally-shaped trees soften the lines of the house and complement the curves of the landscape. By positioning these trees at the front edge of the property and in the center of the walkway, the designer buffered the view of the house from the street, creating a sense of privacy while framing the home. Evergreen foundation shrubs used near the house match the traditional style of the architecture. Elsewhere, flowering shrubs provide seasonal color.

This landscape design works successfully because the gentle, repetitive lines and forms, which remain apparent even in the winter, unify the property, making it seem larger than it is. Also shown here is home plan HPB657 by Home Planners. For information about ordering blueprints for this home, call 1-800-521-6797.

Plan View

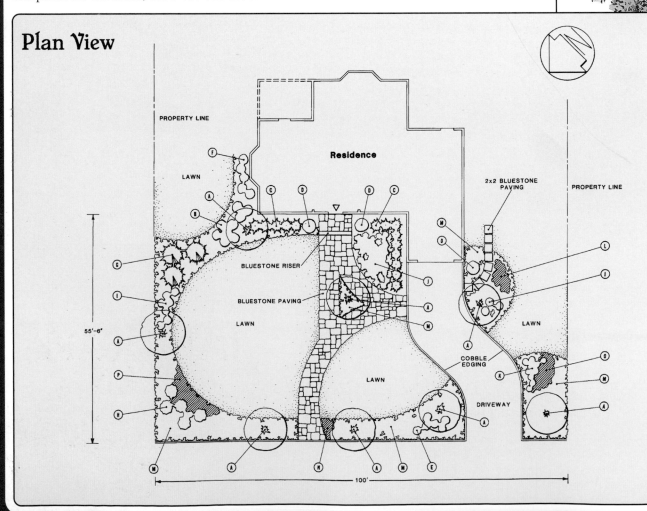

Repetition of forms, curves and paving unifies the landscape design for this traditional New England-style home.

LANDSCAPE PLAN
HPT110052
Shown in Spring
Design by
James Morgan

Gambrel-Roof Colonial

With two entries close to each other at the front of the house, it is imperative that the landscaping for this gambrel-roof Colonial home defines the formal or dominant entry—the one to which a visitor should go. This is accomplished by framing and blocking views.

Notice how small ornamental trees frame the large entry court that leads to the main door. The tree nearest the house blocks the view of the door leading to the family room while it also frames the walk and adds color and interest to the landscape. A low-growing evergreen hedge behind the tree aids in screening, so the visitor perceives only one walkway and one door. Access to the secondary door from the backyard, garage or driveway is by a walkway at the back of this screen planting.

The weeping evergreen and summer-flowering shrubs bordering the outside of the front walkway direct the view up the walk and to the front door. This bed extends into a curving border of trees, shrubs, perennials and groundcovers, which is echoed on the other side of the property. These border plantings provide privacy from neighbors or a side street and, since one cannot see behind the house, further define the front garden. Also shown here is home plan HPB131 by Home Planners. For information about ordering blueprints for this home, call 1-800-521-6797.

Plan View

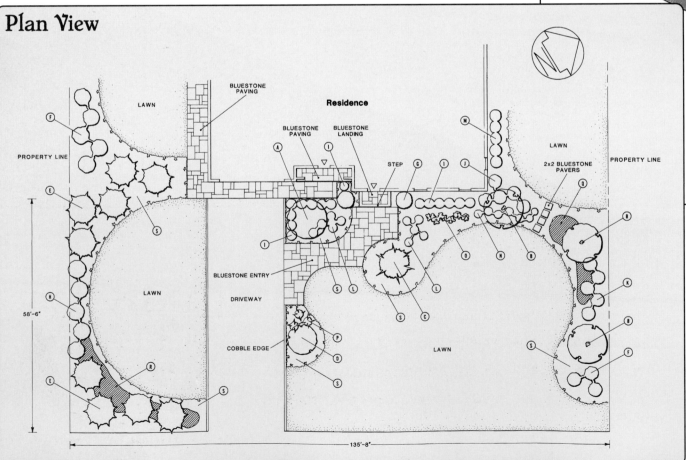

The skillful placement of ornamental trees and shrubs in this landscape design frames the walk and front door, leading the eye and visitors past the secondary entrance and directly to the main entrance.

LANDSCAPE PLAN
HPT110053
Shown in Spring
Design by
Michael J. Opisso

Brick Federal

The architecture of the brick Federal house might remind you of a trip to Colonial Williamsburg, and so too does the formality and grandeur of the landscape design. The key to the success and beauty of this design is its simplicity and symmetry, reflecting the symmetrical and repetitive lines of the house. If you fold the plan in half, it is identical on both sides with the exception of the driveway.

The symmetry is carried out in two ways. One is by mirror-imaging from left to right—note the placement of the large shade trees on either side of the house, the repetition of the foundation plants and the border plants, and the symmetrical paved area in front of the entry, flanked by two circular lawn areas. In the second way, the lines of symmetry go from the front of the landscape to the back—note the repetition of the same trees on either side of the two-foot-high wall, the use of brick in the wall to match the brick of the home, and the repetition of stone piers on each end of the wall. These, in turn, exactly line up with the stone piers at both sides of the entry, creating a feeling of a courtyard in the circular driveway.

The plants used in this design provide a graceful setting that gives the home a sense of performance. Here and there, flowers, berries and fall foliage provide spots of seasonal color, but the overall feeling is one of quiet, cool greenery. The elegance of this design matches the elegance of the house, reflecting well upon the good taste of the owners. Also shown here is home plan HPB662 by Home Planners. For information about ordering blueprints for this home, call 1-800-521-6797.

Plan View

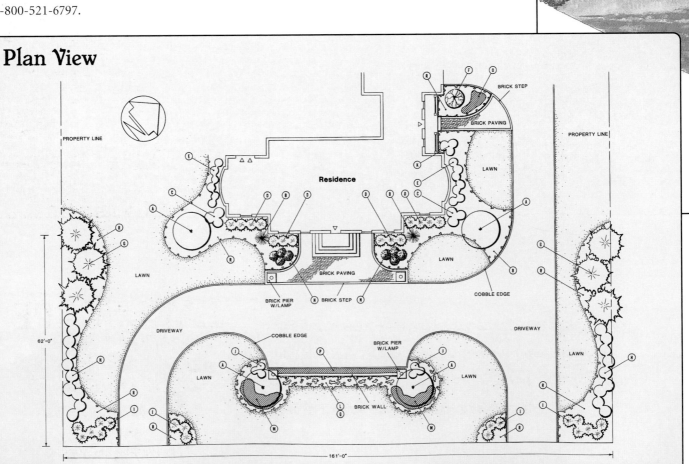

The success and beauty of this landscape design come from the clean lines and symmetry of the plantings, which reflect the formality of the brick Federal home both from left to right and from front to back.

LANDSCAPE PLAN
HPT110054
Shown in Spring
Design by
David Poplawski

Basic Yet Special

The basic ranch house with its clean, simple lines makes a perfect starter house, retirement retreat or home for small families. Its small size dictates an understated landscape design. In answer, the designer created an attractive yet straightforward plan that sets it apart from similar homes in the neighborhood.

Access to the front door is easy and appealing by way of the curved brick paving—a more attractive choice than a straight walkway. The semicircular foundation planting creates a homey setting while extending the architecture forward, making the house appear larger than it is. Within this bed, a small flowering tree softens the corner while adding seasonal color. Because space is limited, an espalier grows flat against the wall near the entrance, providing sculptural interest and color while taking up minimal space.

Although the plan is asymmetrical, the informal repetition of forms on each side of the driveway balances the design. The brick walk leading to the front door is echoed by the walk leading to the back of the house. On each side of the driveway entrance, a decorative fence, whose horizontal boards respond to the horizontal siding on the house, ties the two sides of the design together. Along the property line, an elongated oval of lawn bordered by shrubs and flowering perennials creates an attractive alternative to the strip of lawn so commonly seen in side yards. This bed is picked up on the other side of the driveway and continued along the street, visually unifying the entire landscape. Also shown here is home plan HPA920 by Home Planners. For information about ordering blueprints for this home, call 1-800-521-6797.

Plan View

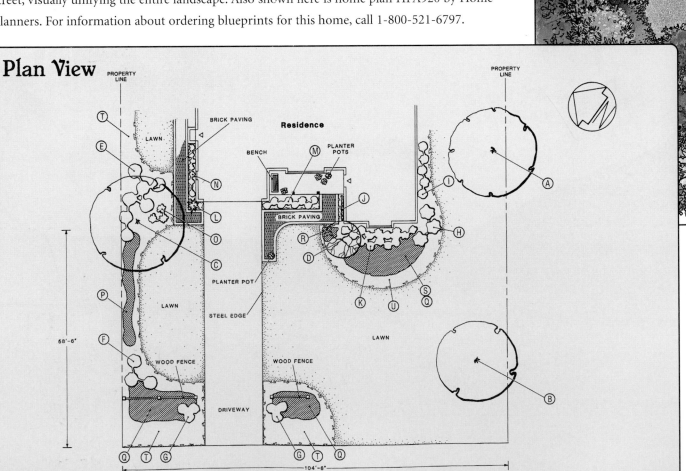

Basic, yet special, the landscaping for this ranch house fits it perfectly, creating a homey setting and making the property appear larger than it is because of the open design. Finished with a fence that echoes the clapboard siding, this house will stand out among similar homes in the neighborhood.

LANDSCAPE PLAN
HPT110055
Shown in Spring
Design by
Michael J. Opisso

Classic Colonial

The success of this landscape design relies on using simple, clean lines and forms to balance the squareness and flat facade of this classic New England home. The foundation planting curves around and extends beyond the house, making it appear longer. The outlines of the shrub borders on both sides of the property transcribe a huge circle, enclosing a circular lawn area that perfectly balances the mass of the house. The curved walkway leading from the driveway provides a graceful entrance to the house, while the brick inlay at the front of the driveway announces the transition from public street to private residence.

Large trees situated in both the lawn and the planting borders integrate the two areas, soften the facade of the house, and provide privacy and cooling summer shade. Flowering, deciduous and evergreen shrubs are used along both property lines for spring color. Rather than using an underplanting of groundcovers to unify the planting beds, the designer chooses to dress up the beds with an organic mulch of wood chips, in keeping with a tidy, neatly groomed New England look.

Fencing on each side of the house separates the front yard from the backyard and helps to elongate the lines of the house. It is partly camouflaged by three small trees, which help to block the view beyond the front of the house and balance the visual weight of the garage. Also shown here is home plan HPB731 by Home Planners. For information about ordering blueprints for this home, call 1-800-521-6797.

Plan View

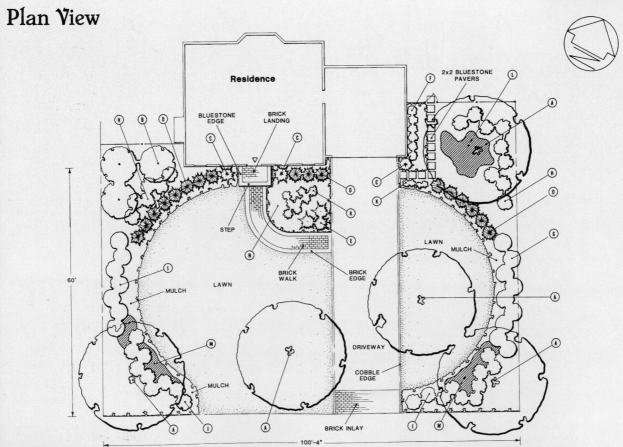

The uncomplicated sweeping lines of this front yard reflect the tidy, neatly groomed appearance one expects to find in Colonial New England, while at the same time softening the flatness and "saltbox" look of the house.

LANDSCAPE PLAN
HPT110056
Shown in Spring
Design by
Damon Scott

Center-Hall Colonial

Devoid of shutters and other ornamentation, this handsome center-hall Colonial home could look austere without the right kind of landscaping. The design presented here uses soft-textured shade trees and a deep bed of shrubs accented with perennials and groundcovers to alleviate any sense of starkness posed by this huge formal home.

The straight driveway and front walk were designed to be functional as well as to match the clean lines of the home's architecture. To create interest and contrast with these straight lines, the brick entry court is circular. The brick inlay at the front of the driveway matches the brick paving on the walkway, defining the entrance to the driveway while unifying the design. Strong, curved planting beds and lawn shapes further relieve the symmetry and formality of the house and walkway. Notice how the curving line of the lawn carries through to the foundation planting in front of the garage to complete the sweeping line. By mounding the soil in the front bed into a berm and planting a small ornamental tree there, the designer adds height, interest and a third dimension to the flat facade of the house. The lawn trees also soften the flatness of the house and partially block the view from the street, providing privacy and scale. Also shown here is home plan HPB610 by Home Planners. For information about ordering blueprints for this home, call 1-800-521-6797.

Plan View

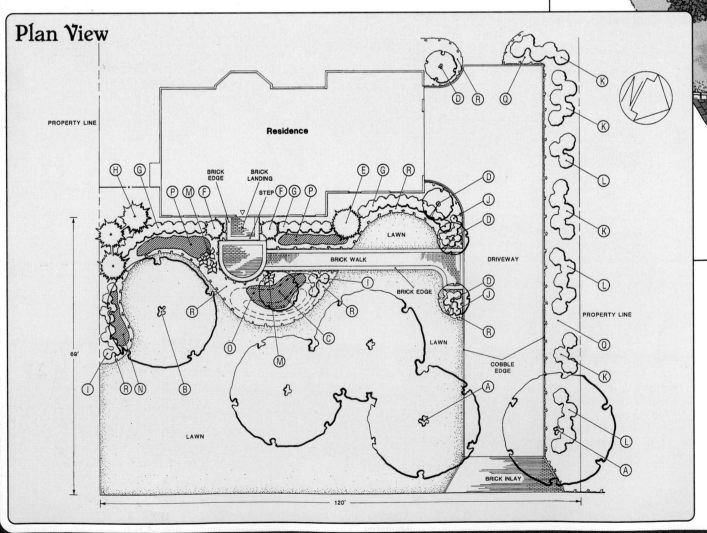

The landscape designer transforms this large, formal straight-lined house into a warm, welcoming home with the artistic use of soft-textured trees and shrubs combined with colorful perennials in gracefully curving beds. The resulting landscape brings the house to life.

LANDSCAPE PLAN
HPT110057
Shown in Summer
Design by
Damon Scott

Country-Style Farmhouse

Set in a friendly and homey landscape brimming with flowers from spring through fall, this farmhouse's country atmosphere is now complete. Masses of perennials and bulbs used throughout the property create a garden setting and provide armloads of flowers that can be cut for indoor bouquets. But the floral beauty doesn't stop there; the designer artfully incorporates unusual specimens of summer- and fall-blooming trees and shrubs into the landscape design to elevate the changing floral scene to eye-level and above.

To match the informal mood of the house, both the front walkway and driveway cut a curved, somewhat meandering path. A parking spur at the end of the driveway provides extra parking space and a place to turn around. Fieldstones, whose rustic character complements the country setting, pave the front walk. The stone piers and picket fence at the entrance to the driveway frame the entry and match the detail and character of the house's stone foundation and porch railing. The stone wall at the side of the property further carries out this theme.

Large specimen trees planted in the lawn set the house back from the road and provide a show of autumn color. Imagine completing the country theme in this tranquil setting by hanging a child's swing from the tree nearest the front porch. Also shown here is home plan HPB774 by Home Planners. For information about ordering blueprints for this home, call 1-800-521-6797.

Plan View

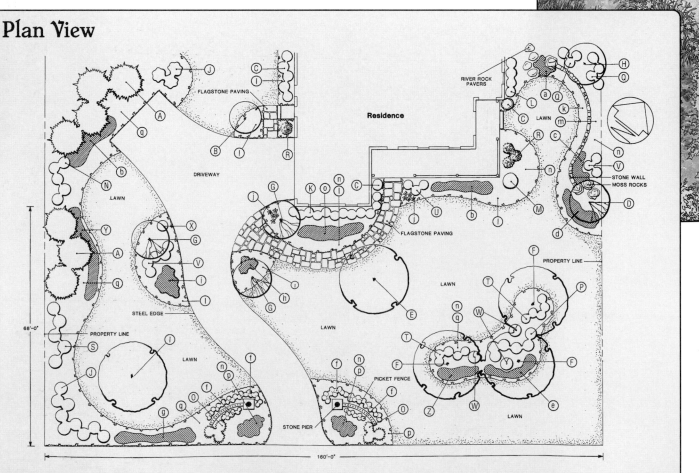

Graceful trees, curving lines and bursts of flowers blooming from spring through fall complement this comfortable country retreat. The friendly landscaping creates the perfect finishing touch that says: here's a place to hang up a hammock and relax.

LANDSCAPE PLAN
HPT110058
Shown in Summer
Design by
David Poplawski

New England Style

A charming flower court complete with a fish pond is the highlight of this landscape design. Visible through two sets of sliding glass doors—one set leading from the dining room and the other from the playroom—the courtyard garden can be enjoyed even when the weather isn't fine enough to venture outdoors. When days are balmy, however, the courtyard makes a cozy spot in which to sit outside and relax in the afternoon sun. A board fence encloses the garden space and matches the architecture of the barn-style house. Planters set out on the terrace can be filled with colorful annuals and changed to match the seasons.

Because the courtyard is at the front of the house, it is screened from the driveway and front walk by a small flowering tree and shrubbery. Two additional flowering trees of the same type are located across the entry walkway from the first tree, casually marking the way to the front door. To match the informality of the house, the stone walkway is laid out in an irregular pattern, which allows a soft interplay with the groundcover plants.

Four shade trees underplanted with shade-loving shrubs and groundcover frame the house near the street. Three of these trees are grouped in a free-standing bed whose gracefully curving outline invites one's eye to follow the lawn around to the side of the house. There one would expect to discover another pretty garden scene.

Plan View

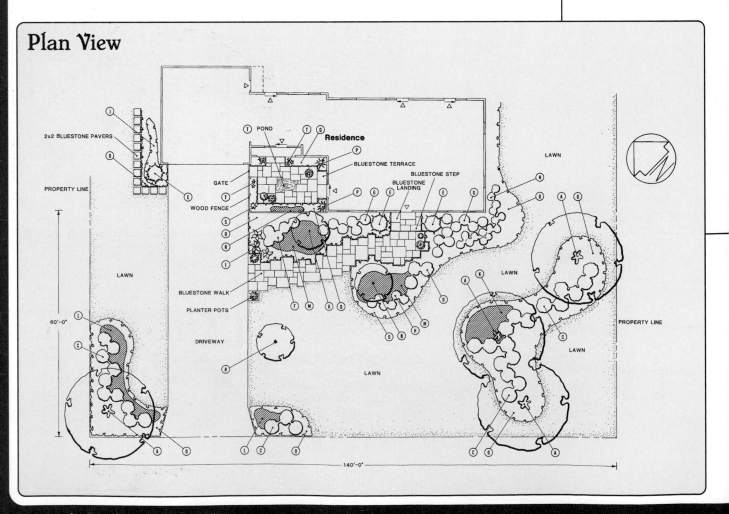

Curved planting beds, randomly laid paving stones and skillfully placed trees and shrubs create an informal private setting for this barn-style home. Note the ornamental pond included in the courtyard garden.

LANDSCAPE PLAN
HPT110059
Shown in Spring
Design by
Damon Scott

Raised-Porch Farmhouse

The style of this house with its raised and covered front porch is reminiscent of a time when streets were wide and children played beneath the shade of large, stately trees whose branches overhung the street. The symmetrical period design of this farmhouse calls for a straightforward, traditional landscape design. To reflect that period, the design for this corner lot uses a perimeter planting of large trees whose canopies frame the view of the house from overhead, providing a sense of tranquility.

A traditional front walk leads from the street to the steps and the front porch; the straightness of the walk is in keeping with the symmetry of the house and the clean lines of the landscape design. Low-growing, spreading shrubs frame the entrance to the front walkway along with fragrant, summer-flowering perennials, which offer a pleasing aroma to greet visitors.

The foundation planting features low-growing, flowering shrubs and perennials so that the handsome stone piers and latticework along the porch foundation remain visible. Taller spring- and summer-flowering shrubs provide easy-care beauty in the borders along the driveway and at the property line. To contrast with the tall trees around the perimeter of the property, small informal trees soften the corners of the house near the side doors. At the other corner, a large tree balances the design. The entire landscape is unified with the same groundcover used throughout. Also shown here is home plan HPB694 by Home Planners. For information about ordering blueprints for this home, call 1-800-521-6797.

Plan View

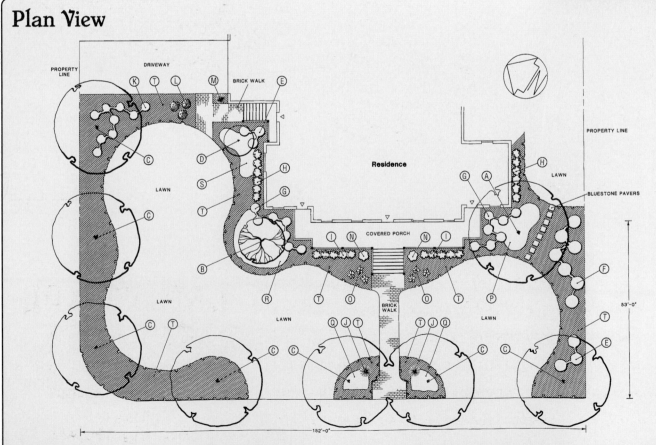

In this plan, the landscape designer re-creates the feeling of an earlier, simpler time that brings to mind cookies and milk on the porch and the sound of children's laughter. This bucolic setting is achieved by the simple lines of the traditional front walk, an overhead canopy of stately trees and an open arrangement of flowering shrubs and perennials.

LANDSCAPE PLAN
HPT110060
Shown in Autumn
Design by
Michael J. Opisso

Wood-Sided Contemporary

A combination of sharp angles and circular and sweeping lines creates a dramatic setting for this wood-sided contemporary. The angled landing before the main entry looks more interesting than would a more typical squared-off walkway and entry. Angled as it is, the wooden landing becomes an extension of the modern architecture, projecting the house into the landscape.

In contrast to the angled paving and entry deck, sweeping curved lines are used in the planting beds across the front of the house. The designer maintains a flowing feeling while preventing the sprawling house from seeming longer than it is. Lawn areas placed on both sides of the walkway complete and unify this circular line, which is further strengthened by the circular planting bed that flows into the paving and integrates the softscape and hardscape features of the design.

Rather than employing a circular drive to bring visitors to the front of the house, a parking court is used instead to leave more room for plantings in the front of the house. To hide the asphalt leading to the garage, three large evergreens are placed at the corner of the house. These are repeated at the opposite corner for balance and they strengthen the front of the house by adding a vertical element to contrast with the horizontal lines of the architecture. More evergreens border the driveway to provide privacy and a windbreak. Soft in texture, these evergreens, together with the circular lines of the design, contrast nicely with the straight lines of the house and the landing and paving. Also shown here is home plan HPB781 by Home Planners. For information about ordering blueprints for this home, call 1-800-521-6797.

Plan View

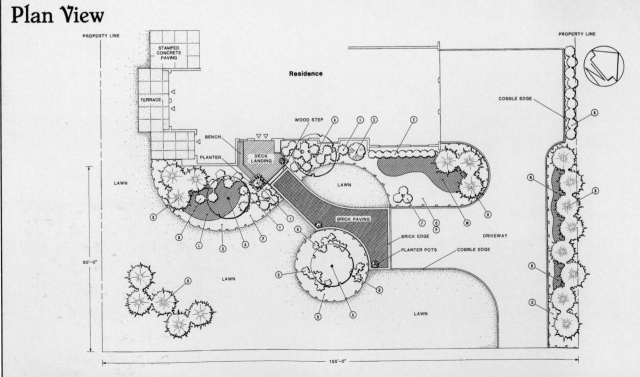

In this landscape, the designer created an unusual angled landing and walkway leading to the front door to add visual excitement to the straight lines of the architecture.

LANDSCAPE PLAN
HPT110061
Shown in Spring
Design by
Michael J. Opisso

Mission-Tile Ranch

The low, sprawling lines of this ranch house and its red-tile roof evoke the Spanish Mission style reminiscent of the easy-living, comfortable nature of Southwestern life. The landscape designer chooses both hardscaping and softscaping to complement the house and the climate. Exposed aggregate walks, simple yet attractive, lead to both main and secondary entrances and blend well with the contemporary Southwestern architecture.

The bed bordering the walkway to the secondary entrance is bermed slightly to block the view of the walkway used by the homeowner, preventing the visitor from approaching the wrong door. The V-shaped driveway provides a convenient parking spur and the angles of the driveway create visual excitement in the design. Three flowering trees spaced out near the corners of the driveway reinforce the V-shape and provide welcome summer color. The tree on the right frames the entrance to the garage; the one on the left frames the view to the door; and the one in the center buffers the view to the secondary entrance. Together, the three balance each other, forming a pleasing triangle. The planting border running in front of the garage wing continues on the other side of the driveway, strengthening the lines of the bed and creating a transition between front and back. Without the continuation of the planting area, the landscaping would abruptly end; with it, the sight line gracefully continues. At the end of a second sight line, the small flowering tree at the left corner of the house creates a view for a visitor strolling up the walk. Also shown here is Home Planners design HPB670. For information about ordering blueprints for this home, call 1-800-521-6797.

Plan View

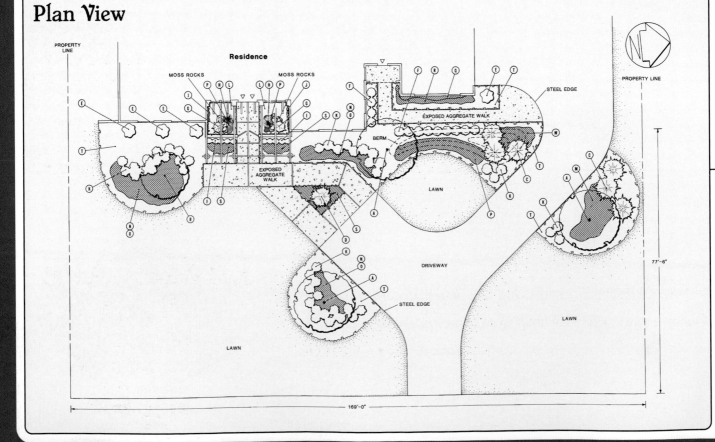

An effective landscape design matches the climate—here, heat-tolerant plants work together to create a perfect cooling combination for a hot climate.

LANDSCAPE PLAN
HPT110062
Shown in Summer
Design by
Damon Scott

English-Style Cottage

Follow the example set by the designer of this English-style cottage landscape, and you will learn several tricks about how to make a small property appear larger. Space is limited, but a small entry court was created at the end of the driveway; the paving that extends across the front of the house and the garage harmonizes with the house and unites the entire area. The bench and planter pots overflowing with flowers lend an informal atmosphere and extend the living space into the garden. The lawn sweeps around the side of the house, with curved lines defined by planting beds filled with masses of flowering shrubs and perennials. Pavers leading through the planting bed welcome visitors into the yard to enjoy the flowers. Although more pavers provide access to the backyard, the two areas are clearly separated, leaving the impression of greater space and creating curiosity about what lies beyond.

Narrow, upright evergreens placed at the corner of the garage balance and interplay with its low roofline and its strong horizontal lines. These are echoed and balanced by an evergreen screen on the right side of the property. Tall shade trees, chosen for their pleasing shape and seasonal color, form a garden ceiling. The trees towering over the one-story house give a woodsy feeling to the scene, enhancing its cottage charm and matching the rustic character of the home's natural wood siding. Also shown here is home plan HPB606 by Home Planners. For information about ordering blueprints for this home, call 1-800-521-6797.

Plan View

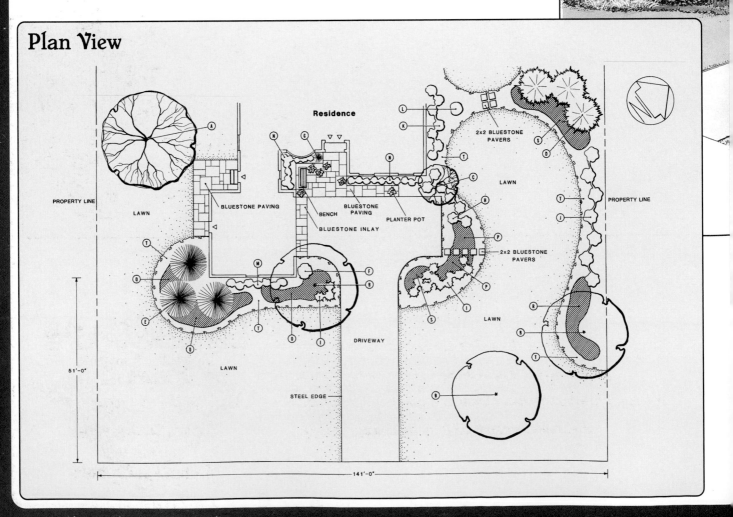

The tall trees shading the property contract with the size of the cottage, emphasizing its cozy appearance. A well-defined entry court further enhances the friendly atmosphere created by the landscape design.

LANDSCAPE PLAN
HPT110063
Shown in Summer
Design by
Michael J. Opisso

Elizabethan Tudor

The romance of the English countryside comes alive in this setting created for an Elizabethan Tudor home. The designer chooses rough stones for walls and walkways, reminiscent of the historical English landscape where stones and cobbles pave many roads and walks. The sixteen-inch-high retaining wall creates an outdoor vestibule where flowering shrubs, perennials and a groundcover chosen for its dramatic color and texture delight the eye. The wall is circular to unify the many different angles and lines of the house and parallels the curved planting line of the trees surrounding the home. Repetition of curves throughout the design helps the entire landscape to flow easily to both sides.

The five formally shaped trees around the perimeter loosely define the boundaries of the design while separating the home from the road. Four clumped trees provide contrasting shape and texture. The designer places an ornamental flowering tree before the large window at the front of the house to provide privacy from the front walk. When in bloom, this showy tree becomes a focal point and creates a stunning view through the nearby window.

Designed for a corner lot, this plan provides access to the garage from the side street. Visitors parking in front are greeted by a walk with a broad entrance. To adapt this plan for a lot without a corner, swing the driveway toward the front and link the walk to it with a sweeping curve. Adapt the trees and shrubs to border the driveway. Also shown here is home plan HPB356 by Home Planners. For information about ordering blueprints for this home, call 1-800-521-6797.

Plan View

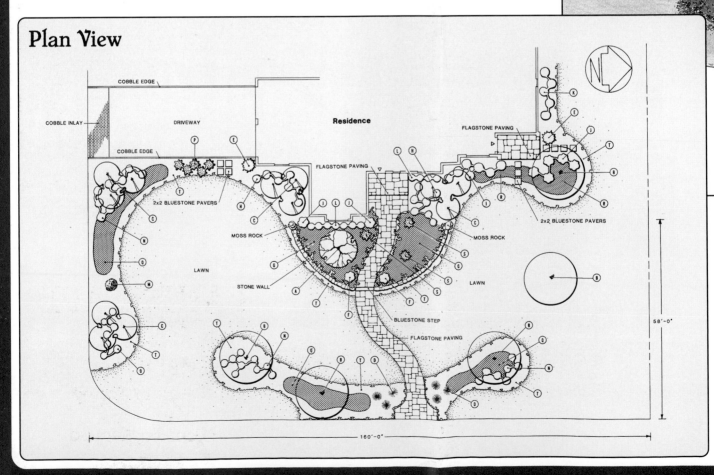

Beautiful trees, shrubs, perennials and groundcovers in this landscape provide an ever-changing show of soft colors and textures throughout the year.

LANDSCAPE PLAN
HPT110064
Shown in Spring
Design by
Michael J. Opisso

Traditional Country Estate

The problem facing the landscape designer of this one-story home is to create intimacy and friendliness where a three-car garage near the front entrance necessitates a lot of pavement. The designer turns what could have been a barren driveway into a functional and attractive space by using trees and the sides of the L-shaped house as the walls of an airy entrance court. Cobble inlay marks the main garage and entrance to the home, and at the same time provides an interesting change in texture. The second garage is blocked from immediate view from both sides by a peninsular bed, which clearly separates it from the primary garage

Enclosing a more intimate courtyard, a low picket fence and bluestone walk define the front door while bringing an informal, homey feeling to the setting. Small grassed areas within this doorstep garden, and in the semicircular area along the rest of the house, provide a green carpet that carries the perimeter lawn into the interior court. The small tree before the window of the master bedroom creates a pretty, ever-changing view through the window and blocks headlights from shining inside.

Graceful trees, masses of cheerful flowering perennials, and the flowing lines of the circular planting beds work together to create a friendly setting for this country home. It's simply pretty as a picture! Also shown here is home plan HPB921 by Home Planners. For information about ordering blueprints for this home, call 1-800-521-6797.

Plan View

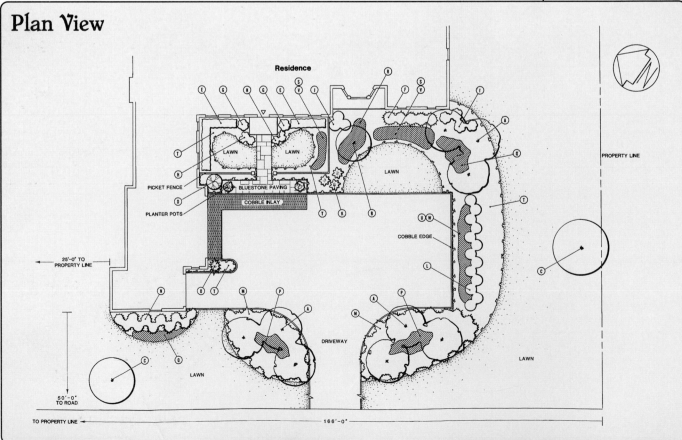

A canopy of trees draws visitors inside the courtyard here, and the doorstep garden outlined by a picket fence and carpeted in green provides a friendly greeting on an intimate scale.

LANDSCAPE PLAN
HPT110065
Shown in Spring
Design by
David Poplawski

Ample Parking

The layout of this L-shaped home presents several landscaping challenges. The landscape design must provide cars with easy access to the two-car garage and enough turnaround space so they needn't back out of the driveway. The home's three front entrances need to be distinguished one from another, and plantings should counter the elongated look of the house.

Though the driveway is large and comes close to the house, the inlaid cobblestones transform what could otherwise resemble a parking lot into an entry court that escorts visitors to the main entrance. A curving line of ornamental trees bordering the driveway leads the eye directly to the door, blocks headlights from glaring into the windows, screens the view into the front rooms and camouflages the private entrance that leads from the master suite to the covered porch and private garden. A low picket fence keeps this lovely garden even more private. Though, of necessity, the driveway is up close to the house, the view from the inside looking out is of beautiful flowering trees rather than asphalt.

A wide landing of bluestone paving further highlights the main entrance. Once on the landing, visitors notice that the paving also leads to the service entrance beside the garage, which was hidden from direct view by a latticework trellis. Covered with a flowering vine, the lattice complements the home's country feeling. Also shown here is home plan HPB615 by Home Planners. For information about ordering blueprints for this home, call 1-800-521-6797.

Plan View

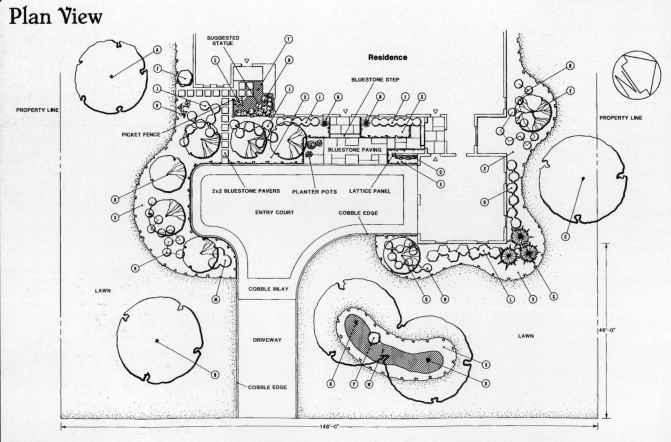

Here, the landscape designer offers an attractive way to provide ample parking space in front of the house by creating an entry court with inlaid cobblestones. The courtyard effect is reinforced by a border of ornamental trees, which can be enjoyed from a private garden encircled by a picket fence.

LANDSCAPE PLAN
HPT110066
Shown in Spring
Design by
Michael Opisso

Balance the Scale

The major challenge in designing the landscape for a large house with straight, rather symmetrical lines is to bring the scale and style of the architecture into the landscape while retaining a sense of human scale in the design. The four formally shaped flowering trees in front of the house achieve this goal, while defining the dominant area of the house and echoing the four columns supporting the portico. Colorful perennials and planters brimming with annuals achieve the second objective.

Because the garage is set at the side of the house, a circular driveway is designed to lead visitors directly to the front entrance in style. Brick inlay marks the space at the front door where cars should stop. Three large evergreens at the corner of the house block the view of the rear parking area and the garage, and they contrast in color and texture with the perennials planted under them. The secondary door can be reached by a walkway, which has a jog in it for added interest. Because of the skillful placement of trees, foundation plants and paving, it is obvious to any visitor which door is the main entry.

An island bed in the lawn bordering the circular driveway contains large evergreens and a shade tree of grand proportions to provide needed privacy. Other evergreens along the street buffer the view of the house from the street and the driveway. The size of the island planting is balanced with the rest of the landscape by the bed on the left of the house, which sweeps around until it disappears out of sight. Also shown here is home plan HPB889 by Home Planners. For information about ordering blueprints for this home, call 1-800-521-6797.

Plan View

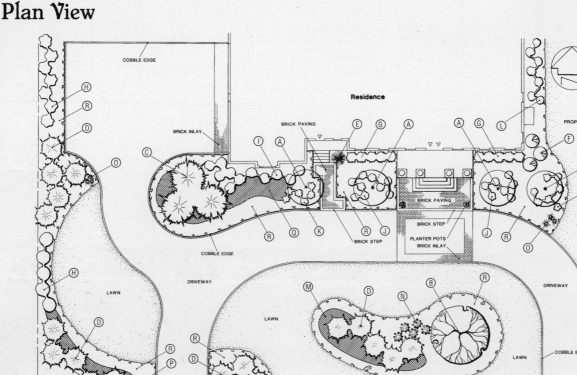

Large evergreens and tall trees balance the scale of this grand-portico Georgian home. The plantings also provide screening from the street, enhancing the view of the house from the driveway and blocking the garage from immediate view.

LANDSCAPE PLAN
HPT110067
Shown in Summer
Design by
Michael J. Opisso

Southern Colonial

The grand size of a traditional Southern Colonial home demands an equally grand landscape whose scale and style balance the house's imposing size and massive columns. The designer uses six tall shade trees to shelter the house and create a parklike setting for the home. The terrace at the front of the house creates a formal entry court that reflects the stateliness of the architecture, while planter pots positioned at each side of the courtyard provide a human scale to an otherwise large-scale house and landscape.

The large trees and planting bed at the entrance to the driveway buffer the view of the drive and the house and create a feeling of anticipation as one enters the property. The driveway splits, leading back to the side-entry garage and also swinging around front to deliver guests in style to the main entrance and a conveniently located parking bay. The canopy of trees at the entrance to the secondary driveway and the repeated semicircular lawn areas announce that this is the entry. Three decorative trees with colored foliage underplanted with low-growing shrubs screen cars parked in the parking bay from the street, while giving the entire entry area a sense of privacy and enclosure. For the convenience of family members, a brick walk, screened from view by a hedge, leads from the garage to the secondary entrance.

Plan View

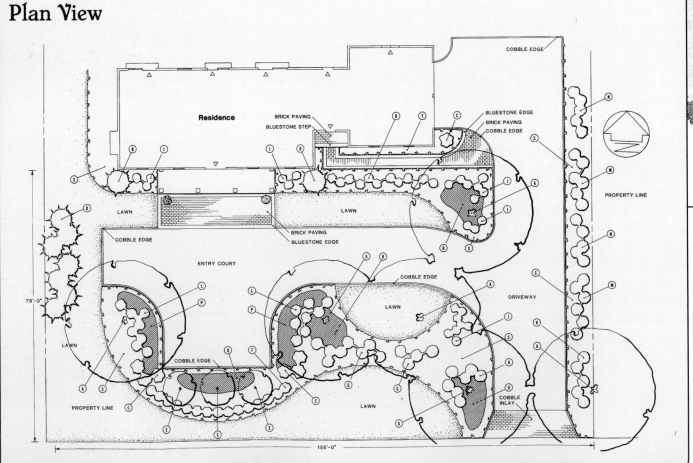

A massive house such as this one demands an equally impressive landscape. The parklike setting and formal entry court created for this Southern Colonial home balance the scale of the architecture in grand style.

LANDSCAPE PLAN
HPT110068
Shown in Summer
Design by
Damon Scott

Symmetrical Layout

The British have influenced more than one style of architecture, including this Georgian-style manor house. While many of these styles tend to be informal, the Georgian style appears formal and stately. Here, the designer creates a beautifully symmetrical landscape that offers a dramatic parklike setting, perfectly suited to the country manor house of an English lord and lady.

Because of the vast size of the house and property, a circular driveway swings in front of the main entrance for easy access. The entry court, clearly defined by the brick inlay that matches the facade of the house, allows room to park several cars. This parking court is hidden from the street by a berm and an evergreen hedge; the hedge actually serves as a low privacy wall but appears more friendly than a brick wall would in the same position. Brick piers are placed on each end of the hedge and at each side of both driveway entrances to emphasize the symmetry of the design.

Majestic shade trees placed along the street and entry court create a transition from the public space to the home's private space. The large size of the trees also helps to scale down the size of the house, helping it to seem at home in its setting. Closer to the house, flowering trees in front of the large windows soften the facade and block the view into the house while providing those inside with a lovely sight in spring. Also shown here is home plan HPB683 by Home Planners. For information about ordering blueprints for this home, call 1-800-521-6797.

Plan View

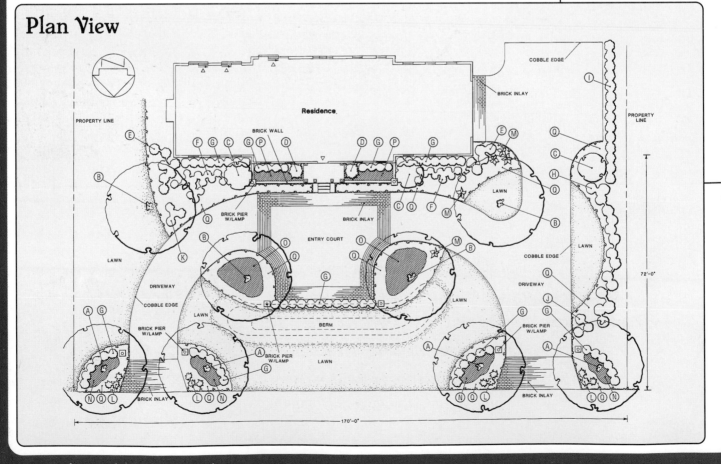

The symmetrical layout of this landscape design perfectly
matches the character of the grand Georgian house.
Overhanging trees create a quiet, private setting, while
the circular driveway and grassy berm hide the
entry court from immediate view, revealing the
full impact at the final moment.

LANDSCAPE PLAN
HPT110069
Shown in Spring
Design by
Damon Scott

Tudor One-Story

The design for this charming Tudor-style home employs a repetitive theme of curved shapes throughout the landscape. Beginning with the circular driveway, the theme can be seen in the rounded outlines of the lawn areas before and on each side of the driveway, and in the curved edges of the front walk and bordering beds. These lines sweep across the design, playing up the horizontal lines of the one-story house.

The front walk, which branches toward the garage, is bordered by low-growing shrubs and flowering perennials and made even more intimate by decorative trees. This area offers a special welcome because it is intensely populated with plants that provide color throughout the year. The highlight of this garden is the ornamental tree, which is visible from the breakfast nook. It ties together the irregularly patterned paving leading to both segments of the driveway and camouflages the blank garage wall.

Drifts of flowering perennials located throughout the landscape provide friendly bursts of color during summer and well into fall. Fall too brings a stunning display of autumn foliage. If for some reason a circular driveway would be undesirable, this plan is easily adapted without compromising any of the design elements. The circular part of the driveway can be eliminated and turned into a parking spur that ends in front of the entrance. The circular border to the left of the property can be merged into the front border to complete the curve, and lawn can fill in the rest of the area to create a picture-perfect design. Also shown here is home plan HPB802 by Home Planners. For information about ordering blueprints for this home, call 1-800-521-6797.

Plan View

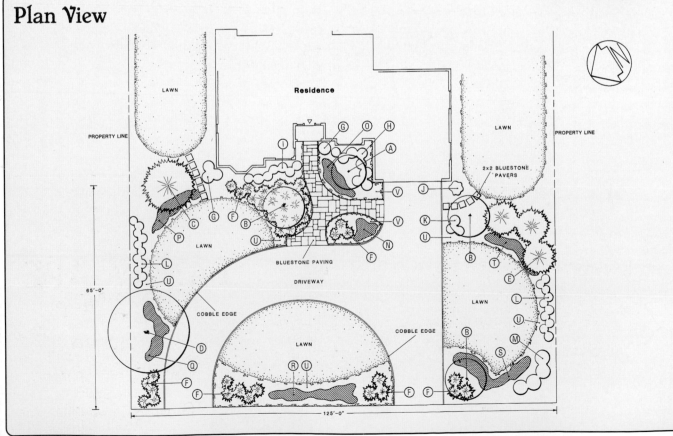

Although the circular driveway separates the lawn and planting borders into three distinct zones, these areas are visually linked because they sweep across the property in continuous lines. This visual trick makes the property appear much larger.

LANDSCAPE PLAN
HPT110070
Shown in Summer
Design by
David Poplawski

Queen Anne Victorian

This Victorian house ought to be the home of a large family where children delight in playing hide-and-seek and exploring its many nooks and crannies. The very large all-wood house is of monumental scale and makes a significant presence on the property. In keeping with that, the designer presents a landscape plan that complements the uniqueness of the architecture and balances its weight and scale.

A circular driveway solves the problem of the garage being set so far to the back of the house and allows easy access to the front door. The driveway brings the visitor to a wooden platform that links the house to the drive and extends the wraparound porch into the landscaping. The smooth, flowing lines of the landscape extending around the house and to the street are clean and pleasing to the eye, while not competitive with the many angles of the house. Low-growing plants are chosen for the front of the house, in order not to hide the home's interesting architectural features. A large tree at the front right corner anchors the house and is repeated in three other areas to frame the view and balance the massive scale.

The uniqueness of the architecture demands that drama be carried through to the landscaping, which is accomplished with the pond and foundation on the outside of the driveway. Berms were added around the pond to enhance its setting. The weeping tree beside the pond also emphasizes the unique nature of the house and adds special interest. Also shown here is home plan HPB953 by Home Planners. For information about ordering blueprints for this home, call 1-800-521-6797.

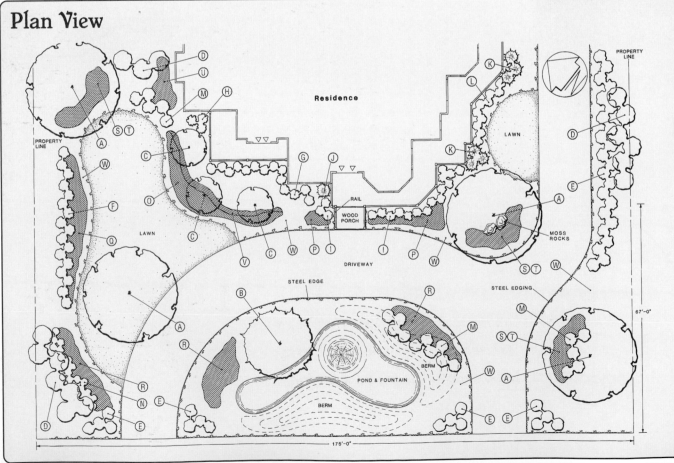

Plan View

The massive size and drama of this Victorian house demand a dramatic landscape, created here by majestic trees, a garden pond and a fountain.

LANDSCAPE
PLAN
HPT110071
Shown in Spring
Design by
Damon Scott

Drought Tolerant Garden

This design proves that "drought tolerant" and "low maintenance" don't have to mean boring. This attractive backyard looks lush, colorful and inviting, but relies entirely on plants that flourish even if water is scarce. This means you won't spend any time tending to their watering needs once the plantings are established. Even the lawn is planted with a newly developed turf grass that tolerates long periods of drought.

The designer specifies buffalo grass, a native grass of the American West, for the lawn. The grass has fine-textured, grayish-green leaf blades, tolerates cold, and needs far less water to remain green and healthy than most lawns. It goes completely dormant during periods of extended drought, but greens up with rain or irrigation. To keep the lawn green throughout summer, all you need do is water occasionally if rainfall doesn't cooperate. And mowing is an occasional activity, too! This slow-growing grass needs mowing only a few times in summer to about one inch high. To keep the grass from spreading into the planting borders—and to reduce weeding and edging chores—the designer calls for a decorative brick mowing strip surrounding the lawn.

Deciduous and evergreen trees and shrubs interplanted with long-blooming flowering perennials—all drought tolerant—adorn the yard, bringing color every season. Against the fence grow espaliered shrubs, which offer flowers in spring and berries in winter. The vine-covered trellis shades the roomy, angular deck, where you can sit in cool seclusion and relax while your beautiful backyard takes care of itself.

Plan View

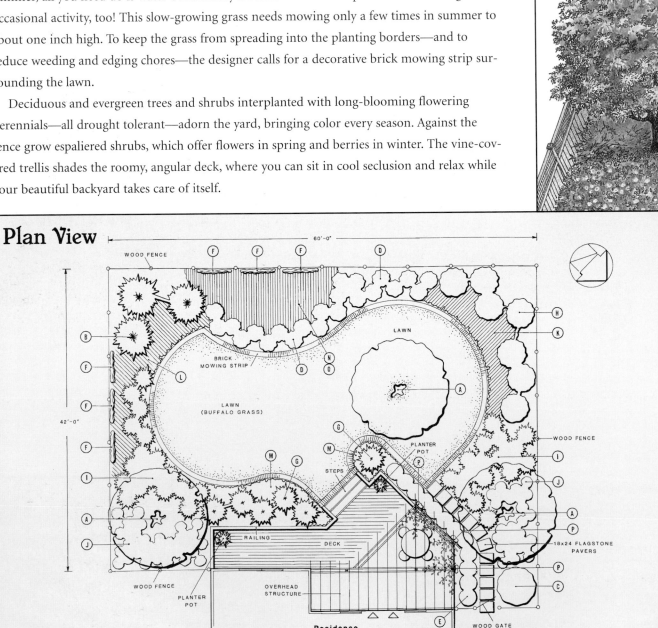

This environmentally sound landscape plan won't strain the local water supply or burden you with gardening chores, because all the plants used here—from grass to flowers to trees—are easy-care, trouble-free kinds that flourish without frequent rain or irrigation.

LANDSCAPE PLAN
HPT110072
Shown in Summer
Design by
Damon Scott

Weekend Retreat

This colorful backyard serves as a special weekend retreat where you and your family can spend your free time relaxing and entertaining. Enjoy a quiet afternoon reading or lounging in the hammock under the romantic arbor, or host a cookout for your friends on the spacious patio complete with an outdoor kitchen.

Both the patio and the hammock provide refuge from the hot summer sun—a vine-covered overhead trellis and leafy trees protect the patio, and the hammock hideaway tucked in the corner of the yard can catch a breeze while reflecting the sun's hot rays. Just right for a lazy afternoon snooze, the hammock structure nestles within an intimate flowery setting that encloses and enhances the space. Flagstone pavers lead the way from the patio to the hammock, following the gentle curve of the border, and flagstones mark the entrance from the gates at each side of the yard for easy access.

Privacy-protecting evergreen trees and shrubs fill the rear of the property, and all are gracefully set off by a purple-foliaged weeping specimen tree located on sight lines from both the patio and the arbor. (In some regions, another type of eye-catching specimen tree is substituted for the purple-foliaged tree.) For color contrast, long-blooming, yellow-flowering perennials surround the tree. The designer includes large patches of other easy-care perennials that punctuate the rest of the landscape with splashes of color from spring through fall to create a welcoming backyard retreat.

Plan View

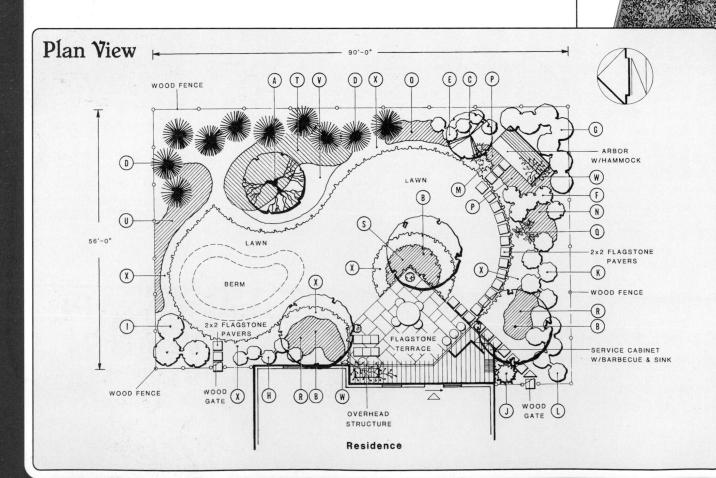

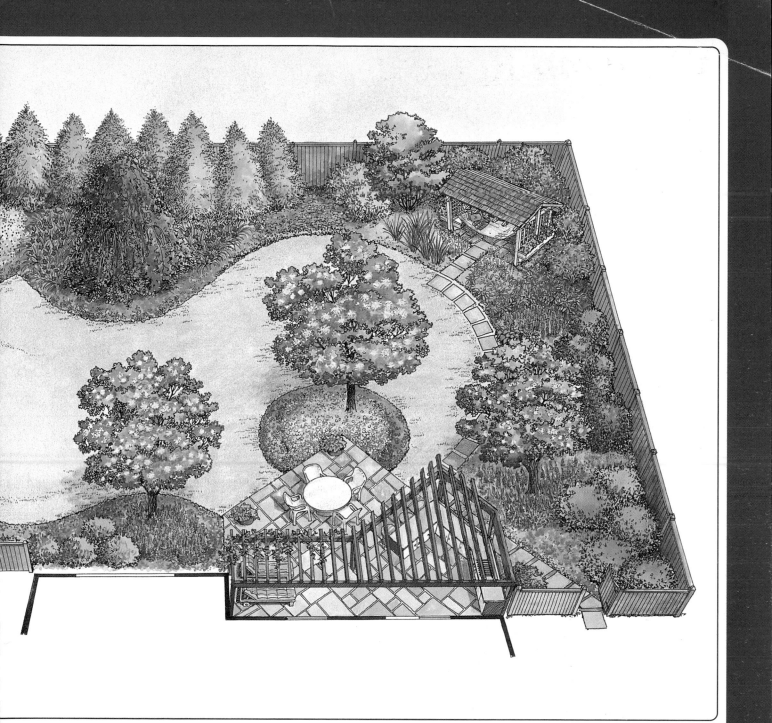

An arbor-covered hammock and a spacious patio with a kitchen provide comfortable spots for relaxing outdoors while enjoying the colorful flowering perennials.

LANDSCAPE PLAN
HPT 110073
Shown in Summer
Design by
Michael J. Opisso

Backyard Play Courts for Action Games

*I*f your family is the energetic kind that never stops moving, this backyard plan provides the perfect solution for soaking up all their enthusiasm. Three play courts are permanently installed: shuffleboard, badminton and hopscotch. All are discreetly integrated with other elements of the landscape to create a beautiful, but functional, backyard.

In the center of the lawn, the outer dimensions of a volleyball or badminton court are marked inconspicuously with landscape timbers laid on edge and flush with the ground. Set this way, they don't interfere with mowing or cause anyone to trip, yet they remain as clear markers. You can make bolder, temporary official court lines in the lawn with garden lime, gypsum or flour—none of which will harm the grass.

The shuffleboard and hopscotch courts in the perimeter of the yard are made from poured concrete. Both are partially hidden behind shrubs and trees and are surrounded by an evergreen groundcover to soften their hard edges. Younger children will delight in the circular timber-edged sandbox, which can be turned into a flower or strawberry bed when the kids outgrow sand-castle and fort building.

The brick patio, attractively curved to mimic the shape of the lawn, allows plenty of space for adults to relax in the sun, dine outdoors and enjoy a commanding view of all the sports action.

Plan View

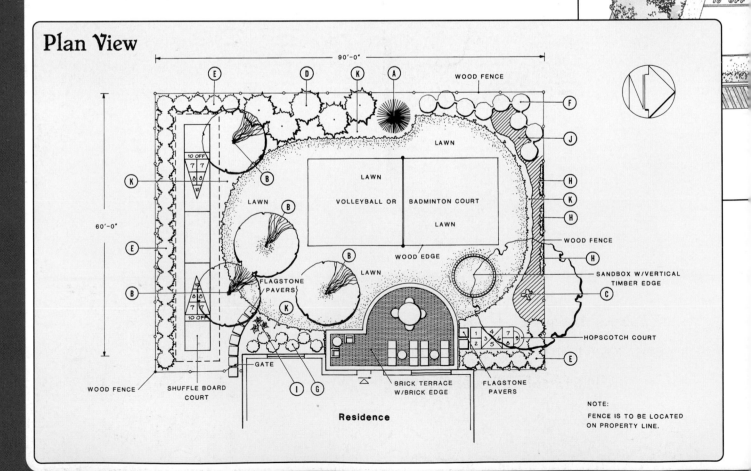

The ideal backyard for a sports-minded family, this design features three permanent playing fields to provide children and adults alike with plenty of play options.

LANDSCAPE PLAN
HPT110074
Shown in Summer
Design by
Michael J. Opisso

Abundant Flowers

Colorful butterflies will flock to this floriferous backyard, which is planted with flowering shrubs and perennials irresistible to these welcome winged visitors. A butterfly's needs are simple: a sunny spot out of the wind to perch on, a puddle of water to drink from, nectar-rich flowers to sip from and food plants for the caterpillar phase to munch on. The designer incorporates all these needs into this landscape plan, while also providing for human visitors.

The flagstone patio, nestled among the flowers near the center of the yard, brings you away from the house right out where the butterflies congregate. This is a perfect place for a table and chairs, where you can sip coffee during a sunny spring morning or dine during a summer evening, all the while keeping an eye out for a visiting monarch, red admiral or swallowtail feeding on the nearby flowers or perching on the flat rocks near the puddle. The swing and arbor (not included in the plan) provide a cool spot to relax.

Instead of a pure grass lawn, the designer specified a lawn composed of mixed clover and grass. The clover provides nectar for the adult butterflies and forage for the caterpillars. Keep in mind that, as beautiful as they are, butterflies are insects. To enjoy the elusive winged stage, you'll have to tolerate a little feeding damage from the caterpillar stage. It's best to garden organically, steering clear of all insecticides—whether chemical or biological—in this garden, or you're likely to have few butterfly visitors.

Plan View

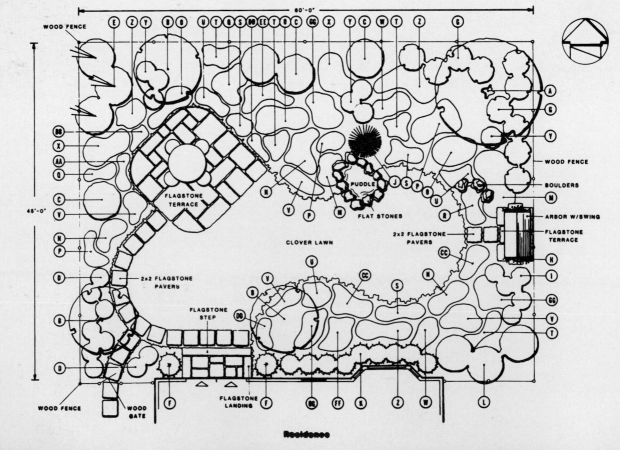

The abundant flowers in this backyard turn it into a paradise for butterflies as well as for garden lovers. Dozens of different kinds of nectar-rich plants, blooming from spring through fall, provide the necessary blossoms to lure the ephemeral beauties not only to stop and pay a visit, but perhaps to stay and set up a home.

LANDSCAPE PLAN
HPT110075
Shown in Summer
Design by
Tom Nordloh

Backyard Apple Orchard

Your backyard can be both productive and beautiful if you create an edible landscape by planting attractive fruit-bearing trees and shrubs according to recognized landscape design principles. The designer arranged the fruit trees and shrubs in clusters and groups to create a lovely landscape that will fool anyone into thinking the garden was designed for its beauty alone. The delicious harvest is an added bonus. Evergreen groundcovers and swaths of summer-flowering perennials planted beneath the curving line of apple trees turn this into an ornamental planting, while providing easy access for both maintenance and harvest. The curving border defines the lawn and yard, creating a pleasing shape, yet proves to be a practical plan for fruit growing. The apple varieties selected are disease resistant, reducing the need for pest-control measures. Included are several types that will cross-pollinate and ripen their fruit at different times. The designer uses semi-dwarf trees because they bear earlier, are easier to harvest, and need less care than standard-sized trees.

Also featured are a nut tree to shade the deck, an island bed planted with a groundcover of strawberries and a dwarf fruit tree, and berry plants flanking the apple trees. Backyard gardeners will appreciate the handsome storage shed, where tools can be conveniently kept. Concealed behind several lengths of fencing, the compost piles are also right at hand for recycling garden and kitchen refuse into a valuable soil amendment.

Plan View

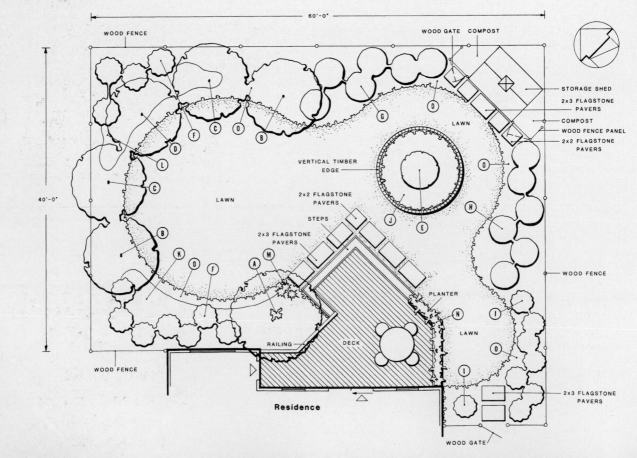

Your friends will be surprised and delighted when you harvest baskets of delicious apples, berries and nuts from this beautiful yard in summer and fall. The simple curved lawn and angular deck set off the surrounding orchard of fruiting trees and shrubs.

LANDSCAPE PLAN
HPT110076
Shown in Summer
Design by
Damon Scott

Backyard Meadow Garden

If you yearn for the look and feel of a flower-drenched meadow, this low-maintenance landscape plan can help you create it in your very own backyard. The small lawn needs normal mowing maintenance, but once established, the wildflower meadow requires only once-a-year mowing to a height of 6 inches in late fall or winter to keep it blooming and to prevent woody plants from invading.

The designer creates the wildflower meadow from native field grass and sun-loving perennial wildflowers—those at home on America's prairies and open meadows. You'll be assured of success with this garden, because you start it from container-grown flowers planted together with seed-sown meadow grass. Unlike totally seeded meadow gardens, which are difficult at best to get established, this method ensures that the flowering plants become quickly rooted and spread year after year into a gorgeous spectacle of blossoms set against wavy green grass. You'll have to weed between plants the first season or two until the desirable flowers and grass become established enough to crowd out weeds.

A rustic stacked-rail fence, in keeping with the bucolic theme of the garden, separates the manicured lawn from the meadow, taming its wildness just a bit. Plantings near the house include informal plants, such as ornamental grasses, that echo the wilder look of the plants in the meadow. Drought-tolerant evergreen trees, grouped strategically in the meadow, provide privacy and wind screening while giving the yard a permanent structure and year-round beauty.

Plan View

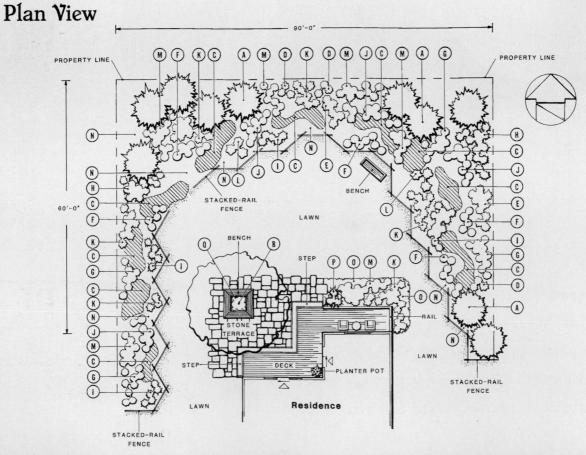

This plan re-creates one of Nature's great spectacles: a grassy meadow brimming with blooming flowers. A deck of wood planking rises above the level of the yard so you can appreciate the view from above. Steps lead down to naturalistic stone paving that feathers into the lawn.

LANDSCAPE PLAN
HPT110077
Shown in Summer
Design by
Damon Scott

Woodland Wildflowers

Large trees create the woodland look of this plan, which provides exactly the right environment for the native shrubs and the delicate wildflowers and ferns that need a bit of shade to flourish. If you're lucky enough to have several large trees on site and perhaps are despairing over what to grow in their shade, this plan is your answer. If you have a sunny yard but yearn for shade, plant the largest slow-growing trees you can afford, balanced by a few fast-growing kinds. Plan on removing the faster, shorter-lived trees in a few years when the more desirable trees gain some stature. Ideal slow-growing trees to consider include native oaks and sugar maples. Fast growers that can be used to create shade and scale in a hurry include alder, poplars and willows.

Wood-chip pathways throughout the mulched wildflower border make movement through the garden easy and inviting, creating vignettes at their corners and curves. The pond and the bridge that spans it anchor the design and lend the garden its unique character. Evergreen and deciduous trees and shrubs, including many natives, provide year-round structure.

At first, the wildflowers will grow in the spaces where you plant them, in exciting drifts of color. Over time, however, they'll grow mingle and reseed, creating a more natural unplanned look. Please be sure to purchase nursery-propagated wildflower plants and seeds; never transplant them from the wild or buy them from sources that gather them in the wild, since doing so further endangers the beauty of our natural heritage.

Plan View

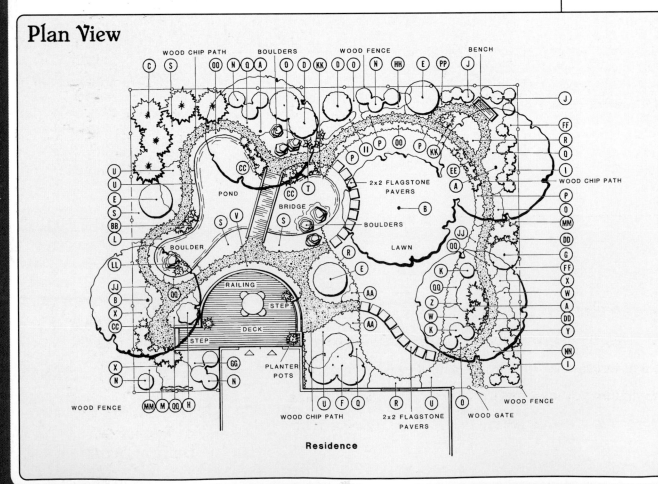

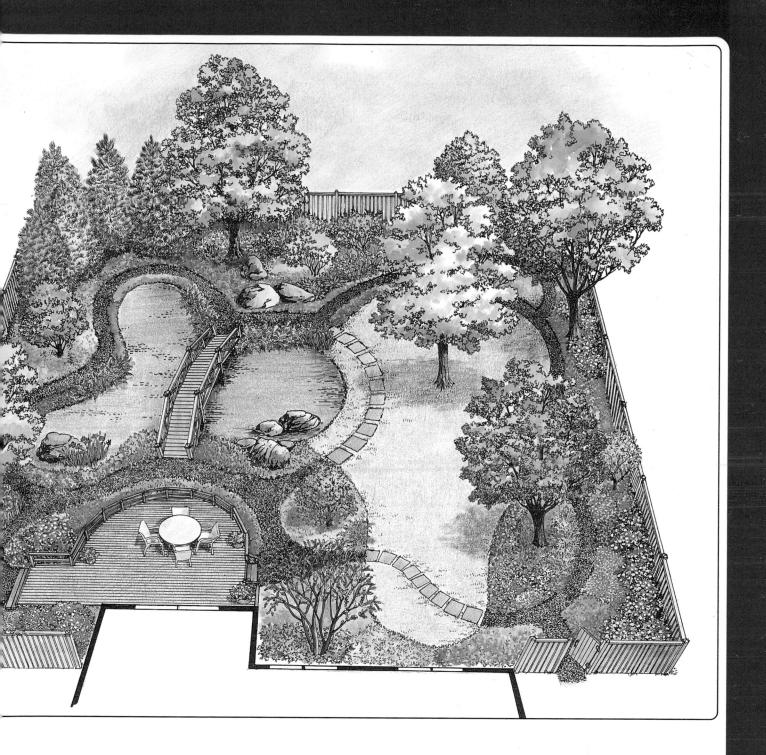

Admire your lovely woodland on a summer evening from the convenience of the raised deck, or at midday from the shaded, secluded bench in the far corner. Gentle curves, punctuated by wildflowers, boulders and trees, invite a peaceful stroll through the woodland.

LANDSCAPE PLAN
HPT110078
Shown in Spring
Design by
Damon Scott

Serene Simplicity

The simplicity of the curving lines in this design helps create a private backyard of informal grace. Cornerless and nondirectional, the sensual lines of the pool emphasize neither its width nor its length. As a result, the garden's sense of space is enhanced by forcing the eye to scan the beautifully planted edges. To further connect the pool to the landscape, the shapes of the brick terrace, wood deck, stone path and two bermed areas bordering the lawn echo the pattern.

In addition to the sound-buffering berms, the groupings of background trees behind and across from the pool enhance the sense of seclusion and privacy. The designer specified three vase-shaped, deciduous shade trees for the garden to balance the visual weight of the pool. Needled evergreens provide privacy by wrapping around the rear corner of the property behind the pool. Note the specimen shrub planted on the pool's edge and set off against the dark foliage of the evergreens. The gracefully spreading plant makes a spectacular sight when in bloom in spring and again in fall and winter when colorful fruits decorate its branches.

Blooming just in advance of the flowering tree near the pool are three spectacular small flowering trees along the patio; these are located near the house for maximum enjoyment because weather may still be chilly in early spring. Extravagant patches of long-blooming perennials provide color during the summer, when you'll be outside enjoying the pool and the generous outdoor living space.

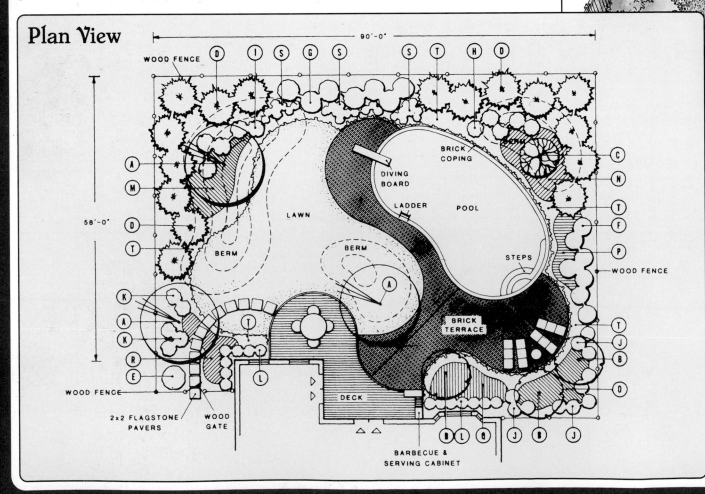

Plan View

This serene design creates a private, comfortable, quiet and carefree mood for relaxing with family and friends. Vase-shaped shade trees block the hot sun on the deck and patio while letting the sun warm the swimming pool.

LANDSCAPE PLAN
HPT110079
Shown in Summer
Design by
Tom Nordloh

Love Outdoor Living?

The perfect setting for an outdoor party—or for simply relaxing with family and friends—this backyard features an elegant wooden deck and brick patio that run the length of the house. The deck area on the right (not included in the plans) acts as an outdoor kitchen, featuring a built-in barbecue, serving cabinet and space enough for a dining table and chairs. For those who opt to mingle with the other guests, rather than chat with the cook, a separate area has been provided at the other end.

Built at the same level as the house, and easily accessible from inside, the deck extends the interior living space to the outdoors. Three lovely flowering trees shade the deck and house, while creating a visual ceiling and walls to further reinforce the idea that these areas are outdoor rooms.

Down a few steps from the deck, the brick terrace makes a transition between the house (and deck) and the garden. Open on two sides to the lawn, this sunny terrace feels spacious and open, creating a great place in which people can mingle and talk during a cocktail party or sunbathe on a Saturday afternoon. From here, it's possible to enjoy the garden setting close at hand. The plantings around the perimeter of the yard feature several kinds of tall evergreens to provide privacy. In front of the evergreens, large drifts of flowering perennials are perfectly displayed against the green background. Between the evergreens, masses of shrubbery provide a changing color show from early spring through fall.

Plan View

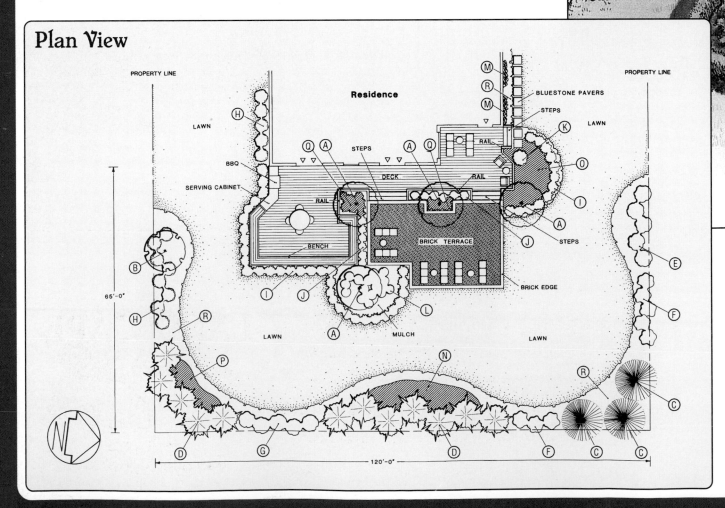

Designed for families who love outdoor living, this backyard features a deck and patio combination that is perfect for entertaining. It features an area for cooking and dining, as well as space for intimate conversations and relaxing in the sun.

LANDSCAPE PLAN
HPT110080
Shown in Spring
Design by
Michael J. Opisso

Naturalistic Swimming Pool

*I*f you look at this landscape design and ask yourself, "Is that really a swimming pool?" then the designer is to be congratulated because he succeeded in his intention. Yes, it is a swimming pool, but the pool looks more like a natural pond and waterfall—one that you might discover in a clearing in the woods during a hike in the wilderness.

The designer achieves this aesthetically pleasing, natural look by employing several techniques. He creates the pool in an irregular free-form shape and paints it "black," actually a very dark marine blue, to suggest the depths of a lake. Large boulders form the waterfalls, one of which falls from a holding pond set among the boulders. River-rock paving—the type of water-worn rocks that line the cool water of a natural spring or a rushing stream—surrounds the front of the pool. The far side of the pool is planted right to the edge, blending the pool into the landscape. If you want to make a splash, you can even dive into this pool—from a diving rock rather than a diving board.

Although the pool is the main attraction here, the rest of the landscape offers a serene setting with abundant floral and foliage interest throughout the year. For security reasons, a wooden stockade fence surrounds the entire backyard, yet the plantings camouflage it well. The irregular kidney shape of the lawn is pleasing to look at and beautifully integrates the naturalistic pool and landscaping into its man-made setting.

Plan View

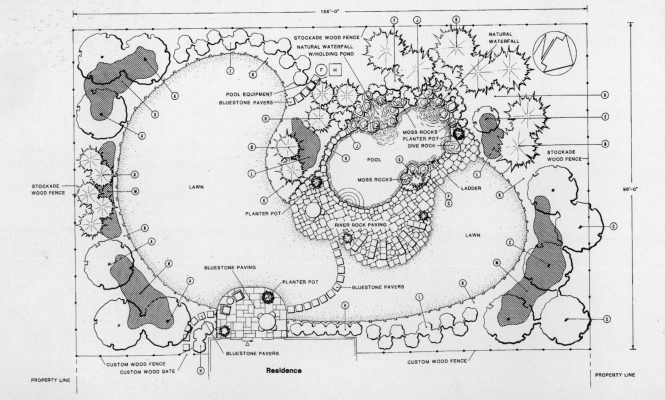

Resembling a tranquil country pond high in the mountains, this swimming pool, with its waterfalls, river-rock paving and border planting, brings a wonderful, natural setting to your own backyard.

LANDSCAPE PLAN
HPT110081
Shown in Summer
Design by
Damon Scott

Elegant Lap Pool

Designed primarily for exercise, a lap pool is much longer than it is wide, although it does allow two people to swim comfortably side by side. It's also shallower than pools designed for high diving. This long, narrow pool fits economically into a small backyard, because it takes up less space and costs less to build. Although intended for a healthy workout, the pool will certainly provide cooling relief from sultry summer days for all family members, not just the athletically minded.

The lap pool not only serves as a recreational feature, but it also organizes the space in the landscape, acting as the main point of interest. The designer situated the pool easily within the confines of a modest-sized backyard by locating it off-center and at the focal point of a line of sight leading between two oval flowering trees and ending with a small specimen tree on the other side of the pool. The brick patio offsets the visual weight of the pool, balancing the design. The designer worked to vary the pattern and direction in the brick paving around the rectangular, hard-edged shape of the 35-by-10-foot pool to avoid an overly formal result.

A path of flagstone pavers, leading from the gate to the brick terrace and from the terrace to the pool, provides easy circulation through the landscape. Swimmers can reach the pool from two doors of the house. Although the perimeter plantings ensure privacy for the swimmer, a variety of flowering shrubs and perennials creates a spring-through-fall display of flower and leaf color for all to enjoy.

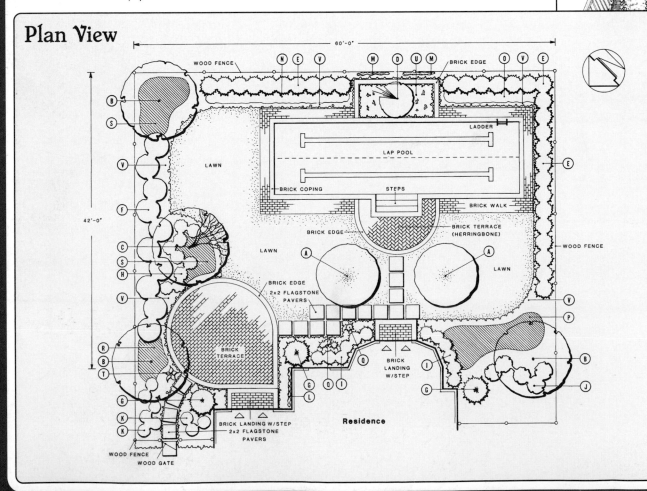

Plan View

Even modest-sized backyards have room for a lap pool for the athletically minded and those seeking a refreshing dip. This elegant backyard plan incorporates a lovely patio and pool with a generous lawn, evergreens for privacy, and flowering trees and shrubs for spring beauty.

LANDSCAPE PLAN
HPT110082
Shown in Spring
Design by
Tom Nordloh

Play Yard for Budding Gymnasts

Your young, active children and their friends will enjoy hours of engaging play in this wonderful backyard. The elaborate play structures, which are designed to exercise every growing muscle a kid has to develop, features many different elements—a hanging tire, pull-up bars, slides, swings and rings, as well as platforms for game playing. With so many choices, a child's short attention span is sure to be accommodated. Besides the obvious play structures, the yard includes secret hiding places nestled behind the shrubs and under the trees in the yard's corners—these will lure any child in need of a quiet, contemplative moment.

The repeating circles beneath the play structure create the landscape's main design feature. These are actually giant sand pits. They're bordered by easy-to-install vinyl strips that keep the sand from spilling onto the lawn. With the play structures set off center of the yard, plenty of lawn area remains for running games and visual beauty.

Although a wood fence at the property line borders the yard for security reasons, the densely planted trees and shrubs enhance the sense of privacy and enclosure, while providing colorful flowers and softening greenery. The wood deck, accessible from the house through sliding glass doors, balances the visual weight of the play structure. The deck's diagonal lines and squared-off shape make a happy contrast with the circular sand pits.

Plan View

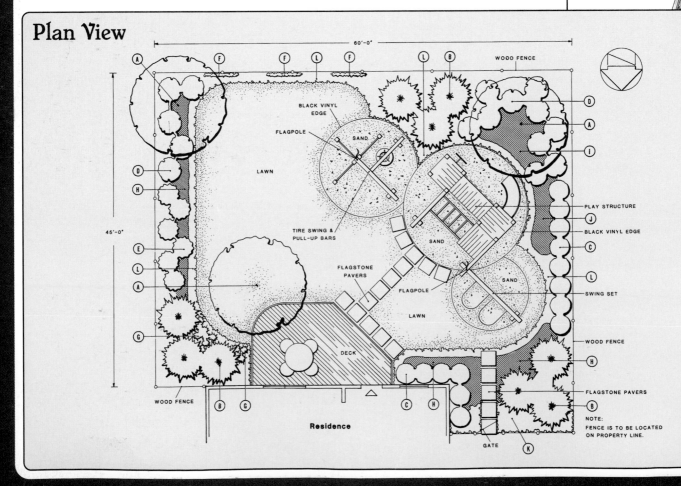

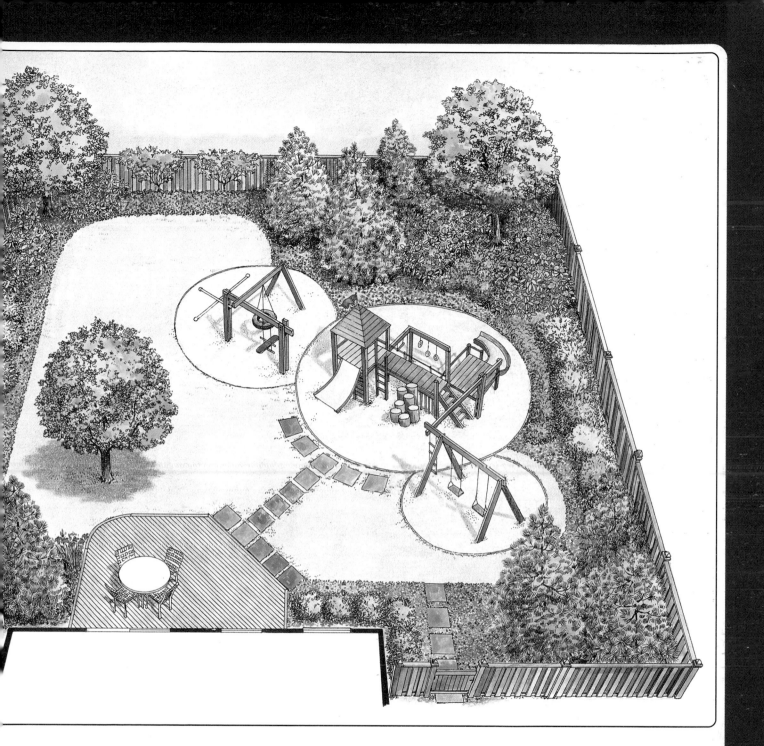

Could any child resist this wonderful backyard?
Circular sand pits—designed for both play and safety—
combined with fabulous play structures make this
backyard as exciting as the local park.

LANDSCAPE PLAN
HPT110083
Shown in Spring
Design by
Damon Scott

Naturalistic Flowers and Grasses

Designed with the flower-lover in mind, this oasis of flowers and grasses looks great all year. Bright flower colors during spring and summer are followed in fall by the pale, elegant flowers and seed heads of the ornamental grasses. The seed heads and foliage persist until the following spring, decorating the winter landscape with their delicate flower-like plumes and wheat-like fronds. Don't cut the dried grasses back to the ground until just before the new growing season begins, so you can enjoy them all winter.

The garden is formed from three connecting beds, with three paths leading into a central paved area between them. Flagstone pavers, which are interplanted with scented groundcover plants, lead into this central patio. A medium-sized deciduous tree in each bed shapes the flagstones and puts on a brilliant show before dropping leaves in fall. This allows you to add a table and chairs, so you can sit quietly and enjoy the trio of colorful garden beds. Be sure to site this lovely design so that the path is visible from a distance. That way, visitors will be tempted to come and enjoy the patio and surrounding plantings.

Plan View

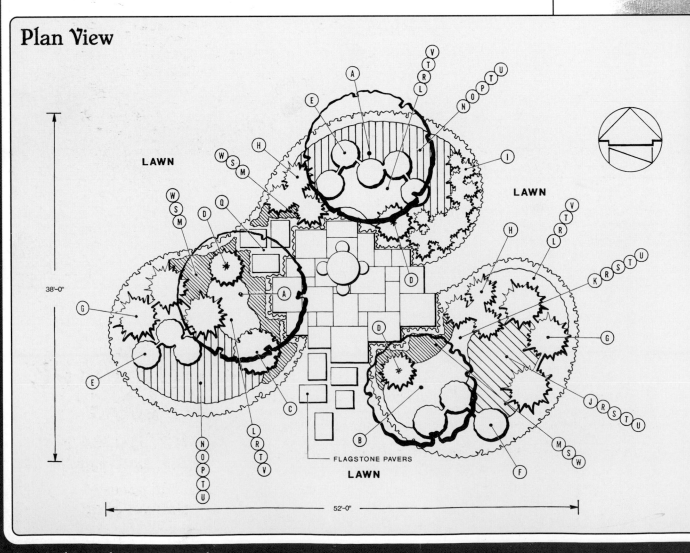

LAWN

LAWN

LAWN

FLAGSTONE PAVERS

38'-0"

52'-0"

You won't be worrying about your gardening chores while sitting on this pretty patio—the flowers and ornamental grasses used here thrive in poor soil and low moisture.

LANDSCAPE PLAN
HPT110084
Shown in Summer
Design by
Damon Scott

Bird Friendly

This attractive border does double duty, because it serves both as a beautiful landscape planting as well as an effective wildlife sanctuary. Offering natural food sources, shelter and water, the planting brings birds to your property throughout the year, while its informal but tidy design looks right at home in any suburban setting. Although they serve a practical purpose as well, the birdhouses, bird feeders and birdbath add interesting architectural elements to the design.

The shrubs and trees used in the border—and even many of the perennials and ornamental grasses—produce berries and seeds that attract birds. They are arranged informally and should be left unpruned to form a dense shelter for nesting sites. Because most berried plants produce best when cross-pollinated by another similar plant, the designer masses specimens together and repeats plants.

You can site this border along the property lines in either your front- or backyard, or round off its corners and use it as an island planting. Then sit back and enjoy the birds and birdsongs that fill your garden.

Plan View

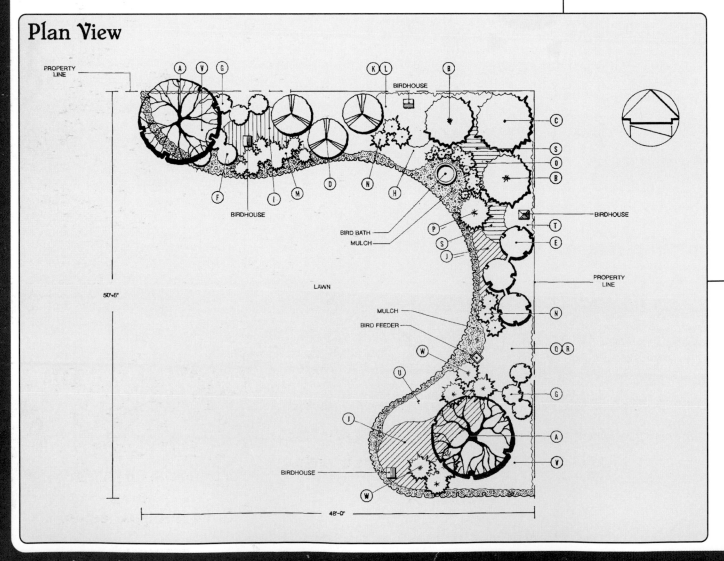

Filled with fruiting shrubs, trees, ornamental grasses and perennials that provide food for birds, this border is as beautiful as it is bird friendly.

LANDSCAPE PLAN
HPT110085
Shown in Autumn
Design by
Salvatore A. Masullo

Privacy Berm

This naturalistic berm is planted with a season-spanning design that can transform a suburban yard into a quiet haven. The berm rises to three feet high—tall enough to make you forget that your neighbor's yard lies just beyond. Staggered plantings cover the berm and create baffles that muffle sound, while the diverse mix of plants provides color and interest all year long.

Intended for a backyard, the berm allows you to enjoy the remaining lawn in privacy. Tall berry-producing evergreens located at the top of the berm provide immediate screening, while perennials and bulbs, ornamental grasses, and small flowering trees at the front provide seasonal bursts of brilliance. A flowering groundcover on the berm helps hold the soil in place and makes a graceful transition between the slope of the berm and the flat lawn area.

Wherever you decide to site the berm, be sure to maintain the original grade of the yard at the property line, to avoid violating zoning regulations. Also, be sure to add a two- to three-inch-thick layer of mulch to help the slope retain moisture and to discourage weeds.

Plan View

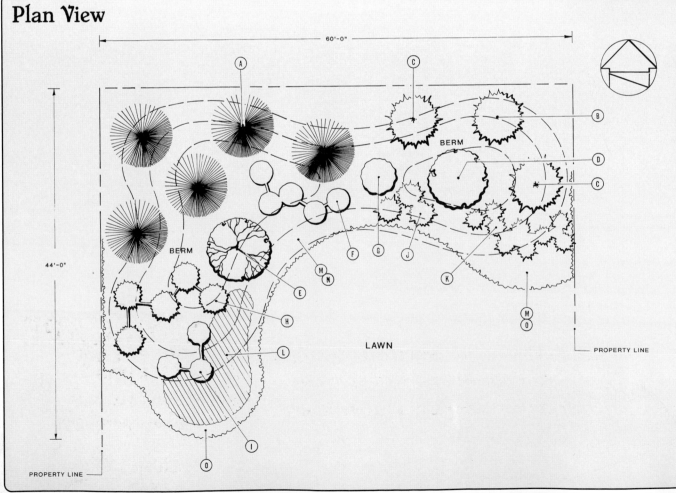

*This privacy planting gets a head start on creating an
effective screen by beginning with a berm,
which gives young plants a height advantage.*

LANDSCAPE
PLAN
HPT110086
Shown in Spring
Design by
Michael J. Opisso

Easy-Care Mixed Border

When small trees, flowering shrubs, perennials and groundcovers are planted together, the result is a lovely mixed border that looks great throughout the year. The trees and shrubs—both evergreen and deciduous types—provide structure and form in winter, while also offering decorative foliage and flowers in other seasons. Perennials and bulbs occupy large spaces between groups of woody plants and contribute leaf texture and floral color to the scene.

Even though this border contains a lot of plants, it is easy to care for. That's part of the beauty of a mixed border—the woody plants are long-lived and need little pruning if allowed to grow naturally. By limiting the number of perennials and blanketing the ground with weed-smothering groundcovers, maintenance is kept to a minimum without sacrificing beauty.

You can install this mixed border in a sunny location almost anywhere on your property, though it's intended to run along the back of an average-sized lot. If your property is larger or smaller than the one in this plan, you can alter the design by either increasing or decreasing the number of plants in each grouping.

Plan View

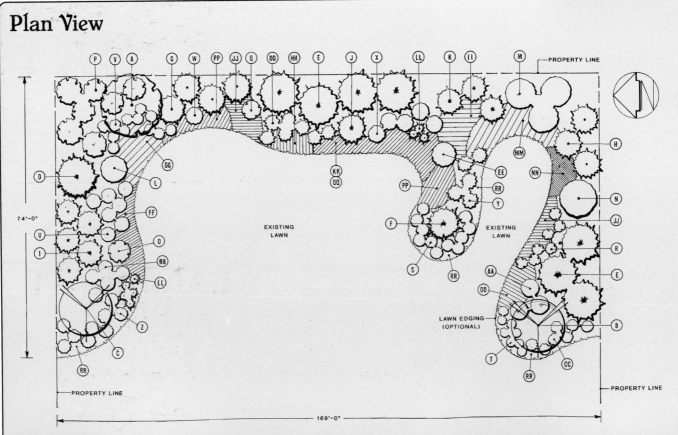

Evergreen and deciduous shrubs and small trees, mixed with drifts of bulbs and flowering perennials, create an ever-changing border that's gorgeous every month of the year.

LANDSCAPE PLAN
HPT110087
Shown in Spring
Design by
Jim Morgan

Privacy Border

If you'd like to create a private haven in your backyard without putting up a fence, this plan is for you. This backyard border relies solely on massed plantings of evergreen and deciduous trees and shrubs to screen out neighboring properties and to buffer noise. The designer also includes a charming circular bench where you can sit and enjoy a peaceful yard under the shade of a tree. Edged with flowering groundcovers and bulbs, the circular bed and the main border fit together naturally, like the pieces of a puzzle.

Starting with spring-flowering bulbs, this border design offers varied color and texture throughout the year. Broad-leaved and needle-leaved evergreens at the back of the border provide a permanent structure, effective screening and a pleasantly neutral color that sets off the vibrant perennials and bulbs planted in the front. The stepping stones leading through the flowering groundcovers at the tree's base encourage visitors to meander across the lawn to get a closer look at the abundant plantings in the main border.

Plan View

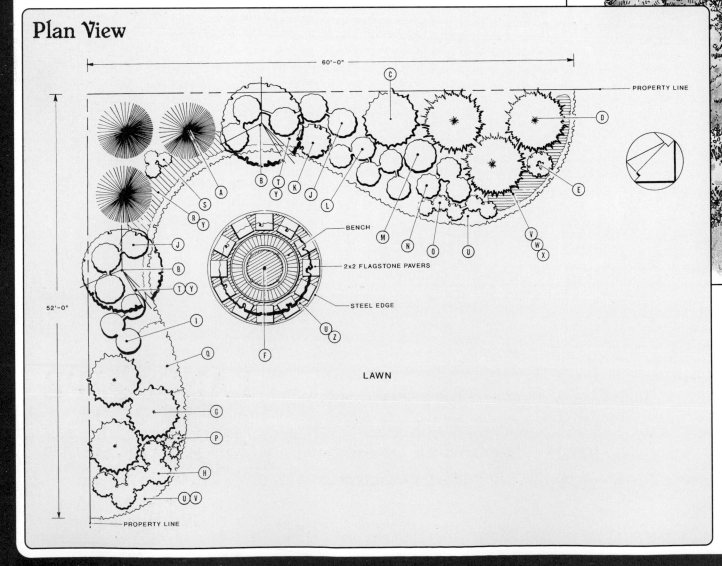

Here, a dense planting of assorted evergreens, set off by a changing show of flowering deciduous trees and shrubs, creates privacy from a neighboring property and also effectively muffles noise.

LANDSCAPE PLAN
HPT110088
Shown in Spring
Design by
Jim Morgan

Colorful Evergreen Border

Here's a border garden much richer in texture and color than most traditional evergreen hedgerows. Although evergreens are a common choice for defining private space because they provide year-round screening, their green color can be boring and monotonous. The designer overcomes that problem here by using many evergreen trees and shrubs that are available in shades of gold, blue and green to create a luxuriant privacy border.

The various colors and textures of the foliage plants, which vary from feathery to bold, are skillfully combined to form a striking and harmonious composition. Unlike deciduous trees and shrubs, which put on a colorful but brief show, the evergreens that form the mainstay of this design hold their elegant jewel-toned colors all year. The evergreens also attract birds, which make nests in the dense, lush foliage and feast on the berries and cones.

An ever-changing show of bulbs, perennials, groundcovers, ornamental grasses and flowering shrubs placed at the border's front edge, stands out against the backdrop of evergreens. The border's free-form curves and natural shapes nicely balance the formality of single clipped hedge.

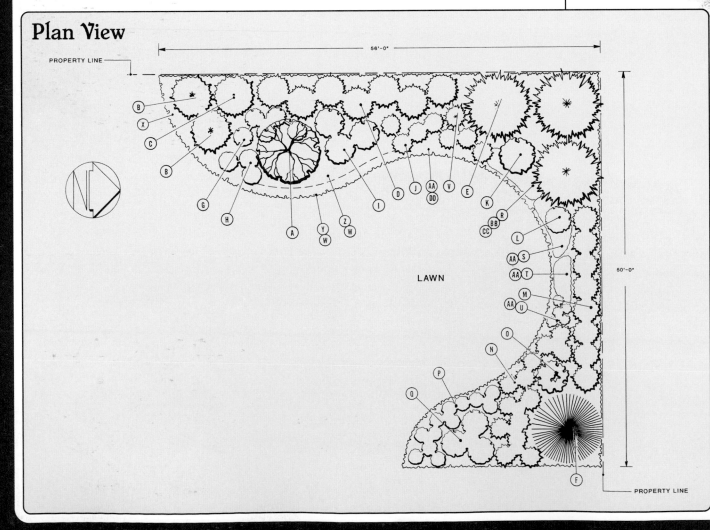

Plan View

This privacy border relies on an assortment of evergreens with colorful needles to provide year-round screening while also creating a landscape scene that's always interesting to look at.

LANDSCAPE PLAN
HPT110089
Shown in Summer
Design by
Gary J. Martin

Edible Landscape

The suburban food gardener needn't worry about turning the backyard into unattractive rows of vegetables when following this innovative design. Here is a backyard that looks good enough to eat! It is designed to produce abundant and fresh home-grown produce and still be a beautiful spot for relaxing and entertaining. Though the main feature of the property is a central vegetable garden, many of the landscape plants used in the border plantings and along the house produce edible fruit as well. These plants were especially chosen because they can perform double duty, acting both as ornamentals and as food-producers.

The vegetable garden is accessible by way of a short path around the lawn. The garden is designed in a round form for greater interest and has gravel paths dissecting it for ease of working and harvesting. Even in winter, when bare of plantings, this garden will continue to be attractive because of its geometrical layout. The designer has left the choice of vegetables up to the gardener and chef, but there is plenty of space to grow the family's favorite choices. Off to the side, a storage shed provides needed space for storing gardening paraphernalia. A compost pile is conveniently located behind the shed.

The outdoor kitchen area on the brick patio contains a barbecue, a sink and a serving cabinet that doubles as a bar. Covered with an overhead lattice to set off the chef's culinary preparation area, this part of the patio provides a comfortable spot in which to lounge and dine out of the sun. For sunning, move out from under the lattice and soak up the rays. Deck Plan HPT110171 is shown on page 272.

Plan View

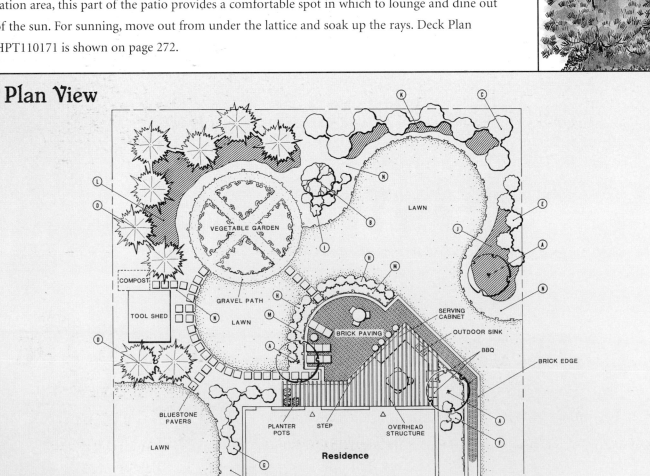

COMPOST

TOOL SHED

VEGETABLE GARDEN

GRAVEL PATH

LAWN

LAWN

LAWN

LAWN

BLUESTONE PAVERS

PLANTER POTS

STEP

OVERHEAD STRUCTURE

BRICK PAVING

SERVING CABINET

OUTDOOR SINK

BBQ

BRICK EDGE

Residence

A cook's garden, this backyard provides fruits and vegetables for the family to eat. This garden is integrated into the yard in a manner more attractive than usual vegetable gardens, and the shrub borders feature berry plants and fruit trees.

LANDSCAPE PLAN
HPT110090
Shown in Summer
Design by
Michael J. Opisso

Raised Perennial Border

The yard and garden pictured here would delight any flower lover, since they are designed to bloom from early spring into fall. During spring, flowering trees and shrubs, which border part of the property, provide seasonal color.

The main feature of the property, however, is a dramatic perennial border designed to bloom from summer through fall. The key to creating a successful display of flowering perennials lies in choosing and combining plants that bloom together and in sequence, so the garden is never bare of flowers. When so orchestrated, the border displays a fascinating, ever-changing collection of colors. The perennials grow in large drifts to create the most impact when viewed from across the lawn. The planting beds surround an irregular, bow-shaped lawn, a pretty way to add interest to an uninspiring squared-off property.

A low stone wall raises the planting beds several steps up, bringing the flowers closer to eye level and emphasizing the contours of the design. The low retaining wall also provides an attractive way to deal with a sloping property so the lawn can be level. If your property is flat, the wall can be eliminated without altering the basic design. Behind the perennial garden, evergreens form a background that sets off the colors in summer. When sitting on the patio of this beautiful yard, the eye is drawn toward the gazebo. Accessible by a stepping-stone walk, the gazebo makes a wonderful place to sit and relax in the shade while enjoying the beauty of the perennials from a different perspective.

Plan View

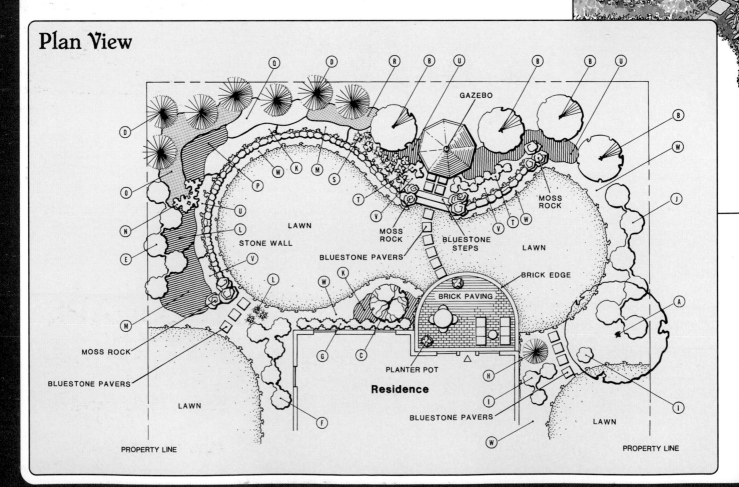

Here is a yard that is alive with flowers from spring through fall. In winter, the pretty stone wall, shrubs, evergreen trees and groundcovers keep the yard looking bright and beautiful.

LANDSCAPE PLAN
HPT110091
Shown in Summer
Design by
Michael J. Opisso

Secluded Fountain Planting

Designed to be a backyard oasis, this mixed garden bed features a gently curving path that leads to a secluded patio and fountain. Deciduous trees and shrubs, evergreens, ornamental grasses and perennials blend together to create a privacy screen around the seating area. The sense of enclosure is further enhanced with a low berm behind the wall surrounding the fountain. In this intimate setting, you can sit and relax while listening to the music of the splashing fountain.

The designer edged the semicircular fountain basin with stone that matches the patio and walkway to visually unite the design. The varied and dense plantings of this design are attractive to wildlife. As an added bonus, this heavily planted garden leaves little room for pesky weeds to take hold. And because this is a naturalistic garden, there's no need to keep a rigid maintenance schedule. Occasional deadheading and pruning to maintain plant health are the only gardening musts.

Plan View

FLAGSTONE TERRACE &
FOUNTAIN W/ RAISED FLAGSTONE WALL (18")

MOSS ROCK

MOSS ROCK

FLAGSTONE WALK

LAWN

LAWN

MOSS ROCK

52'-0"

80'-0"

Sit here in solitude, or with friends and family, and enjoy the sounds of splashing water and singing birds. This bed can be placed almost anywhere on your property to create a beautifully private scene.

LANDSCAPE PLAN
HPT110092
Shown in Summer
Design by
Jeffery Dieffenbach

Fence-Line Planting

T his appealing border is designed especially for a backyard that needs to be enclosed by a privacy fence. Here, the designer chooses a handsome fence to define the property line and provide screening, while creating a backdrop for a brilliant mixed border of sound-absorbing plants. The fence features a solid lower part that provides privacy and a lattice top that allows air to circulate and light to shine around the garden. This design creates a healthier growing environment than a solid fence—and it's prettier, too.

The colorful planting softens the wooden fence behind it, enhancing it rather than concealing it. Flowering vines, easily trained to grow on a fence, make a strong visual connection between the hardscape and softscape. Evergreens, perennials, bulbs, flowering shrubs and vines all contribute color and interest throughout the year, while the fence provides a comforting sense of enclosure and permanence. The strategically placed groups of evergreens also create additional privacy and help to anchor the design without obscuring the fence.

Plan View

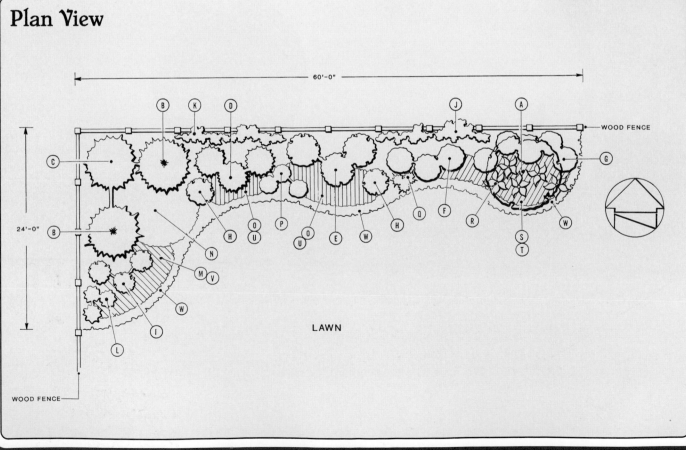

This design turns a necessary privacy or security fence into a landscape asset by softening it with vines and using it as a backdrop for a colorful garden.

LANDSCAPE PLAN
HPT110093
Shown in Spring
Design by
Damon Scott

Corner Property Planting

An expansive front lawn is nice if you live on a quiet, secluded lot, but on a busy corner lot, you'll need a more substantial planting to create privacy. This L-shaped bed effectively screens the front yard from the street, yet also allows visibility for traffic at both corners. And it looks just as good from the street side as it does from the yard side.

The designer chooses landscape plants that are all tough enough to retain their good looks despite the onslaught of car exhaust and road salt. Bulbs that will naturalize and spread, compact shrubs that won't need pruning, and tough perennials and pollution-resistant trees that aren't daunted by a difficult growing site put on a year-round show with minimum maintenance.

All you'll need to do is deadhead spent blossoms from time to time to encourage more flowers, and add mulch annually to control weeds and save on watering. Be sure to leave a wide mulched strip at the curb to allow maintenance access from the street side, leave the view open for drivers and accommodate snow piles in cold-winter climates.

Plan View

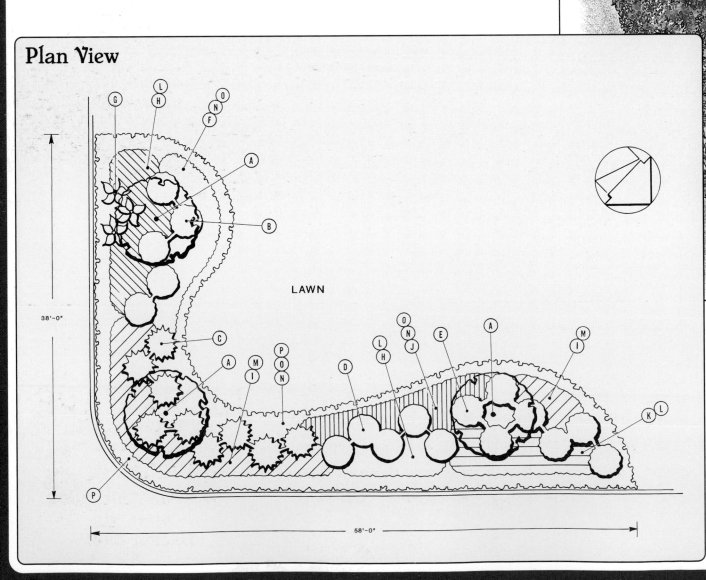

38'-0"

LAWN

58'-0"

An attractive landscape along the edges of a corner property not only beautifies the community, but it goes a long way toward creating a peaceful setting where the house and yard have increased privacy from street traffic.

LANDSCAPE PLAN
HPT110094
Shown in Summer
Design by
Damon Scott

Country French Rambler

This country French home has elegant horizontal lines and a symmetrical facade that the designer accentuates with the long lines of the drive, lawn and walkway. The elongated, narrow lawn panel in front of the house continues past the corner tree, giving the impression of a long, sweeping vista.

A circular driveway is not used in this plan, yet to make provision for adequate parking near the front door, a parking spur was added. An exquisite weeping tree accents the horizontal sight line from the parking spur and directs the eye toward the front door. This elegant tree is also the first thing seen upon leaving the front door. Large evergreens screen the garage and rear parking areas as well as provide landscape interest, color and texture. These are balanced at the other side of the house by a tall flowering tree, which is a surprise addition to the otherwise symmetrical planting scheme.

A small inner courtyard at the front door greets visitors and creates a transition from semi-public to private space. Defined by a low brick wall, the courtyard features symmetrically placed shrubs and a pair of ornamental trees, in keeping with the sophisticated ambiance of the house—Home Planners design HPB779. For information about ordering blueprints for this home, call 1-800-521-6797.

Plan View

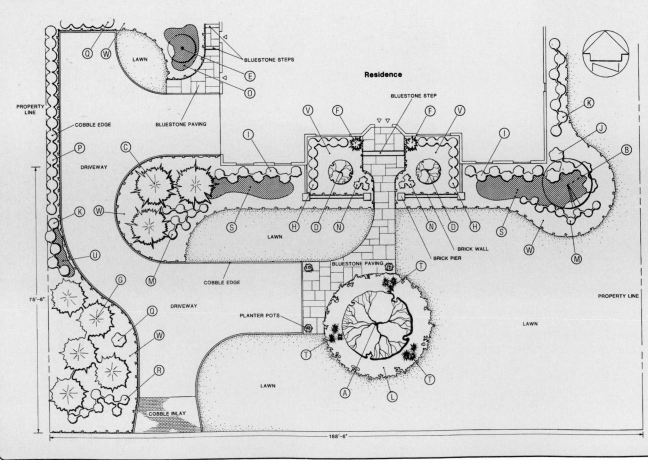

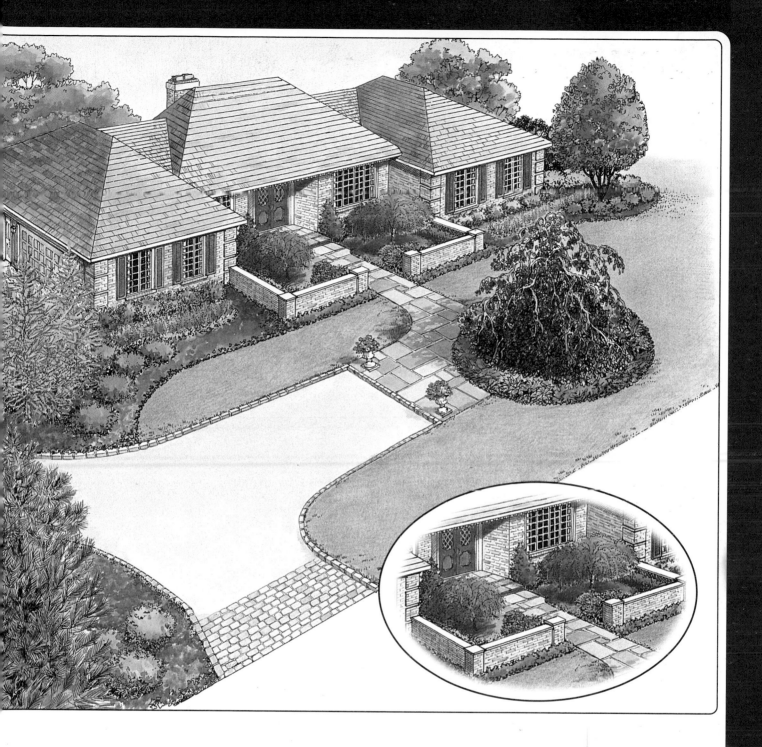

The walled courtyard garden featured in this design creates a formal entrance in keeping with the elegant architecture. Sweeping lines used in the planting beds and driveway carry the eye past the house on either end, complementing the low lines of the house.

LANDSCAPE PLAN

HPT112001
Shown in Summer
Design by
Michael J. Opisso

Imaginative Projects:

57 gliders, gazebos, garden sheds & more

Building a beautiful or practical outdoor addition in your yard or garden should be like adding icing to a cake. Often, it can become a something-extra, value-added, just-for-fun project from concept through completion. Whether you built your home or had it built—just moved in or have been there for years—take a look around with a "wish list" in mind. Given your lifestyle, what would you and your family use most? A playhouse? A romantic gazebo? A potting shed?

On the following pages are illustrations for 57 stellar projects—some practical, some whimsical, but all designed to enhance your lifestyle and make creative use of your outdoor areas. Take your time browsing through them to find the one that's perfect for you.

The Ornament

PLAN HPT110095
SQUARE FOOTAGE: 144
WIDTH: 11'-8"
DEPTH: 11'-8"

Reflecting the image "gingerbread" is intended to convey, this delightful gazebo will be the focal point of your landscape . . . the icing on the cake . . . the star atop the holiday tree! The floor area of nearly 144 square feet is large enough for a table and four to six chairs. Or, add built-in benches to increase the seating capacity to accommodate twenty people. Painted white with pink asphalt roof shingles, this gazebo has a cool summery appearance. Or, you can build it with unpainted, treated materials and cedar shake shingles for an entirely different effect. Either exterior design will provide an outstanding setting for years of outdoor relaxation and entertainment. The jaunty cupola complete with spire adds a stately look to this single-entrance structure. The plans also include an optional arbor, which can be incorporated into the entrance of the gazebo.

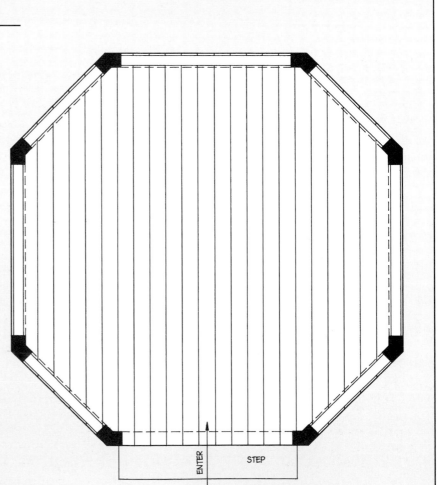

Make It Your Own

PLAN HPT110096
SQUARE FOOTAGE: 114
WIDTH: 12'-0"
DEPTH: 12'-0"

Victorian on a small scale, this gazebo will be the highlight of any yard. With a cupola topped by a weathervane, a railed perimeter and double steps up, it's the essence of historic design. Small enough to fit on just about any size lot, yet large enough to accommodate a small crowd, it is perfect for outdoor entertaining. Choose standard gingerbread details from your local supplier to make it your own.

American Classic

PLAN HPT110097
SQUARE FOOTAGE: 160
WIDTH: 16'-0"
DEPTH: 14'-9"

This all-American single-entrance gazebo is simple to construct and easy to adapt to a variety of styles. All materials are available in most areas with no special cutting for trim or rails. This gazebo is distinguished by its simple design and large floor area. The traditional eight-sided configuration and overall area of approximately 160 square feet allow for the placement of furniture with ample seating for eight to ten people. Build as shown, or modify the trim and railings to give a totally different appearance. If multiple entrance/exit access is desired, simply eliminate the rails as needed. Access to the ground is a single step, which could be easily modified for a low ramp.

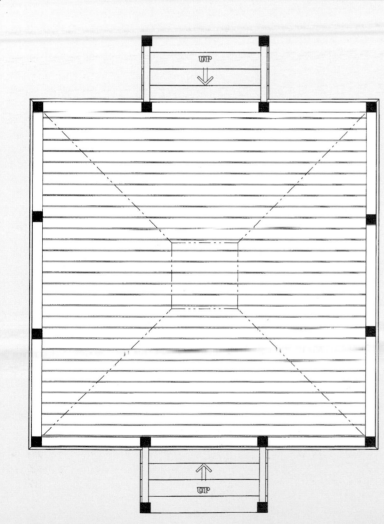

UP

UP

American Bandstand

PLAN HPT110098
SQUARE FOOTAGE: 256
WIDTH: 16'-0"
DEPTH: 22'-4"

Dance the night away in this double-
entrance, pass-through-style gazebo. By day,
the open-air construction provides a clear
view in all directions. The large floor area of
256 square feet seats twelve to sixteen people
comfortably or nicely accommodates musi-
cians or entertainers for a lawn party. The
decorative cupola can be lowered, louvered
or removed to create just the appearance you
want. Or, add an antique weathervane just
for fun. This gazebo has five steps up, which
give it a large crawlspace for access to any
added utilities. Its square shape allows for
simple cutting and floor framing, plus easy
assembly of the roof frame. The trim and
handrails are simple to construct or modify
to achieve several different design effects.

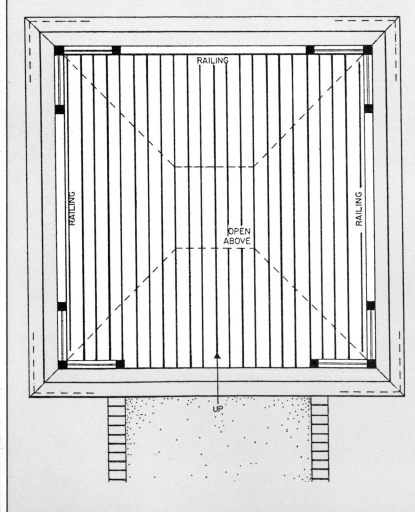

RAILING

RAILING

RAILING

OPEN
ABOVE

UP

Neoclassic Gazebo

PLAN HPT110099
SQUARE FOOTAGE: 144
WIDTH: 12'-0"
DEPTH: 12'-0"

Best suited for larger lots—at least a half acre—this gazebo provides a prime spot for entertaining. It has as much surface space as the average family room. And, topping out at just under 17½ feet, it's as tall as a one-story house! Boasting many neoclassic features—perfect proportions, columns and bases—it blends well with a variety of housing styles: Cape, Georgian, farmhouse and others. The cupola is an added touch that lets light flow to the decking below. Cedar or redwood would be a good choice for building materials.

Trellis-Go-Round

PLAN HPT110100
SQUARE FOOTAGE: 128
WIDTH: 12'-0"
DEPTH: 12'-0"

Up, down and green all around! Light and airy, the unique trellis roof of this innovative single-entrance gazebo is just waiting for your favorite perennial vines. To extend the green-all-around look, modify the railings to a lattice pattern and train vines or grapes—or roses, for a splash of color—to experience nature all around you. The inset corners of the design provide plenty of space for planting. Simple lines make this delightful gazebo easy to construct, with no cumbersome cutting or gingerbread. The large area—128 square feet—provides built-in seating for nine people. This flexible design could be modified to a closed roof with any standard roof sheathing and shingles, and the single-entrance design can be altered to accommodate multiple entrances.

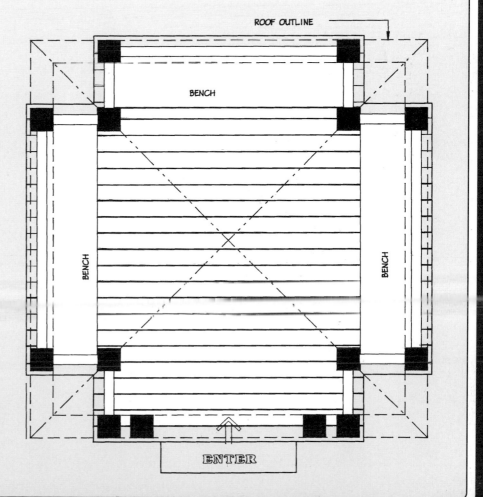

ROOF OUTLINE

BENCH

BENCH

BENCH

ENTER

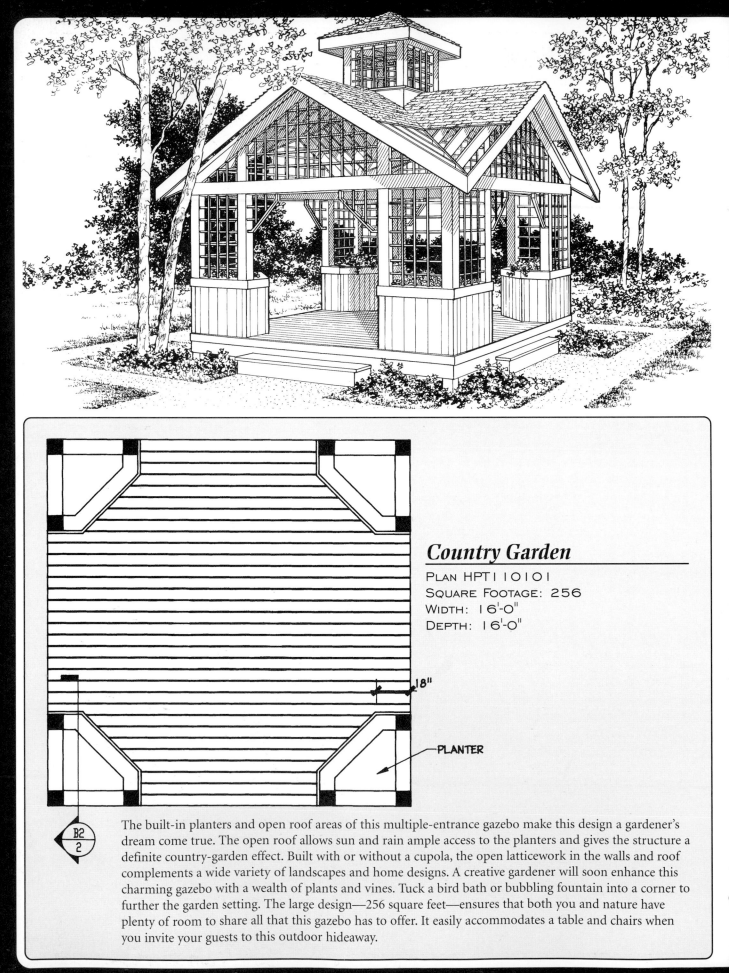

Country Garden

PLAN HPT110101
SQUARE FOOTAGE: 256
WIDTH: 16'-0"
DEPTH: 16'-0"

18"

PLANTER

B2
2

The built-in planters and open roof areas of this multiple-entrance gazebo make this design a gardener's dream come true. The open roof allows sun and rain ample access to the planters and gives the structure a definite country-garden effect. Built with or without a cupola, the open latticework in the walls and roof complements a wide variety of landscapes and home designs. A creative gardener will soon enhance this charming gazebo with a wealth of plants and vines. Tuck a bird bath or bubbling fountain into a corner to further the garden setting. The large design—256 square feet—ensures that both you and nature have plenty of room to share all that this gazebo has to offer. It easily accommodates a table and chairs when you invite your guests to this outdoor hideaway.

Beauty and the Bridge

PLAN HPT110102

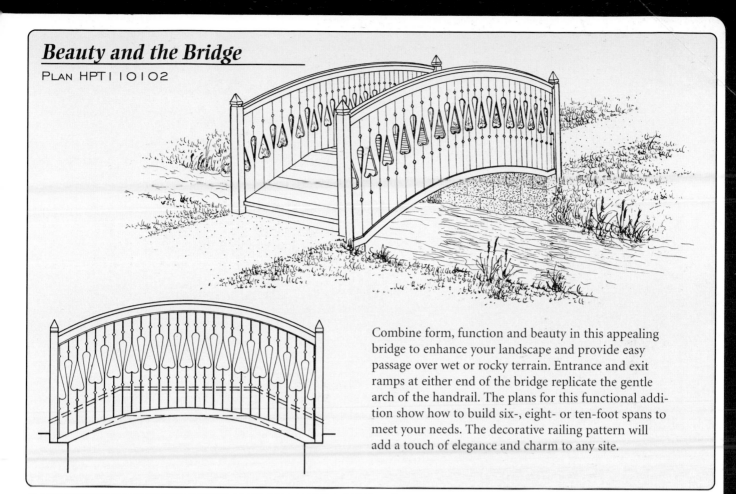

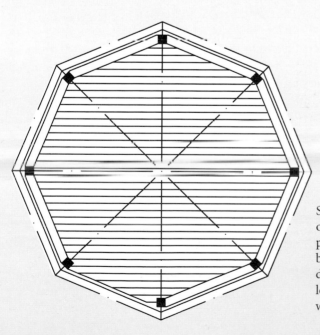

Combine form, function and beauty in this appealing bridge to enhance your landscape and provide easy passage over wet or rocky terrain. Entrance and exit ramps at either end of the bridge replicate the gentle arch of the handrail. The plans for this functional addition show how to build six-, eight- or ten-foot spans to meet your needs. The decorative railing pattern will add a touch of elegance and charm to any site.

Outdoor Leisure

PLAN HPT110103
SQUARE FOOTAGE: 71
WIDTH: 10'-0"
DEPTH: 10'-0"

Simple, yet brisk—this charming gazebo offers a sheltered openness to any yard display. With 71 square feet, this gazebo is petite, yet elegantly rustic for the countryside setting. This gazebo provides a haven and decorative motif to any garden or outdoor arrangement. Add a table and chairs and enjoy afternoon lemonade or tea over a game of cards. Certainly, this structure will encourage outdoor leisure time almost any time of the year.

Trellis Bench
PLAN HPT110104

Build this impressive arbor to cover a garden path or walkway. Add the matching bench inside the arbor as a plant shelf or to provide shaded seating. Use the bench outside as an accent to both the arbor and the surrounding landscape. The 7'-11" patterned back and 5'-11" x 8'-1½" trellis roof are ideal for climbing vines or roses, giving this beautiful arbor even more of a garden effect. The 8'-11" bench is wide enough to seat four or five adults comfortably. The latticework design is repeated on the back and sides of the bench. The arbor is designed to sit on a slab, or you can sink the support columns right into the ground using pressure-treated materials.

Designed for serious entertaining, the size alone—162 square feet—ensures you that this gazebo is unique. The star-lattice railing design, built-in benches and raised center roof with accent trim make this structure as practical as it is attractive. Large enough for small parties, there is built-in seating for about twenty people and enough floor area for another ten to twenty. Ideal for entertaining, the addition of lights and a wet bar make this design an important extension of any home. The rooflines and overhang can be modified to give an Oriental effect, or removed completely to give a carousel-like appearance. Although this double-entrance, pass-through gazebo looks complicated, it is fairly simple to build with the right tools and materials.

Starstruck

PLAN HPT110105
SQUARE FOOTAGE: 162
WIDTH: 18'-0"
DEPTH: 10'-0"

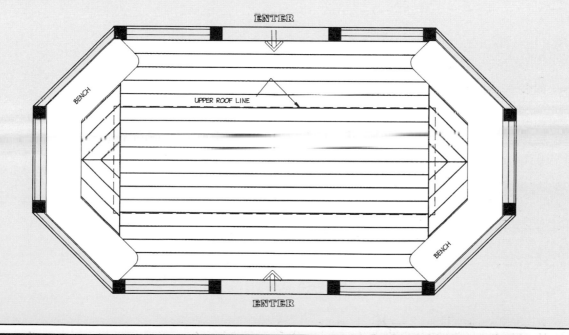

Rustic Retreat

PLAN HPT110106
SQUARE FOOTAGE: 96
WIDTH: 8'-0"
DEPTH: 16'-0"

A rustic blend of cedar shingles and siding accent the exterior of this stylish yard shed. A couple of quick steps lead up to the covered front porch, where a charming window door takes you inside. The interior is enhanced by a large bumped-out window, which illuminates every corner. A built-in work bench is an efficient addition to this design. The whole plan can be utilized as a private workshop—or make it an extra storage space for seasonal outdoor equipment.

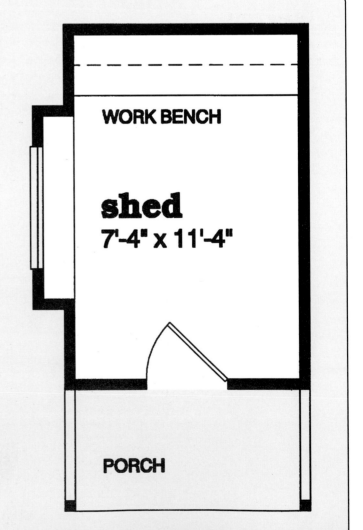

WORK BENCH

shed
7'-4" x 11'-4"

PORCH

Kaleidoscope

PLAN HPT110107
SQUARE FOOTAGE: 585
WIDTH: 19'-10"
DEPTH: 29'-6"

Shining copper on the cupola and shimmering glass windows all around enhance this double-entrance gazebo with dancing light and color. The many windows allow natural light to engulf the interior, making it a perfect studio. Easy to heat and cool, this gazebo contains operable louvers in the cupola to increase the flow of air. An exhaust fan could be added to the cupola to further maximize air flow. The masonry base with brick steps gives the structure a definite feeling of both elegance and permanence. The roof structure is made from standard framing materials with the cupola adorned with a copper cover. If cost is a factor, the cupola roof could be made of asphalt shingles and the glass windows could be eliminated.

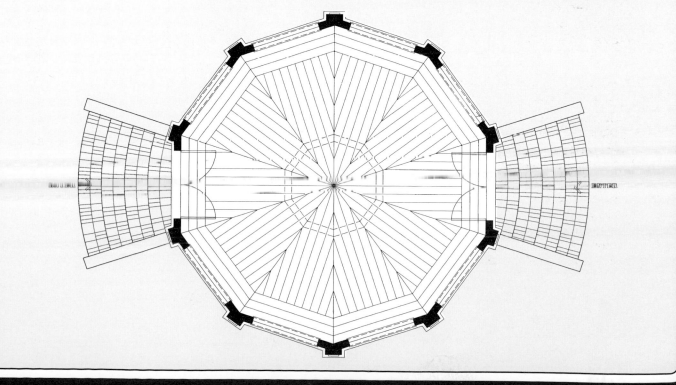

Playhouse Paradise

PLAN HPT110109
SQUARE FOOTAGE: 36
WIDTH: 6'-0"
DEPTH: 8'-0"

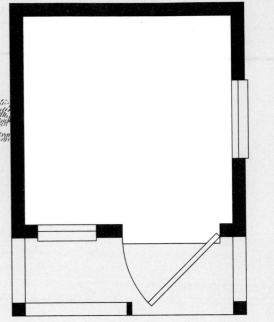

This playhouse paradise is an outdoor haven for any youngster looking for self-made entertainment. It's a place your kids can call their own. Similar to a storybook cottage, make-believe games will become a reality. From the quaint covered porch with a wood railing and square supports, go inside to where this clubhouse is brightly illuminated by two windows. This roomy space can be filled with toy furniture, games, arts and crafts, or anything to entertain on a rainy day.

Petite Pavilion

PLAN HPT110108
SQUARE FOOTAGE: 64
WIDTH: 8'-0"
DEPTH: 8'-0"

REF. SPACE

BAR COUNTER

This petite pavilion design is perfect for private and refreshing entertaining. Build this structure close to a pool area to save trips in and out of the home kitchen. Summer leisure time can be more comfortably spent with this convenience close at hand. A refrigerator space is generously provided alongside a counter preparation area. Above, built-in shelves may be added for extra storage. On the opposite side, a bar counter resides for accessible convenience.

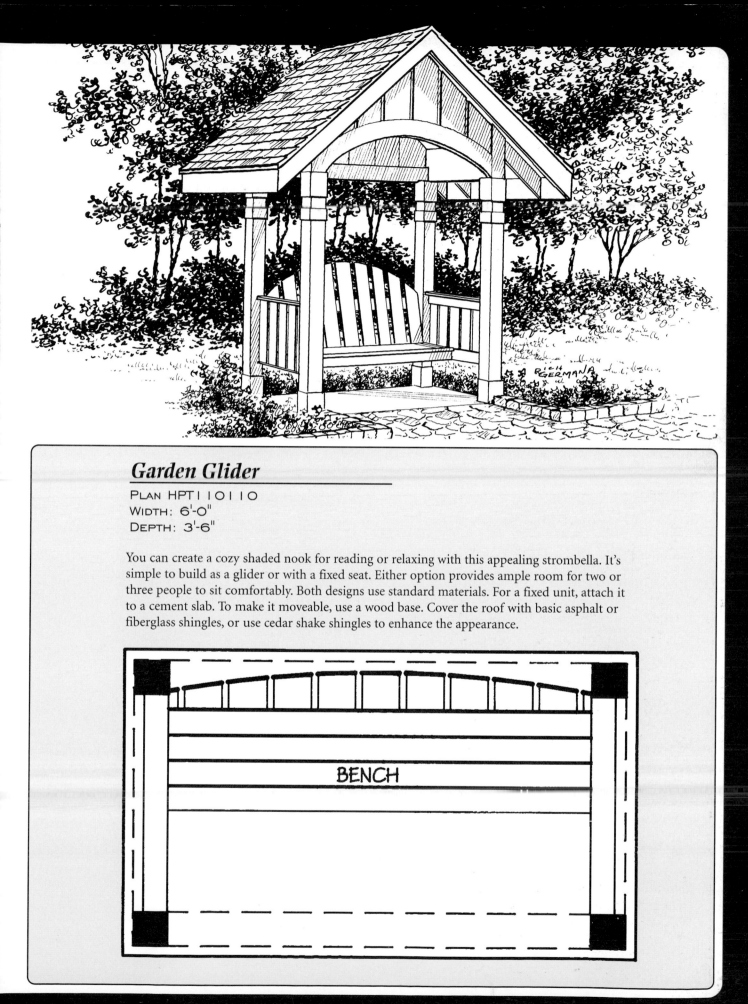

Garden Glider

PLAN HPT110110
WIDTH: 6'-0"
DEPTH: 3'-6"

You can create a cozy shaded nook for reading or relaxing with this appealing strombella. It's simple to build as a glider or with a fixed seat. Either option provides ample room for two or three people to sit comfortably. Both designs use standard materials. For a fixed unit, attach it to a cement slab. To make it moveable, use a wood base. Cover the roof with basic asphalt or fiberglass shingles, or use cedar shake shingles to enhance the appearance.

BENCH

Two-Door Tudor

PLAN HPT110111
SQUARE FOOTAGE: 128
WIDTH: 8'-0"
DEPTH: 16'-0"

Lawn shed extraordinaire, this appealing design can be easily converted from the Tudor style shown here to match just about any exterior design you prefer. In addition to serving as a lawn shed, this versatile structure also can be used as a craft studio, a pool house or a delightful playhouse for your children. The double doors and large floor area provide ample access and storage capacity for lawn tractors and other large pieces of equipment. A handy built-in work bench offers needed space for potting plants or working on craft projects. A separate storage room for craft supplies, lawn-care products or pool chemicals can be locked for safety. Strategically placed on your site, this charming building could be designed to be a reflection of your home in miniature.

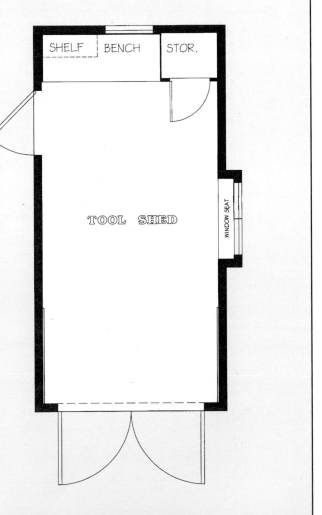

WORK BENCH

garden storage
7'-4" x 11'-4"

playhouse
7'-8" x 7'-4"

COVERED AREA

Practical and Playful

PLAN HPT110112
SQUARE FOOTAGE: 160
WIDTH: 16'-0"
DEPTH: 12'-0"

Efficient for Mom and Dad, while munchkin-sized for little people, this structure boasts practicality and playfulness. The exterior is dazzled in wood siding and cedar shingles—a pleasant display for any outdoor scenery. The garden storage area is separated from the playhouse by a wall and features a sufficient work bench and an illuminating side window. The playhouse resembles a petite version of a country cottage. A tiny covered porch with a wood railing and a window accent the outside and welcome young ones into the petite hideaway. Inside, another window graces the right wall and brightens the interior. There is room enough for a small table and chairs and, most importantly, plenty of toys.

Charming and Classic

PLAN HPT110113
WIDTH: 8'-0"
DEPTH: 8'-0"

This adorable playhouse is great for kids! Any child would enjoy the home-like touches here—a front porch and attractive window boxes where they can grow their own beautiful flowers. Adults will appreciate the classic look of keystone lintels and shutters surrounding the windows, while children will appreciate all of the playing space inside.

Shingled Victorian

PLAN HPT110114
WIDTH: 6'-0"
DEPTH: 6'-0"

A gabled doorway and wooden shingles create an attractive exterior for this petite Victorian-style playhouse, while plenty of windows brighten the interior. In addition to being a warm and friendly place for children to rest and play, this cottage also offers an opportunity for education—children can learn the basics of gardening when they add their own plants and flowers to the window box.

An accent to gracious living, this classic strombrella will create an elegant focal point in any garden or landscape. The bench is large enough to seat up to six people. To increase its function, a half-round pole table could be added to provide a small picnic area or a nook for reading. The generous entrance is four feet wide and could provide space for additional seating if needed.

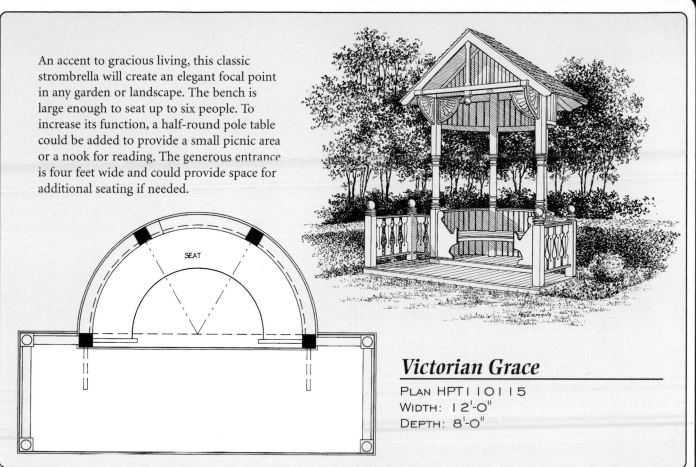

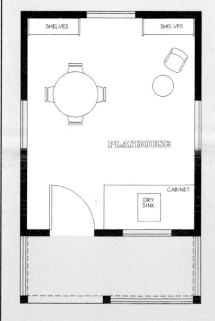

Victorian Grace

PLAN HPT110115
WIDTH: 12'-0"
DEPTH: 8'-0"

Big Kid's Playhouse

PLAN HPT110116
SQUARE FOOTAGE: 104
WIDTH: 8'-0"
DEPTH: 13'-0"

This large Victorian playhouse is for the kid in all of us. With space enough to hold bunk beds, use it for overnight adventures. Four windows flood the interior with natural light, and a single-door entrance provides access from the porch. The 8'-1" overall height will accommodate most adults and the addition of electricity and water would expand the versatility of this unit.

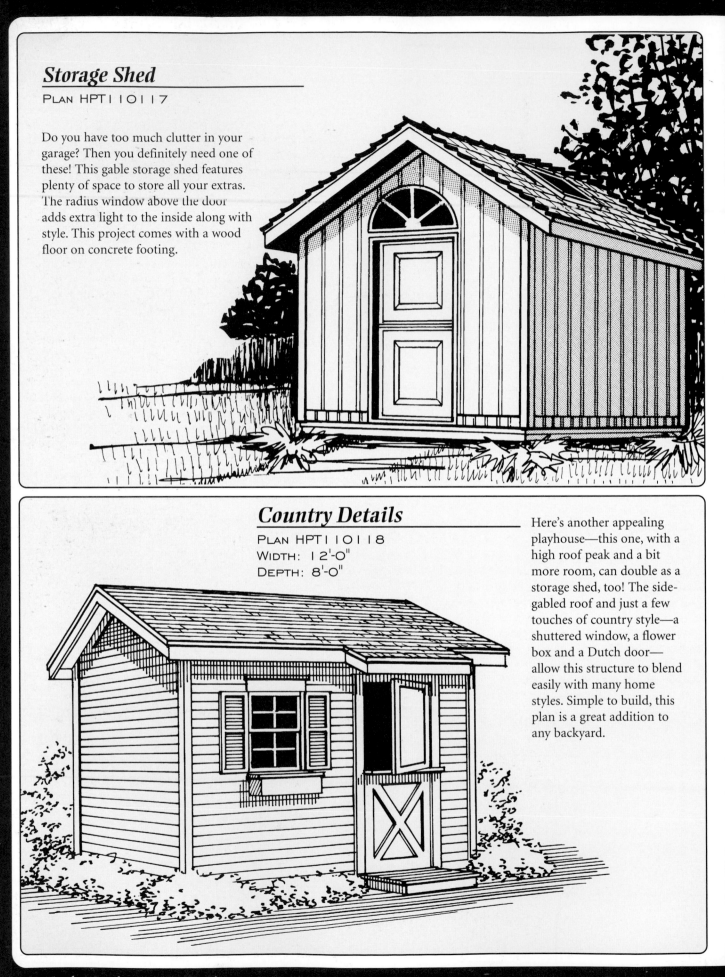

Storage Shed

PLAN HPT110117

Do you have too much clutter in your garage? Then you definitely need one of these! This gable storage shed features plenty of space to store all your extras. The radius window above the door adds extra light to the inside along with style. This project comes with a wood floor on concrete footing.

Country Details

PLAN HPT110118
WIDTH: 12'-0"
DEPTH: 8'-0"

Here's another appealing playhouse—this one, with a high roof peak and a bit more room, can double as a storage shed, too! The side-gabled roof and just a few touches of country style—a shuttered window, a flower box and a Dutch door—allow this structure to blend easily with many home styles. Simple to build, this plan is a great addition to any backyard.

Quaint Chalet

PLAN HPT110120
WIDTH: 8'-0"
DEPTH: 12'-0"

This quaint chalet design is like something you would find in a storybook. It can either be used as a playhouse for children or a storage shed for Mom and Dad—make it a playhouse in the summer and a storage shed in the off-season. The exterior is ornamented by a decorative window with shutters. The interior includes lots of space—choose a wood floor on concrete piers or a concrete floor.

Protect Your Pet

PLAN HPT110119

What a way to show your dog you care! If it's too cold or too hot for you outside, it's too cold or too hot for the dog too—these dog houses are a great way to protect your pet from harsh weather. Choose one of two attractive roofing options—gabled or gently sloping gambrel. This project also comes in two popular sizes.

Jungle Gym Adventure

PLAN HPT110121

Every child loves the adventures that take place on a jungle gym! Either you slide down the slide or swing yourself away and let your mind fly free. The swings and slide can be modified to accommodate the ages of your children. There are countless hours of fun along with plenty of outside enjoyment for everyone in the family as well. This is definitely designed with versatility and easy assembly in mind.

Unique Play Area

PLAN HPT110122

This multi-level jungle gym enjoys platforms, which create a unique play structure. You can bring up some small chairs or tables and have a tea party, or you can spread out some sleeping bags and invite friends for an overnight adventure. Aside from the stairs, there is an even more fun way to go up and down—a net!

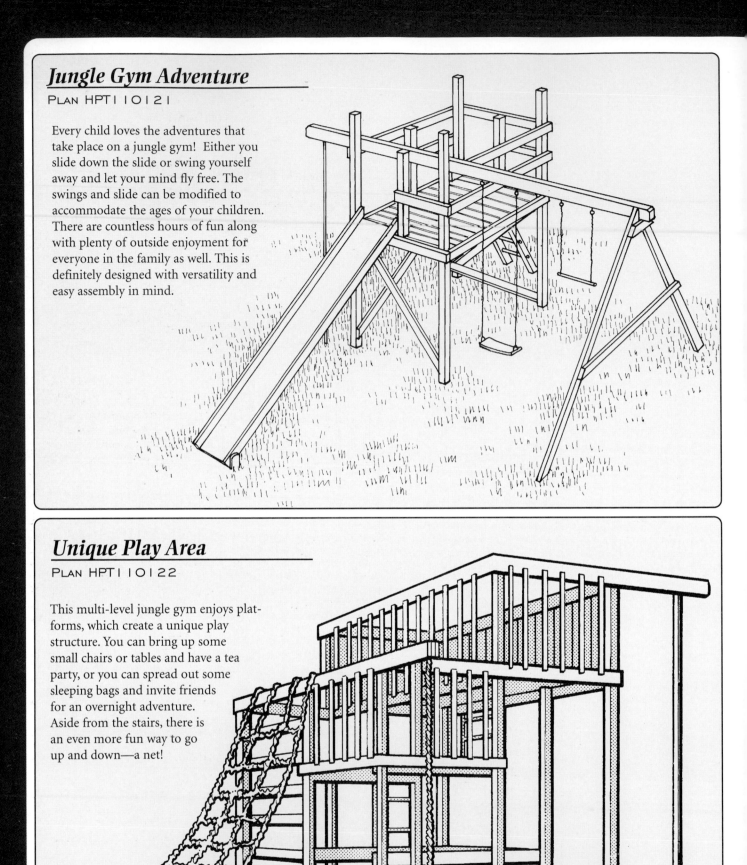

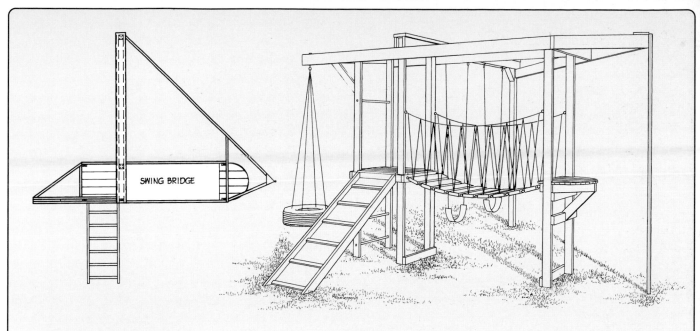

SWING BRIDGE

Swinging Bridge

PLAN HPT110124

The highlight of this delightful playset is the swinging bridge. It is available ready-made in a variety of styles, or you can make it yourself. Designed for kids five and older, this playset includes a ladder inset at an angle to help developmental coordination. Both shelf-style swings and a popular tire swing are provided for variety.

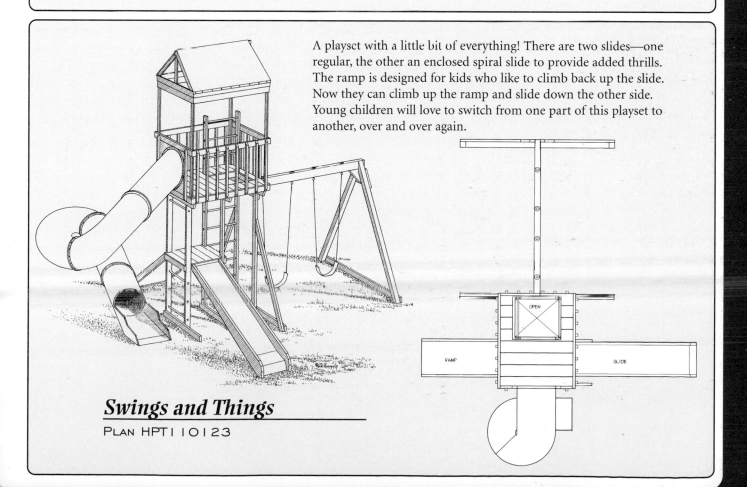

A playset with a little bit of everything! There are two slides—one regular, the other an enclosed spiral slide to provide added thrills. The ramp is designed for kids who like to climb back up the slide. Now they can climb up the ramp and slide down the other side. Young children will love to switch from one part of this playset to another, over and over again.

OPEN

RAMP   SLIDE

Swings and Things

PLAN HPT110123

A playhouse, a tree house, a lookout tower... your children will invent many uses for this mini-gazebo perched almost eight feet above the ground. It's large enough for a small table and chairs for a picnic or a Mad Hatter's tea party. Or, spread out some sleeping bags and invite friends for an overnight adventure—but no sleepwalking! The ladder, swings and slide all add to the fun and can be modified to accommodate the ages of your children. If you have a full-size gazebo on your site, or plan to build one, you could use a similar design in the railings for both units for a surprising "double-take" effect.

The Lookout

PLAN HPT110125
WIDTH: 17'-0"
DEPTH: 11'-8"

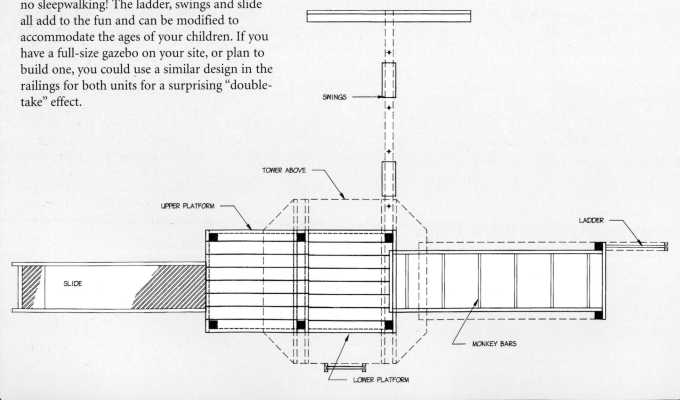

Sail Away

PLAN HPT110126

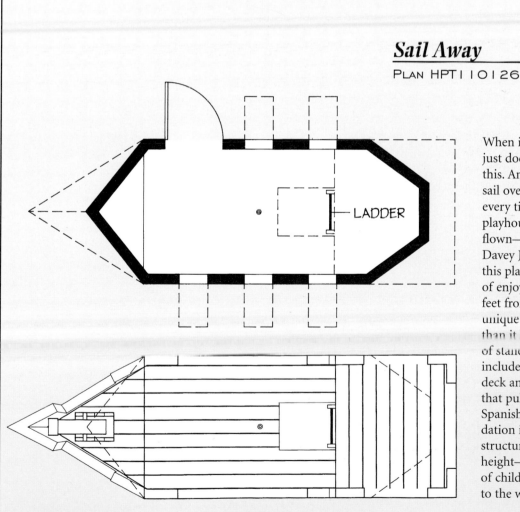

LADDER

When it comes to playhouses, it just doesn't get much better than this. Any child's imagination will sail over mysterious, unknown seas every time he or she enters this playhouse. No matter what flag is flown—that of Captain Hook, Davey Jones or Queen Isabella—this playhouse will offer kids years of enjoyment. More than fifteen feet from stem to stern, this unique playhouse is easier to build than it looks. Constructed entirely of standard materials, the design includes a cannon on the main deck and gun ports in the hold that pull open to simulate a real Spanish galleon. A concrete foundation is recommended for this structure, due to its overall height—9'-5½"—and the number of children who will be sailing off to the wonderful places.

Camelot

PLAN HPT110127
WIDTH: 11'-0"
DEPTH: 10'-0"

Lords and ladies, knights and evil-doers—this playhouse has everything except a fire-breathing dragon! Your children will spend hours re-enacting the days of Kings and Queens and Knights of the Round Table. Surprisingly easy to build, this playset right out of King Arthur's Court uses standard materials. One corner of the playhouse holds a 4' x 4' sandbox. A stairway leads to a 3' x 3' tower with its own catwalk. The area under the stairway could be enclosed to make a storage room for toys...or a dungeon to hold the captured Black Knight. The double castle doors can be fitted with standard hardware, but wrought-iron hinges will make this innovative playhouse look even more like a castle.

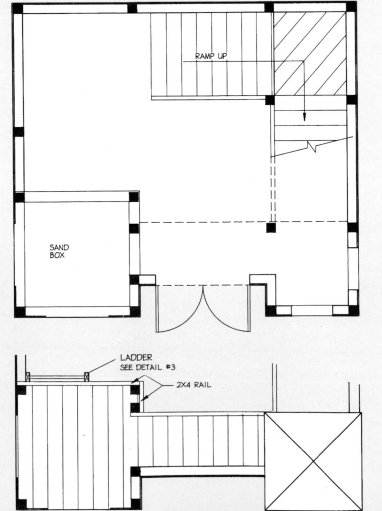

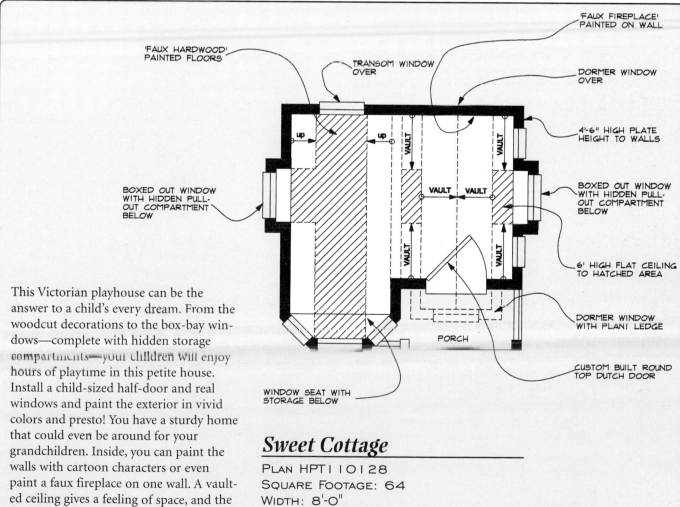

'FAUX FIREPLACE' PAINTED ON WALL

'FAUX HARDWOOD' PAINTED FLOORS

TRANSOM WINDOW OVER

DORMER WINDOW OVER

4'-6" HIGH PLATE HEIGHT TO WALLS

BOXED OUT WINDOW WITH HIDDEN PULL-OUT COMPARTMENT BELOW

VAULT VAULT

BOXED OUT WINDOW WITH HIDDEN PULL-OUT COMPARTMENT BELOW

6' HIGH FLAT CEILING TO HATCHED AREA

DORMER WINDOW WITH PLANT LEDGE

PORCH

CUSTOM BUILT ROUND TOP DUTCH DOOR

WINDOW SEAT WITH STORAGE BELOW

This Victorian playhouse can be the answer to a child's every dream. From the woodcut decorations to the box-bay windows—complete with hidden storage compartments—your children will enjoy hours of playtime in this petite house. Install a child-sized half-door and real windows and paint the exterior in vivid colors and presto! You have a sturdy home that could even be around for your grandchildren. Inside, you can paint the walls with cartoon characters or even paint a faux fireplace on one wall. A vaulted ceiling gives a feeling of space, and the transom windows let sunlight flood in.

Sweet Cottage

PLAN HPT110128
SQUARE FOOTAGE: 64
WIDTH: 8'-0"
DEPTH: 8'-0"

Canopied Swing

PLAN HPT110222

Your backyard will become the favorite hangout of friends and neighbors once you install this charming garden swing—everyone loves to enjoy the outdoors in style! The six-foot bench offers enough space to seat several people, and a wide canopy provides shade from the sun on hot summer days. Five feet wide and over seven feet high, the canopy also allows a bit of extra space for other guests to step into the shade.

Timeless Pleasure

PLAN HPT110129

A timeless pleasure—the porch swing. Chains are included with the swings, so all you need to do is find a good place to hang it. The swing is ideal for attaching to a porch or any outside structure, and provides a place to stargaze or sit and read. Relaxation is the keyword! These swings are comfortable and made for a long, useful life—enjoy!

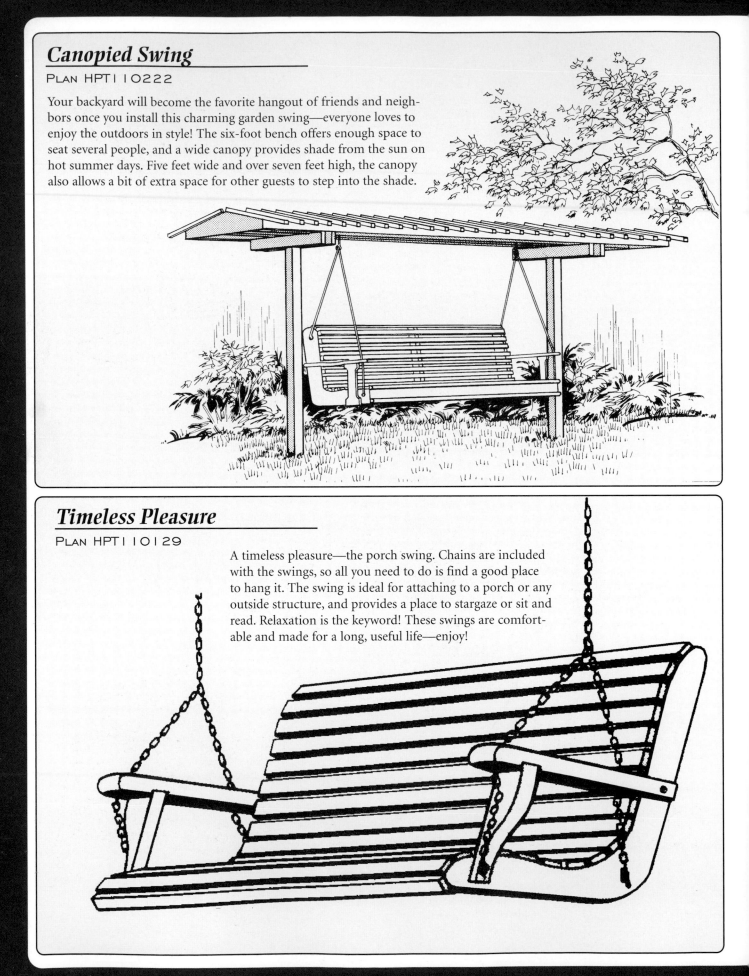

Comfortable Chair

PLAN HPT110130

This fine adirondack chair offers the ultimate in design and comfort—great for outside lounging. The ergonomic design features a deep, contoured seat and a curved, comfortable back. Wide, level arms are positioned sensibly and easily accommodate a drink plus a plate of snacks. This is a project that's very practical and unique with a sturdy construction.

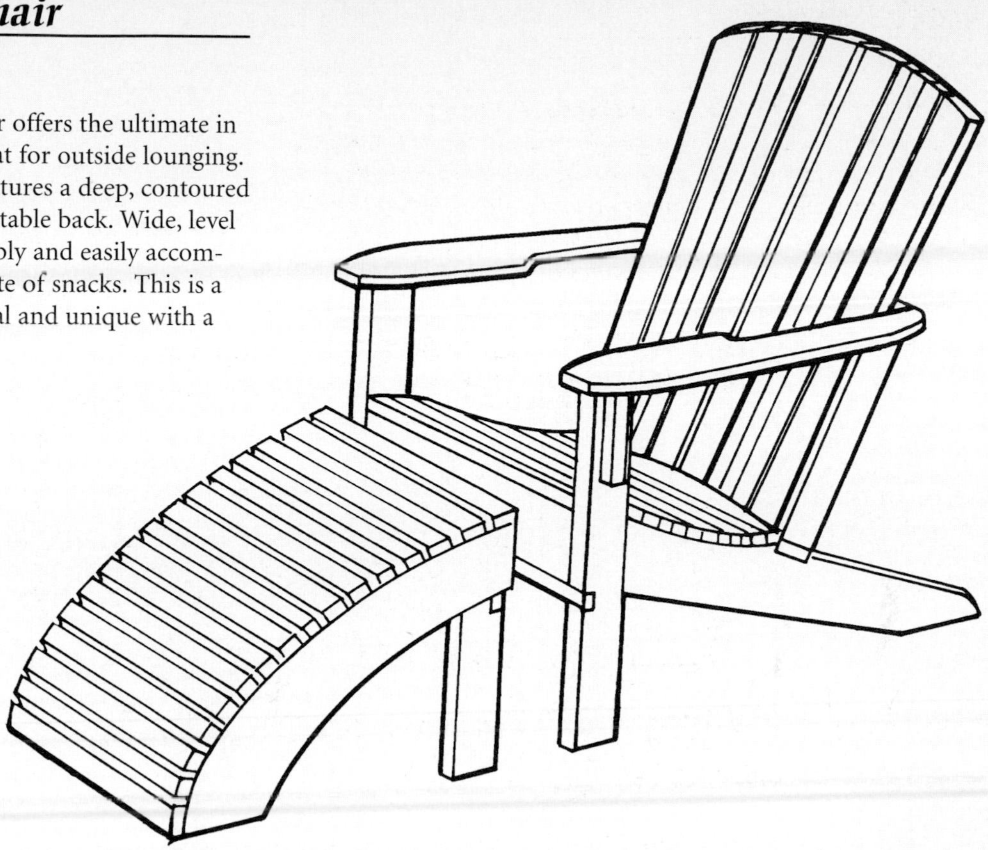

Outdoor Seating

PLAN HPT110131

A picnic table is always a great addition to any backyard, patio or deck! Ideal for outdoor entertaining and backyard barbecues, these tables provide a place where family and friends can sit and enjoy meals. A very attractive design along with reliable construction is what makes this dining set a winner.

Little House in the Garden

PLAN HPT110132
SQUARE FOOTAGE: 72
WIDTH: 12'-0"
DEPTH: 6'-0"

Designed to blend into the garden surroundings, this cozy little building keeps all your garden tools and supplies at your fingertips. This structure is large enough to accommodate a potting bench, shelves and an area for garden tools. The window above the potting bench allows ample light, but electricity could be added easily. To convert this shed design to a playhouse, simply change the window shelf into a planter and add a step with a handrail at the door.

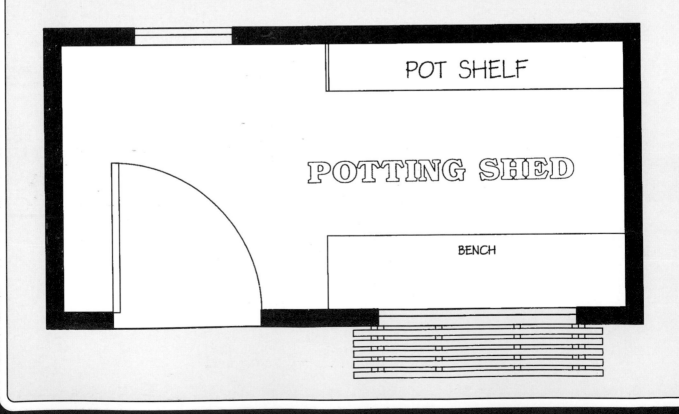

POT SHELF

POTTING SHED

BENCH

Designer Playhouse

PLAN HPT110133
SQUARE FOOTAGE: 183
WIDTH: 18'-0"
DEPTH: 14'-0"

This whimsical, scaled-down version of a full-size house makes a dream-come-true playhouse for kids. Designed by Conni Cross, it features a wraparound front porch with a trellis roof, a "real" front door and a loft that can only be reached by a ladder through a trapdoor! Generous dimensions provide plenty of space for a 7'-4" x 9'-4" playroom and a 5'-8" x 6'-4" bunk room. A 7'-4" x 5'-4" loft overlooks the main play area. Natural light floods all areas of this delightful play center through windows in the playroom, bunk room and loft. A sturdy railing borders the loft and the built-in bunk beds in the bunk room are ready and waiting for sleepovers.

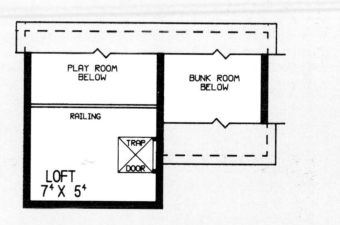

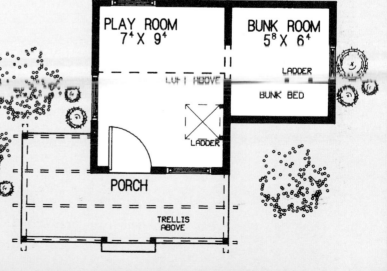

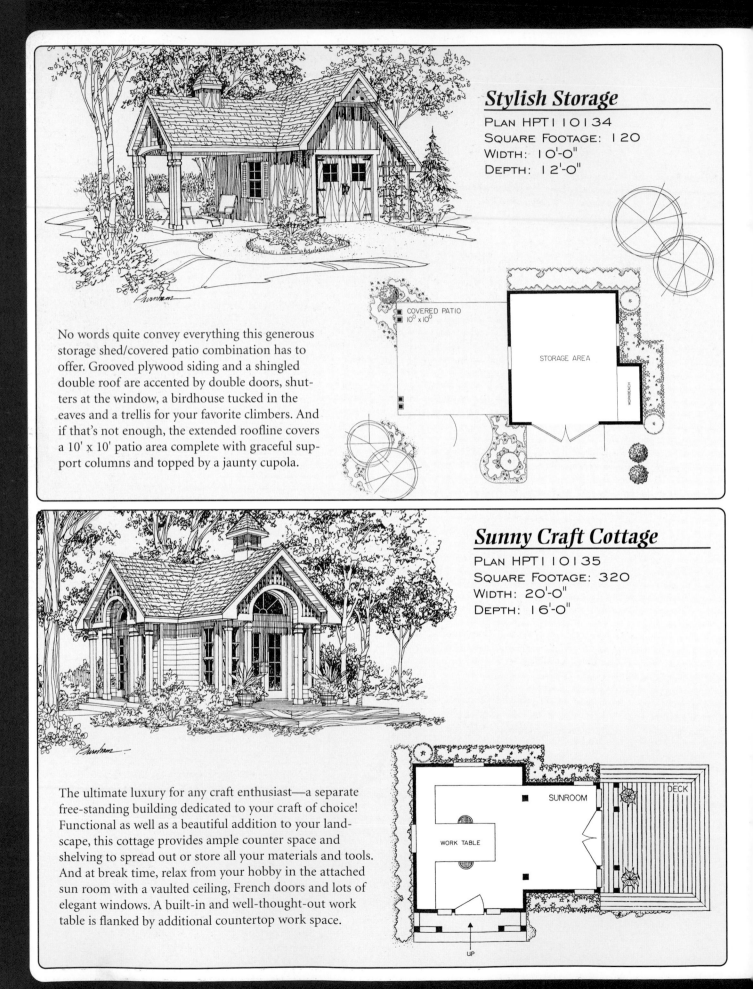

Stylish Storage

PLAN HPT110134
SQUARE FOOTAGE: 120
WIDTH: 10'-0"
DEPTH: 12'-0"

No words quite convey everything this generous storage shed/covered patio combination has to offer. Grooved plywood siding and a shingled double roof are accented by double doors, shutters at the window, a birdhouse tucked in the eaves and a trellis for your favorite climbers. And if that's not enough, the extended roofline covers a 10' x 10' patio area complete with graceful support columns and topped by a jaunty cupola.

COVERED PATIO
10⁰ x 10⁰

STORAGE AREA

WORKBENCH

Sunny Craft Cottage

PLAN HPT110135
SQUARE FOOTAGE: 320
WIDTH: 20'-0"
DEPTH: 16'-0"

The ultimate luxury for any craft enthusiast—a separate free-standing building dedicated to your craft of choice! Functional as well as a beautiful addition to your landscape, this cottage provides ample counter space and shelving to spread out or store all your materials and tools. And at break time, relax from your hobby in the attached sun room with a vaulted ceiling, French doors and lots of elegant windows. A built-in and well-thought-out work table is flanked by additional countertop work space.

SUNROOM

DECK

WORK TABLE

UP

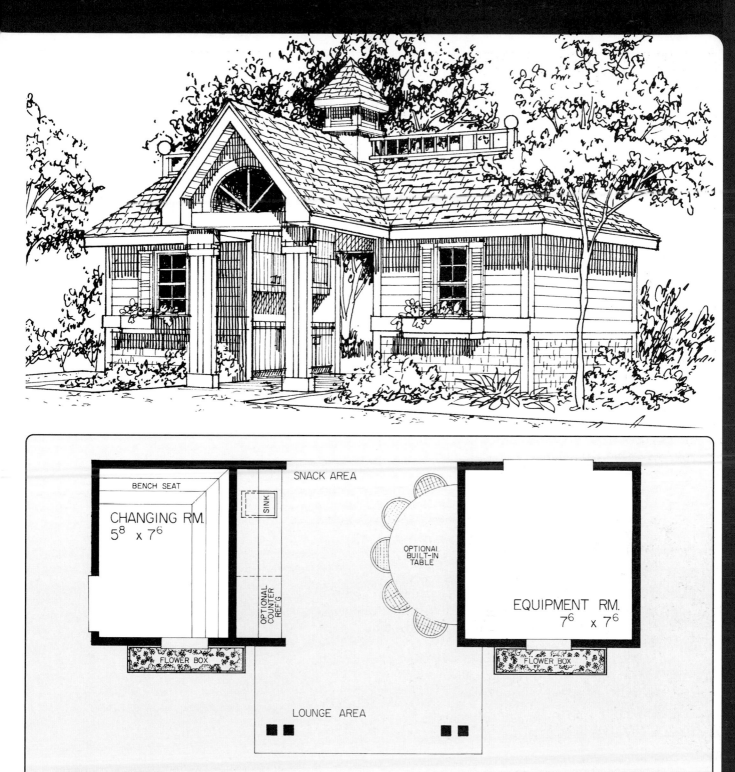

Rain or Shine Pool Cabana

PLAN HPI110136
WIDTH: 24'-0"
DEPTH: 12'-8"

You can enhance both the beauty and the function of any pool area with this charming structure. A mini-kitchen and an optional built-in table are tucked in the breezeway of this double room; you'll have shelter for poolside repasts no matter what the weather. The exterior features include a gable roof with columns in the front, shuttered windows, horizontal wood and shingle siding, decorative flower boxes and a cupola. The two rooms on either side of the breezeway area provide a 5'-8" x 7'-6" changing area with built-in seating and a larger area—7'-6" x 7'-6"—for convenient storage of pool supplies and equipment. This spacious cabana is sure to be a fine addition to an active family's pool area.

Work and Play

PLAN HPT110137
SQUARE FOOTAGE: 152
WIDTH: 16'-0"
DEPTH: 8'-0"

The kids will love this one! This functional, practical lawn shed doubles in design and capacity as a delightful playhouse complete with a covered porch, lathe-turned columns and a window box for young gardeners. The higher roofline on the shed gives the structure a two-story effect, while the playhouse design gives the simple lawn shed a much more appealing appearance. The shed is accessed through double doors. The playhouse features a single-door entrance from the porch and three bright windows. The interior wall between the shed and playhouse could be moved another two-and-a-half feet back to make one of the rooms larger. Remove the interior wall completely to use the entire area exclusively for either the lawn shed or playhouse. The open eaves and porch columns give the structure a country appearance; however, by boxing in the eaves and modifying the columns, you can create just about any style you or the kids like best.

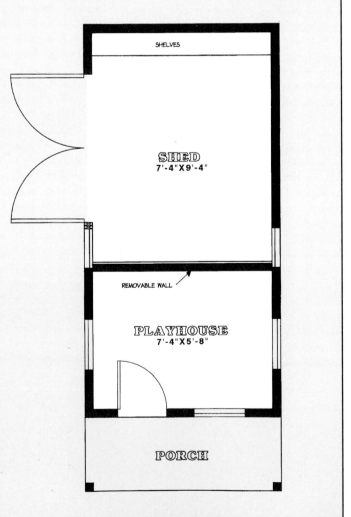

SHELVES

SHED
7'-4"X9'-4"

REMOVABLE WALL

PLAYHOUSE
7'-4"X5'-8"

PORCH

Double Duty

PLAN HPT110138
SQUARE FOOTAGE: 168
WIDTH: 14'-0"
DEPTH: 12'-0"

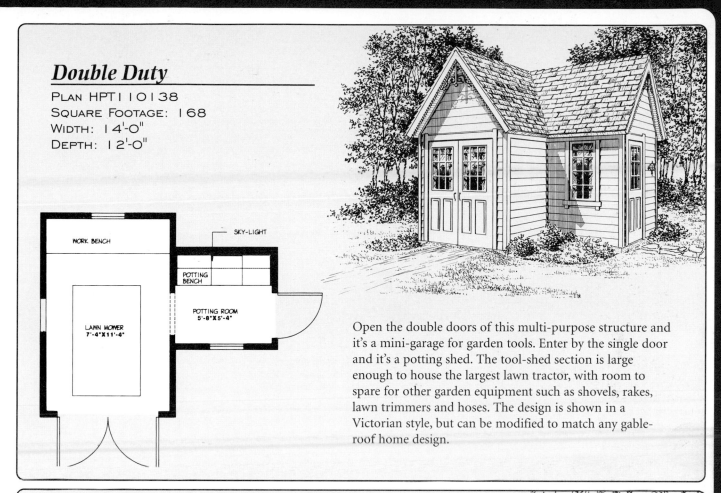

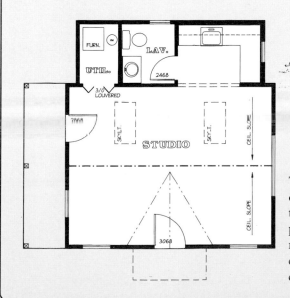

WORK BENCH

SKY-LIGHT

POTTING BENCH

LAWN MOWER 7'-4"X11'-4"

POTTING ROOM 5'-8"X5'-4"

Open the double doors of this multi-purpose structure and it's a mini-garage for garden tools. Enter by the single door and it's a potting shed. The tool-shed section is large enough to house the largest lawn tractor, with room to spare for other garden equipment such as shovels, rakes, lawn trimmers and hoses. The design is shown in a Victorian style, but can be modified to match any gable-roof home design.

Town and Country

PLAN HPT110139
SQUARE FOOTAGE: 320
WIDTH: 20'-0"
DEPTH: 22'-0"

FURN.

LAV.

UTIL.

2468

3/0 LOUVERED

2868

SKY.T.

STUDIO

SKY.T.

CEIL. SLOPE

CEIL. SLOPE

3068

This versatile design features a unique siding pattern: a little bit of country with a pinch of contemporary sophistication. Planned to take advantage of natural light from all sides, this design will make a perfect studio, game room or office. Or, add a shower in the lavatory room and it becomes a guest house. The front porch area is a charming place to relax and put your feet up as you or your guests contemplate the events of the day.

Weekend Cottage

PLAN HPT110140
SQUARE FOOTAGE: 144
WIDTH: 12'-0"
DEPTH: 16'-0"

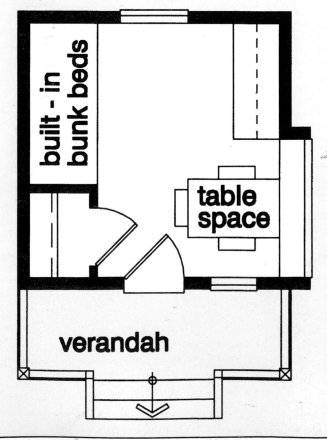

ALTERNATE ELEVATION

For a bare-essentials outdoor structure, this weekend cottage offers a wealth of options for its use. Choose it for handy home office space, craft cottage space, extra room for visitors, a playhouse for the kids or a game room. It features a covered front porch and offers two lovely rustic exteriors from which to choose. The interior has built-in bunk beds, a closet and a bumped-out window that works well for table space. Plans include details for both crawlspace and slab foundation.

Quiet Studio

PLAN HPT110141
SQUARE FOOTAGE: 432
WIDTH: 20'-0"
DEPTH: 30'-0"

Need a quiet place for a home office or studio? You can't go wrong by choosing the plans for this cleverly designed structure. It is filled with amenities that make a small space seem huge. The vaulted ceiling of the main part of the building features clerestory windows to provide ample lighting. Bumped-out areas on both sides are perfect for desks and work areas. A built-in bookshelf along one wall is complemented by a large walk-in storage closet. A half-bath and wet bar round out the plan. The entry is graced by a columned porch and double French doors flanked by fixed windows.

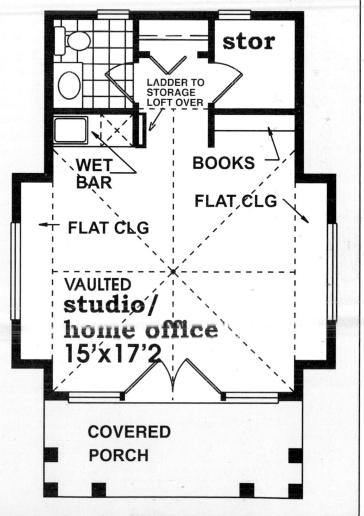

stor

LADDER TO
STORAGE
LOFT OVER

WET
BAR

BOOKS

FLAT CLG

FLAT CLG

VAULTED
studio/
home office
15'x17'2

COVERED
PORCH

Stylish Retreat

PLAN HPT110142
SQUARE FOOTAGE: 128
WIDTH: 16'-0"
DEPTH: 8'-0"

This stylish pavilion is an amusing outdoor retreat for any family. A hipped roof shades the inner area—keep a picnic table close by for outdoor barbecues and entertaining. To the right, a barbecue area is provided for outdoor grilling. A convenient work counter is useful for preparing outdoor meals. A refrigerator space is also provided, next to another counter, for keeping cool foods fresh. The pavilion is completed by a bar counter, large enough to host a wide variety of refreshments. Decorate the outer perimeters with either potted plants or build in a flower bed. Built for the family that excels in entertaining, this structure is a lively addition to any property.

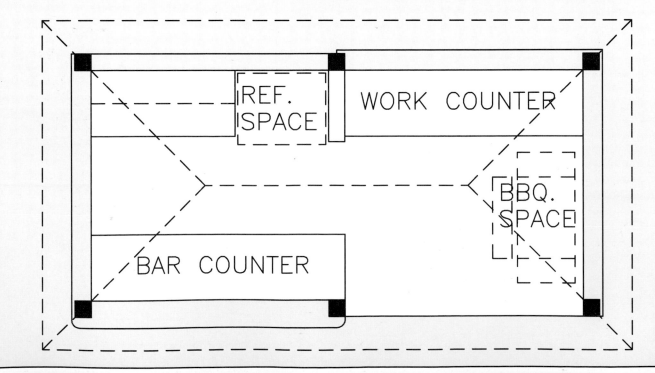

Multi-Functional Ramada

PLAN HPT110143
SQUARE FOOTAGE: 576
WIDTH: 24'-0"
DEPTH: 24'-0"

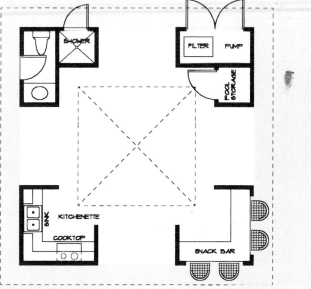

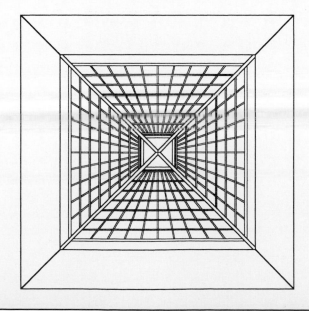

Entertain the possibilities for pool-side parties with this smart, multi-functional ramada. Four corner units are united by open-air walkways and are almost literally tied together by a trellis roof. Pull up a chair to the outside bar in one corner for a refreshing drink or snack. Across the walkway is an efficient kitchenette. In the next corner is a restroom and a shower, each with a separate entrance. The final corner hides all the pool essentials with double doors leading to the filter and pump room and a separate storage room for other pool equipment and toys.

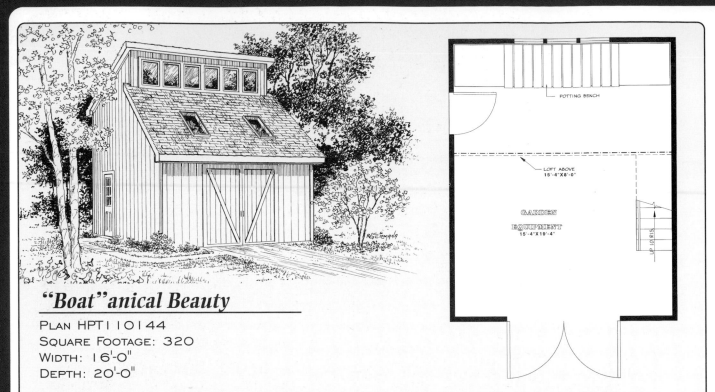

"Boat"anical Beauty

PLAN HPT110144
SQUARE FOOTAGE: 320
WIDTH: 16'-0"
DEPTH: 20'-0"

This large multi-level garden shed can be easily modified to become a boat house if yours is a nautical family. As a lawn or garden shed, there is ample room for all your garden equipment, with a separate area for potting plants. The roomy loft provides 133 square feet of safe storage area for chemicals, fertilizers or other lawn-care products. This practical structure can also be used as a studio or, placed at the water's edge, it can be easily converted to a boat house by adding 4' x 4' columns used as piers in lieu of the slab floor.

Garden Greenhouse

PLAN HPT110145
WIDTH: 12'-0"
DEPTH: 10'-0"

This garden shed, entered through a two-part Dutch door, makes an ideal greenhouse or hobby house with its skylight windows for optimal plant growth. Inside you will find ample room for tool and lawn equipment storage. Whether you are a new or avid gardener, the unique design of this garden shed offers the ultimate in yard flexibility.

Change-Up

PLAN HPT110146
SQUARE FOOTAGE: 32
WIDTH: 8'-0"
DEPTH: 4'-0"

Here's a unique design that can be converted to serve a variety of functions: a tool shed, a barbecue stand, a pool-supply depot or a sports-equipment locker. Apply a little "what-if" imagination to come up with additional ways to use this versatile design to enhance your outdoor living space. As a tool shed, this design features a large potting bench with storage above and below. Second, as a summer kitchen, it includes a built-in grill, a sink and a refrigerator. Third, for use as a pool-supply depot or equipment storage, it comes with a locker to store chemicals or valuable sports equipment safely. This structure is designed to be movable but, depending on its function, could be placed on a concrete slab.

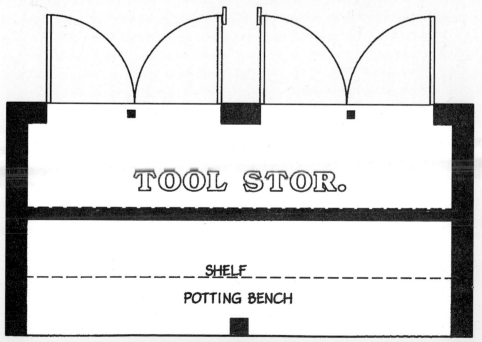

TOOL STOR.

SHELF

POTTING BENCH

Country Shed

PLAN HPT110147
SQUARE FOOTAGE: 144
WIDTH: 12'-0"
DEPTH: 12'-0"

Country living is complete with this barnyard-
style shed, which complements any country or
farmhouse setting as a quaint rural motif.
Double doors open to accommodate and house
any large lawn machinery. Inside this 144-
square-foot wood-siding structure, space can
be divided for tool storage, wood stock storage,
or even a small outdoor workshop area. A window at the rear of the barn shed illuminates the
inside for extra light, making it easier to
maneuver inside during the day.

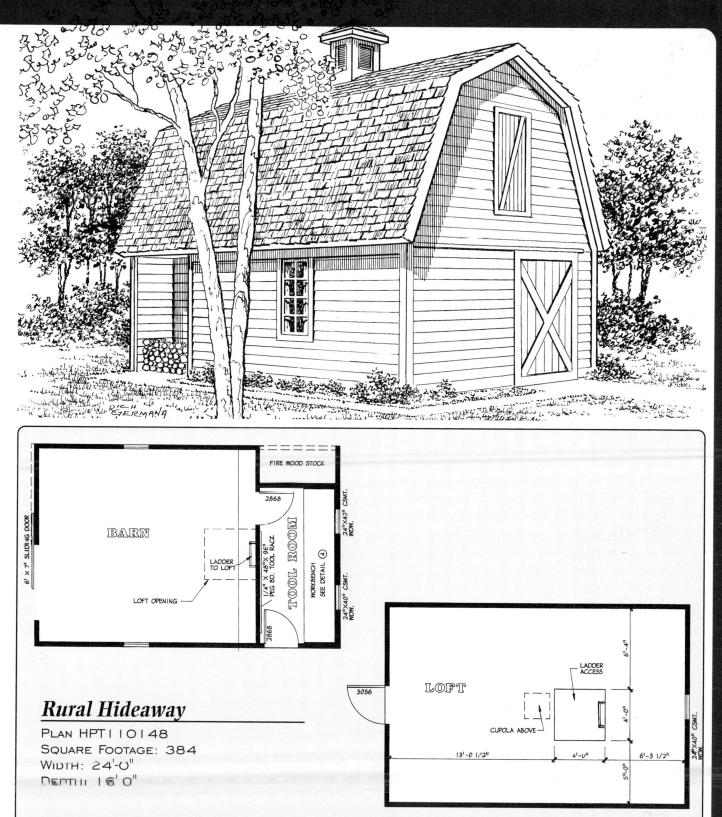

FIRE WOOD STOCK

BARN

6' X 7' SLIDING DOOR

2868

LADDER
TO LOFT

LOFT OPENING

TOOL ROOM

1/4" X 48" X 96"
PEG BD. TOOL RACK

WORKBENCH
SEE DETAIL ④

24"X40" CSMT.
WDW.

24"X40" CSMT.
WDW.

2868

LOFT

3056

LADDER
ACCESS

CUPOLA ABOVE

6'-4"

4'-0"

13'-0 1/2"

4'-0"

6'-3 1/2"

5'-0"

24"X40" CSMT.
WDW.

Rural Hideaway

PLAN HPT110148

SQUARE FOOTAGE: 384

WIDTH: 24'-0"

DEPTH: 16'-0"

This large, sturdy lawn shed is not quite "as big as a barn," but almost! A combined area of 768 square feet—with 384 square feet per floor—includes a 24' x 16' loft area with access by ladder or stairway. The structure is built entirely of standard framing materials requiring no special beams or cutting. An ideal hideaway for the serious artist, this structure could serve a myriad of other uses including a second garage, a game house, or even as a barn for small livestock. Or, expand the design to include utilities and a bathroom to provide a secluded guest room. The large tool room at the back has a built-in work bench with plenty of natural light, plus entrances from inside or outside. If your house has a fireplace, space is provided for a built-in wood stockpile area. The same space could be used to extend the length of the tool room. A louvered cupola and a 6' x 7' sliding-door entrance with crossbars accent the rural effect.

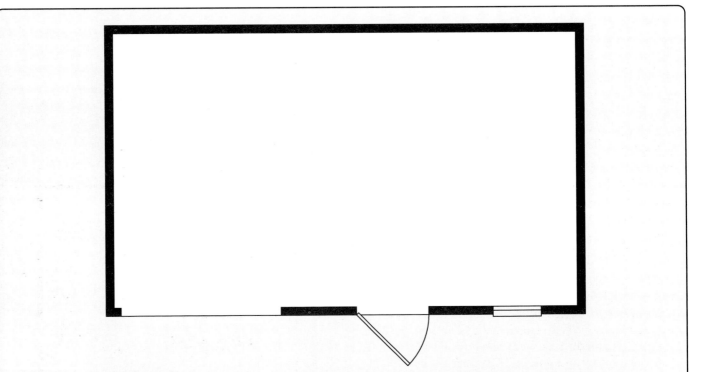

Efficient Design

PLAN HPT110149
SQUARE FOOTAGE: 240
WIDTH: 20'-0"
DEPTH: 12'-0"

This design is meant for the efficient yard organizer. Structured with vertical wood siding and a barnyard-style door, this design thrives in any type of country setting and complements many farmhouse designs as well. Inside, a single window brightens the interior, while 240 square feet of space may be divided among a variety of different yard supplies. Gardening tools and chemicals may be stored safely and efficiently away from the home. Extra firewood may be staked inside or outside during long winter periods. Special yard machinery and tools may be accessed and stored in a separate shed area for convenient use.

El Grande

PLAN HPT110150
SQUARE FOOTAGE: 1,918
WIDTH: 56'-0"
DEPTH: 53'-0"

If you run a large operation, consider this expanded floor plan for your stable requirements. Six 12'-2" x 12' livestock pens with dirt floors feature built-in feed and water troughs and Dutch doors leading either to a fenced exercise area or into either of two conveniently located grooming areas. Both grooming areas have grooved cement floors, sloped for easy hosing and draining. A convenient connecting hall between the grooming areas also has sloped concrete floors for easy maintenance. A central secured tack room with built-in saddle racks and grain bins, a bath with a toilet and sink and a 10' x 17' inside storage area for hay complete the available features. Seven skylights throughout the structure provide an abundance of natural light.

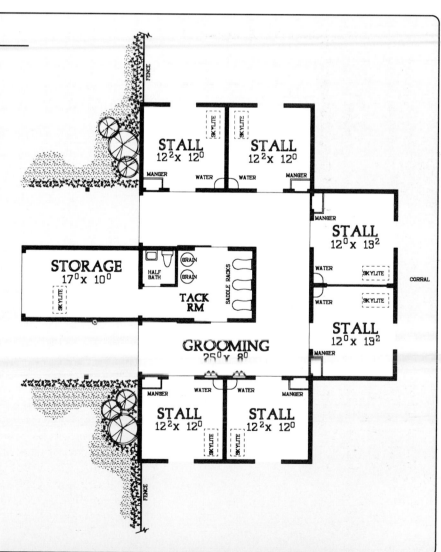

Distinguished Decks:

24 outstanding outdoor living plans

A beautiful deck addition can mean so much—not only to the value of your home, but also to the enjoyment you and your family will share in using this outdoor extension. On the following pages are 24 decks you can actually build. Included with many of the decks are allowances for special amenities such as whirlpool spas, outdoor play equipment for children, and gardening areas. Many also include planters, barbecues, wet bars and benches—everything needed for the perfect outdoor space. You'll also see charming deck details such as gazebos, spiral staircases and secluded conversation areas.

Take a tour through our gallery of deck designs—whether you're looking for a simple outdoor extension or an elegant entertainment area complete with a spa, one of these designs is sure to catch your eye.

Split-Level Sun Deck

PLAN HPT110151

Simple in design, yet versatile in function, this two-level deck provides a striking addition to a backyard landscape where space is at a premium. Covering a total of 540 square feet, the deck can be accessed from indoors at both levels. The upper level can be reached through sliding glass doors at the breakfast room, making it handy to take meals outdoors. Just outside the breakfast room is plenty of space for a table and chairs. A railing wraps around the design, providing safety and interest.

One step down takes you to another level. This level is accessed from indoors via the family room. A built-in bench just outside the sliding doors provides a place for seating and relaxation. The two-step, tiered design provides access to the ground level along its length. Though it is adaptable to any size or style of house, this deck was created to complement Home Planners Design HPB774. For information about ordering blueprints for this home, call 1-800-521-6797.

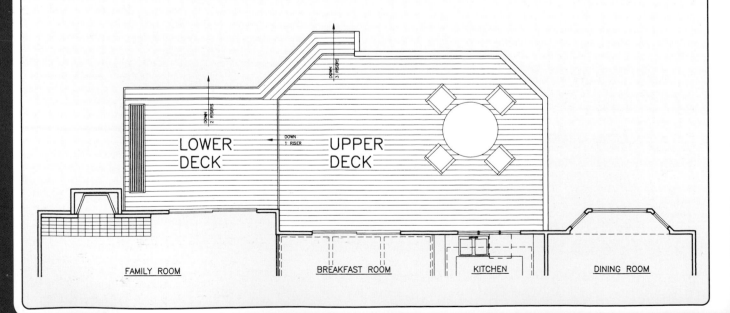

Bi-Level Deck with Covered Dining

PLAN HPT110152

This deck is designed for an active family, as well as for entertaining. With two levels and two accesses from indoors, each area becomes a versatile extension of its adjacent room. The total deck area adds 945 square feet of outdoor living space. Both levels of this deck extend into the backyard. Stairway exits from level one and level two allow easy access to the ground from both the breakfast room and gathering room. Both rooms open onto the deck for open-air enjoyment of meals, entertaining and quiet times of relaxation. Because the gathering room is three steps down from surrounding rooms, the exit to the lower deck is made without stepping down.

An overhead trellis or covered area provides a feeling of privacy and shade, making the deck's sitting area comfortable even during warm periods of the year. Built-in benches provide ample seating for guests. Though it is adaptable to any size or style of house, this deck was created to complement Home Planners Design HPB683. For information about ordering blueprints for this home, call 1-800-521-6797.

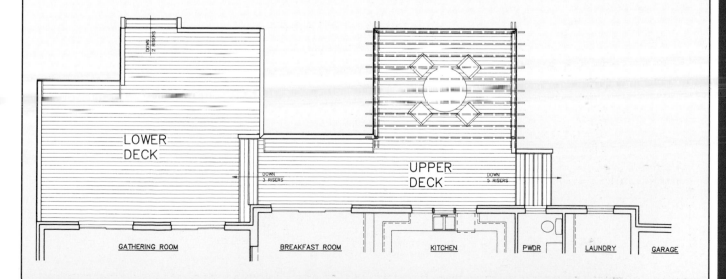

Fresh-Air Corner Deck

PLAN HPT110153

This deck is designed to be built as a simple, rectangular side deck, or to wrap around the corner of a home. Depending on the home's interior layout, it could be modified to allow access from two indoor rooms instead of one as shown here. The wrap design creates some interesting angles, which make the deck seem much larger than its 445 square feet. Separate areas of the deck are natural settings for different activities. For example, the corner directly in front of the dining-room door is more than adequate to accommodate a table and seating for four or more people.

The opposite corner, away from the dining room, is an ideal place for built-in seating, as shown on this plan. The distinct area that is created here works well for conversation, relaxation or for additional seating during meals. Steps allow for quick access to and from the ground level. Railings for safety and appearance provide the finishing touch to this simple, yet versatile deck. Though it is adaptable to any size or style of house, this deck was created to complement Home Planners Design HPB488. For information about ordering blueprints for this home, call 1-800-521-6797.

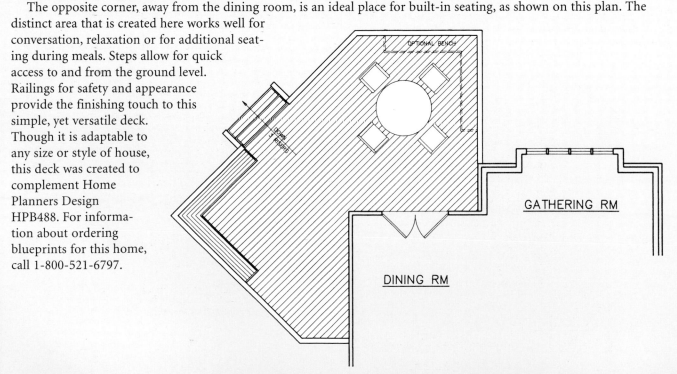

Backyard Extender Deck

PLAN HPT110154

This deck, though not large, allows for an array of uses. Its geometric shape adds interest in a relatively small space—654 square feet. It also permits traffic to flow to and from the kitchen—making it convenient to wander to a deck-side table with a meal or a snack. The plan provides for a table and chairs to be tucked into the corner, just outside the breakfast-room entrance. A short wall (or optional handrail) here maintains privacy and protection. Continuous-level steps around the perimeter allow for complete access to the ground level.

This kind of tiered-step design can be modified—extending the steps so the deck has several levels. Here, the two levels function as steps and can also double as seating for casual parties. Convenient access from the covered porch on two sides means added enjoyment of the deck from that area. Though it is adaptable to any size or style of house, this deck was created to complement Home Planners Design HPB855. For information about ordering blueprints for this home, call 1-800-521-6797.

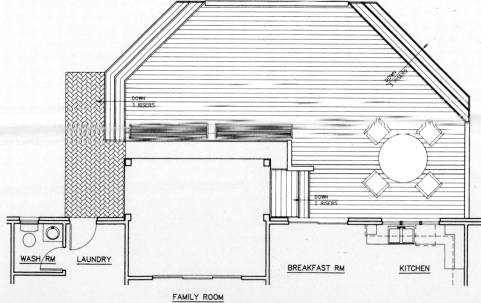

L ooking for a total-living deck design? This plan, with its 1,700 square feet, wraparound shape and multiple accesses, suits any occasion. When a sun room is included, this layout provides a variety of sun-to-shade conditions for almost every season. The sun room, country kitchen and additional room at the rear of the home provide access to the deck. Because so many rooms open to this expansive outdoor space, the possibilities to expand indoor activities—from casual kitchen gatherings to more elaborate entertaining—are numerous. Wrapping around the kitchen and sun room, the deck spans nearly the entire rear of the house.

This interesting wrap design provides practicality and privacy. For example, a quiet meal can be enjoyed near the kitchen, while children play on the built-in swing at the deck's opposite end. Three benches just outside the sun-room access provide multiple seating. Beyond the benches, wide-design stairs lead to ground level. The plans allow for a selection of bright and sunny or cool, shady locations. No matter what the activity or weather, this deck can accommodate. Though it is adaptable to any size or style of house, this deck was created to complement Home Planners Design HPB921. For information about ordering blueprints for this home, call 1-800-521-6797.

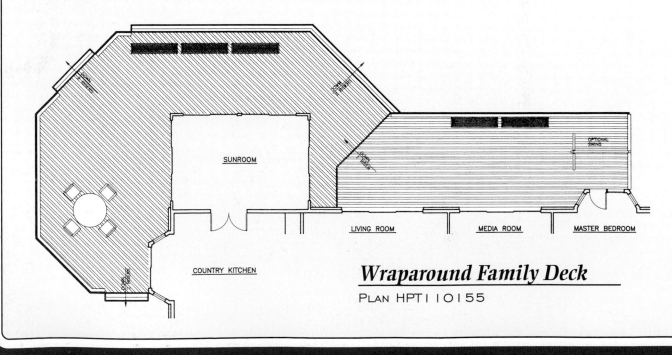

Wraparound Family Deck
PLAN HPT110155

Dramatic Deck
with Barbecue

PLAN HPT110156

There is something special about spiral stairs. They are at once whimsical and practical. In this plan, a spiral staircase is utilized outdoors as a link between a private upstairs balcony and an expansive, first-floor deck. The appearance is dramatic, plus the staircase provides upstairs occupants quick and easy access to the deck below. This is a large deck, stretching twenty feet out from the home and extending forty feet wide for a total of over 700 square feet. The deck can be accessed from the first floor through both the gathering room and dining room. When combined, these rooms span thirty-one feet. When doors are opened to the outdoors, large groups can be accommodated with ease.

The deck's V design reaches an apex at its right-hand side. This shape helps harbor a table and chairs. Just outside the dining-room entrance, a moveable barbecue or sink combination provides handy cooking and cleanup stations for family meals and entertaining. Railings along the perimeter of the deck offer safety and a professional, finished appearance. Two stairways, one directly in front of the balcony and another at the far right, allow for good ground-level access. Though it is adaptable to any size or style of house, this deck was created to complement Home Planners Design HPB711. For information about ordering blueprints for this home, call 1-800-521-6797.

DOWN 3 RISERS

OPTIONAL SPIRAL STAIRS

BALCONY ABOVE

UP

OPTIONAL BAR-B-Q

DOWN 3 RISERS

GATHERING ROOM   DINING ROOM

Split-Plan Country Deck

PLAN HPT110157

Much like a split-bedroom house plan, this is a split-deck design. One deck is more private, located outside the master bedroom. A section in the farthest left-hand deck is elevated to accommodate a whirlpool spa—an area that can be modified to suit manufacturer's specifications. Privacy screening repeats the same lines as this elevated section. In this instance, the screening is a simple construction of vertical boards, while built-in benches provide seating.

Two steps down to the ground level, a brick walk serves as a guide to the family activities deck. The wide expanse between the two decks allows use of both simultaneously without interference between deck areas. This lower level functions as a separate outdoor room, with space for a table and chairs. A wet bar, tucked into an otherwise unusable corner, helps reduce trips indoors for refreshments—a special touch to a highly appealing design. This 950-square-foot deck could be the perfect plan for summer or winter decking. Locate one deck in the shade, such as beneath a large tree; locate the other in a spot that will be bathed in plenty of winter sunshine. Though it is adaptable to any size or style of house, this deck was created to complement Home Planners Design HPB615. For information about ordering blueprints for this home, call 1-800-521-6797.

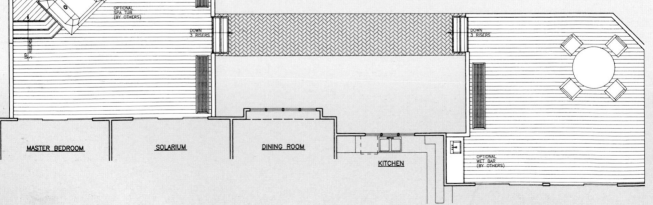

Deck for Dining and Views

PLAN HPT110158

This long, rectangular deck is not only spacious (over 1,100 square feet), its shape allows separate activities to go on simultaneously without interference. Relax, play, catch a meal in the sun—it can all be done on this deck. Access from indoors to out is accomplished by double doors on opposite sides of the gathering room and also from the breakfast room. This encourages the flow of traffic from indoors to outdoors—a real benefit for entertaining or for large families with various interests. A special feature of this deck is the screening that surrounds its perimeter. This is a valuable privacy addition for homes with small lots and nearby neighbors.

Three stairways lead to ground level. Two small stairs are located at opposite ends of the deck; one large set of stairs is positioned in the center, flanked by built-in benches. This triple access to the ground level encourages family members and visitors to make use of the entire lot. To provide plenty of space for a table and chairs, one portion of the deck extends out, which also adds an interesting angle to the design. Don't miss the refreshing hot-tub area, which can be modified to fit any standard spa. Though it is adaptable to any size or style of house, this deck was created to complement Home Planners Design HPB543. For information about ordering blueprints for this home, call 1-800-521-6797.

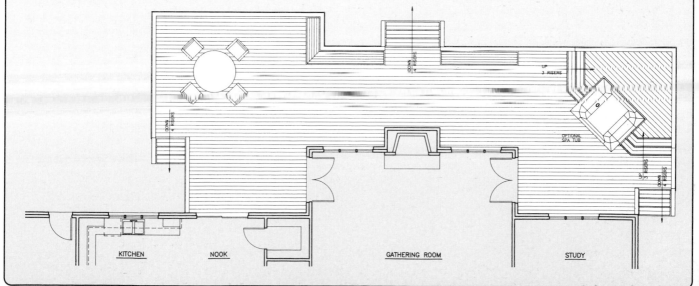

Bold, Angled Corner Deck

PLAN HPT110159

Dramatic—in a big way—describes this deck design. This is a multi-purpose addition that also offers some very specialized features. First, it is an excellent choice for a hillside or slope—it is elevated well above the ground level to accommodate a steep slope or a rugged, rocky surface. Second, if the building lot is flat, it is simple to add a patio below—the upper portion of the deck provides shade from above. Sun, shade and protection from the weather are available just about any time. If a lower-level patio is not desired, the area beneath the deck could be converted to a large storage area.

Because this spacious deck, with its 950 square feet of space, wraps around the entire rear of the house, it has access from the dining room, gathering room and study. The design of this deck, with its sharp angles, would lend itself well to a contemporary or vacation home. Sturdy railings are, of course, necessary with elevated decks. Benches in three separate areas provide adequate seating. A single stairway, located in the far right-hand corner, provides an exit to the ground. Note: This deck is attached to its adjoining house with a ledger strip to make the addition more structurally sound. Though it is adaptable to any size or style of house, this deck was created to complement Home Planners Design HPB511. For information about ordering blueprints for this home, call 1-800-521-6797.

STUDY/BEDROOM

GATHERING ROOM

DINING ROOM

KITCHEN

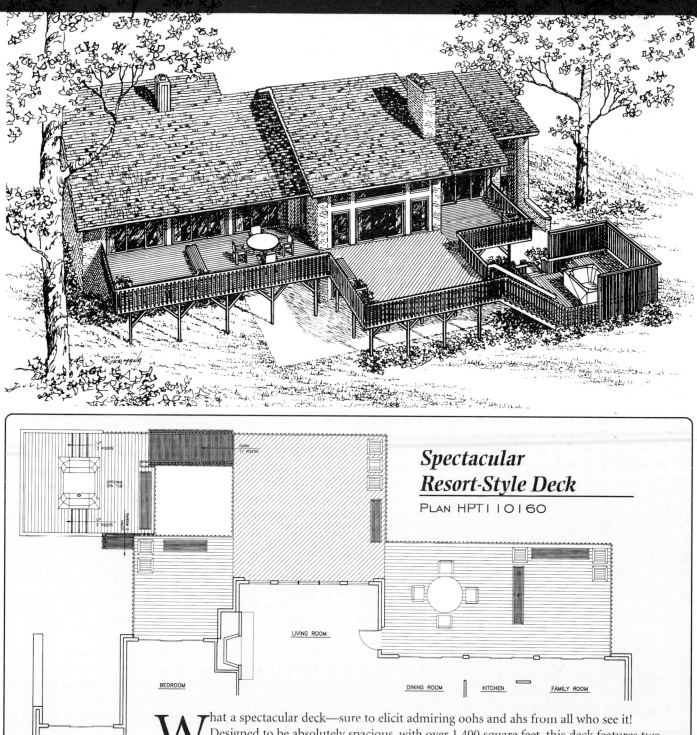

Spectacular Resort-Style Deck

PLAN HPT110160

LIVING ROOM

BEDROOM

DINING ROOM **KITCHEN** **FAMILY ROOM**

MASTER BATH

What a spectacular deck—sure to elicit admiring oohs and ahs from all who see it! Designed to be absolutely spacious, with over 1,400 square feet, this deck features two levels—an upper level and a ground level. A railed staircase links the two levels for convenience. The second-story level is a natural for entertaining. The ground level is designed more for privacy, featuring screening and a secluded spa. The second level is actually three connected decks and can be reached by several rooms. Deck surface patterns change from area to area, reinforcing the feeling of multiple outdoor rooms.

One rectangular deck is adjacent to the family room, kitchen and dining room. Built-in benches and planters are functional finishing touches. Just off the living room is a square-shaped section of deck connected to the family-wing deck. Around the corner is yet another rectangular deck, this one an extension of the master bedroom. It is smaller than the other two decks on this level, providing a more intimate setting.

Taking the stairway down leads to the more private ground-level deck. Tall vertical boards provide screening and promote a sense of enclosure. A built-in bench provides the perfect place to relax. Note: This deck is attached to its adjoining house with a ledger strip to make the addition more structurally sound. Though it is adaptable to any size or style of house, this deck was created to complement Home Planners Design HPB934. For more information about ordering blueprints for this home, call 1-800-521-6797.

Trend-Setter Deck

PLAN HPT110161

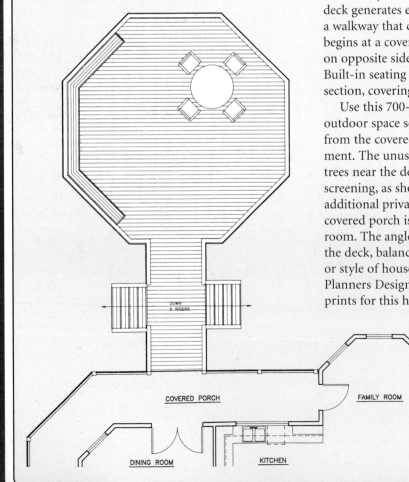

DOWN
5 RISERS

COVERED PORCH

FAMILY ROOM

DINING ROOM

KITCHEN

This is an unusual design that will suit a special home and owners who have a flair for the provocative. It is particularly well-suited to homes with deep, narrow lots. The deck generates excitement from a striking octagon shape, and by a walkway that connects it to the house. This elevated walkway begins at a covered porch attached to the house; matching stairs on opposite sides of the walk provide access to ground level. Built-in seating is extensive—benches wrap around one entire section, covering three of the deck's eight sides.

Use this 700-square-foot design to create a totally different outdoor space separate from the home, so that stepping away from the covered porch is like stepping into another environment. The unusual shape allows for creative use of plants and trees near the deck to provide shade and seclusion. Latticework screening, as shown here around the deck perimeter, provides additional privacy and a sense of enclosure. From indoors, the covered porch is accessed by both the dining room and family room. The angles of the family-room windows repeat those of the deck, balancing the design. Though it is adaptable to any size or style of house, this deck was created to complement Home Planners Design HPB969. For information about ordering blueprints for this home, call 1-800-521-6797.

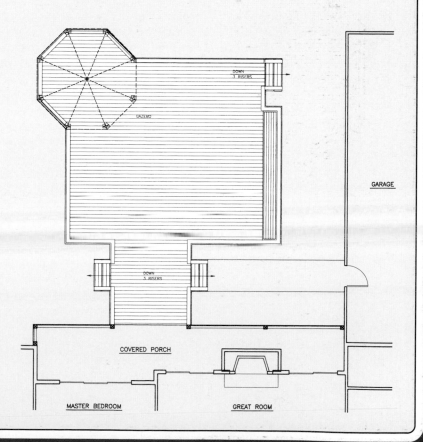

T his creative, 19th-Century deck is designed to provide interest and intrigue to any backyard landscape. It is sure to draw people from indoors to out—inviting exploration of its 800 square feet of deck area and the dramatic octagonal gazebo. Step from either the great room or master bedroom onto a covered porch. From the porch, a bridge leads to the deck itself—located only a short distance away. The bridge also serves as the vehicle for staircase exits on opposite sides. One provides access to the garage via a sidewalk; the other to the ground level.

Designed with entertaining in mind, the deck features a built-in bench that runs along the entire length of one side. The tall peaked gazebo extends the deck outward—an interesting focal point when viewed from indoors or from the covered porch. The gazebo also provides cooling shade and is just the right size for a table and chairs. The railing features a latticework design, repeated in the gazebo roof fascia, providing a unifying effect. A stairway located next to the bench is yet another ground-level access. A truly intriguing deck! Though it is adaptable to any size or style of house, this deck was created to complement Home Planners Design HPB953. For more information about ordering blueprints for this home, call 1-800-521-6797.

Turn-of-the-Century Deck

PLAN HPT110162

GAZEBO

DOWN 3 RISERS

DOWN 3 RISERS

GARAGE

COVERED PORCH

MASTER BEDROOM

GREAT ROOM

Long and angular are two words that help describe this elevated, easy-to-install deck. The 750-square-foot design is contained in a single level, but the many changes in angles along the perimeter provide interest. The deck can be reached from indoors via the dining room and the master bedroom. The deck area outside the dining room extends farther out from the house, creating a perfect spot for setting up a table and chairs for open-air dining or relaxing. Sliding doors from the master bedroom take you out onto a narrower, rectangular sec-

tion of the deck, which is somewhat separate from the dining area.

Benches follow the angles of the perimeter, and are protected with a railing. Two stairways—one near the dining alcove, the other across from the master-bedroom doorway—provide access to the ground level. Though it is adaptable to any size or style of house, this deck was created to complement Home Planners Design HPB941. For more information about ordering blueprints for this home, call 1-800-521-6797.

Weekend Entertainer Deck

PLAN HPT110163

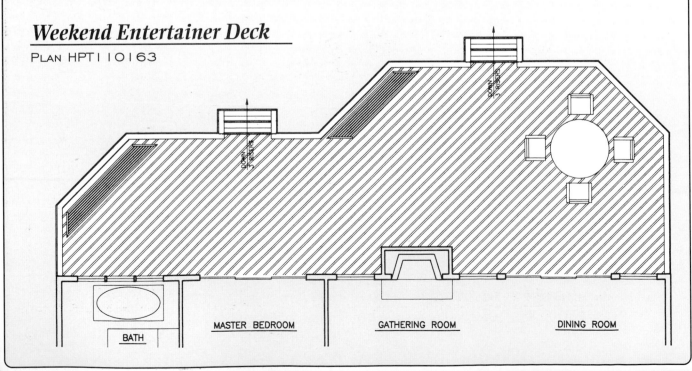

S panning nearly the entire width of the home, this 950-square-foot deck can be accessed from several rooms. The area off the master bedroom is the perfect location for a semi-private gathering spot. Doors from the gathering room open to the center of the deck. And, perhaps most convenient of all, the deck can be quickly reached from the dining room for alfresco dining on the outdoor table and chairs.

Visually, the deck provides impact with its angular chevron or delta design—the most acute angles create an interesting scene from the gathering-room window. Built-in benches vee together for dramatic outdoor seating. Matching stairways on opposite sides of the benches provide dual access to the ground level. Another utilitarian feature of this deck is the garage access, near the chair and seating corner. Moving items to and from the deck for use and storage couldn't be easier. Though it is adaptable to any size or style of house, this deck was created to complement Home Planners Design HPB505. For information about ordering blueprints for this home, call 1-800-521-6797.

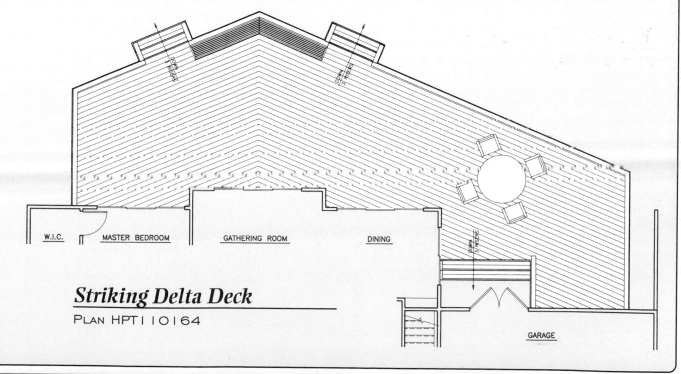

Striking Delta Deck
PLAN HPT110164

Simple, yet possessing interesting design features, this center-view deck would be a valuable and functional addition to any home. Its broad, compact shape provides ample space for gatherings, meals and family activities in over 750 square feet. The deck can be accessed from both the dining room and family room. Special features include space for a bay-window pop-out in the nook between these two rooms. The windows project onto the deck area—providing interesting angles indoors and out. A built-in bench on the deck repeats the angle of the bay window.

Access to the ground is reached via two stairways—one is located front and center, flanked by two raised planter boxes, which will help guide foot traffic to the stair entrance. Another stairway is located nearest the family room, providing quick accessibility to the adjacent mudroom. Railings surround the perimeter for safety. Though it is adaptable to any size or style of house, this deck was created to complement Home Planners Design HPB610. For information about ordering blueprints for this home, call 1-800-521-6797.

Center-View Deck

PLAN HPT110165

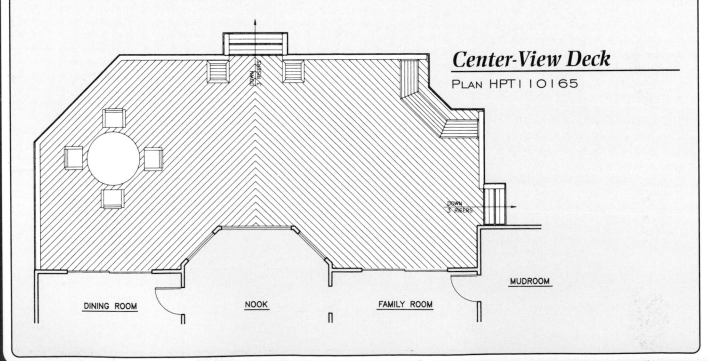

DINING ROOM   NOOK   FAMILY ROOM   MUDROOM

Kitchen-Extender Deck

PLAN HPT110166

Although not a large expanse, just over 525 square feet, this stylish deck makes use of angles and strategic placement to create a sense of spaciousness and room extension. Indoors, a large country kitchen features dual sliding doors opening onto the deck, making the kitchen more accessible to the outdoors. This design is also distinguished by its contemporary wedge shape, and could be a problem-solving design for a small or odd-shaped lot. Built-in benches provide extensive seating—enough for fairly large gatherings. The railing is bolstered by privacy-creating latticework. One set of intricately designed stairs vee outward to ground level, helping guide users, while providing a custom touch to this simple, yet highly functional deck. Though it is adaptable to any size or style of house, this deck was created to complement Home Planners Design HPB682. For information about ordering blueprints for this home, call 1-800-521-6797.

DOWN 3 RISERS

DOWN 3 RISERS

DINING ROOM

COUNTRY KITCHEN

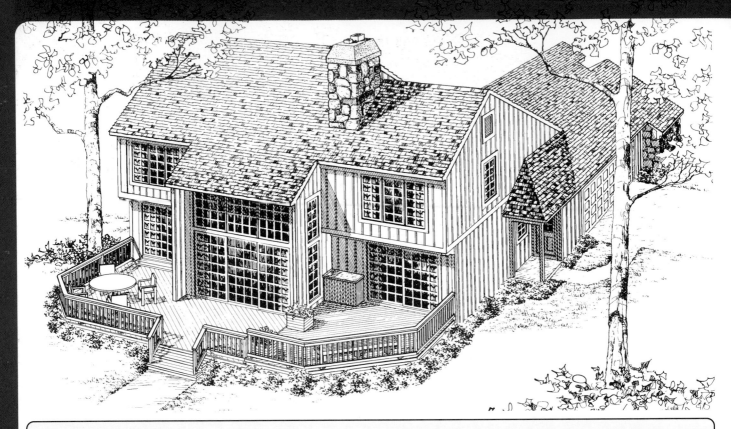

The broad U-shaped design of this bi-level deck places it in the out-of-the-ordinary category. Wrapping around three rooms, the 600-square-foot deck allows multiple views and access. A unique aspect of this deck is the creation of two separate deck spaces. The separation of these two areas is reinforced by using distinctly different decking surface patterns.

This deck also has some custom amenities to make outdoor entertaining a breeze. A wet bar is tucked into a corner created by the adjoining study and gathering room. A built-in bench is aligned with one side of the deck's perimeter, located just outside of the study. Spacious yet intimate, the deck features plenty of room outside of the dining room for a table and chairs, providing a convenient place to relax and enjoy meals. Stairs to the ground level and a safety railing around the perimeter complete this picture-perfect design. Though it is adaptable to any size or style of house, this deck was created to complement Home Planners Design HPB826. For more information about ordering blueprints for this home, call 1-800-521-6797.

Bi-Level Retreat Deck

PLAN HPT110167

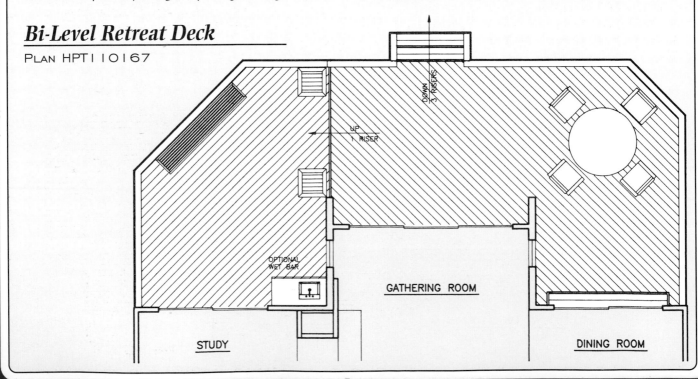

OPTIONAL WET BAR

STUDY

GATHERING ROOM

DINING ROOM

UP 1 RISER

DOWN 3 RISERS

Split-Level Activity Deck

PLAN HPT110168

This spilt-level deck is a pleasing combination of rectangular and octagonal shapes. The result is a functional and highly attractive outdoor living space of over 625 square feet. The two-level design helps promote a two-decks-in-one feeling. In addition, each level can be accessed by separate indoor rooms.

Level one features an octagonal extension, blossoming from one corner of the rectangular section. The octagonal shape is perfect for accommodating a table and chairs. Handily, this area is located just outside of the dining room and kitchen. Stairs near the center of the rectangle lead to the ground. The second level is a single step down from level one. This area has separate access from the family room. Three built-in benches provide plenty of seating for family activities and entertaining. Permanent square-shaped planters flank the stairs, helping identify the stairway and move traffic around safely. Though it is adaptable to any size or style of house, this deck was created to complement Home Planners Design HPA956. For information about ordering blueprints for this home, call 1-800-521-6797.

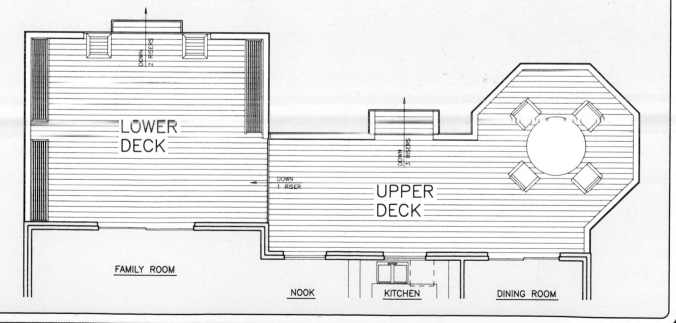

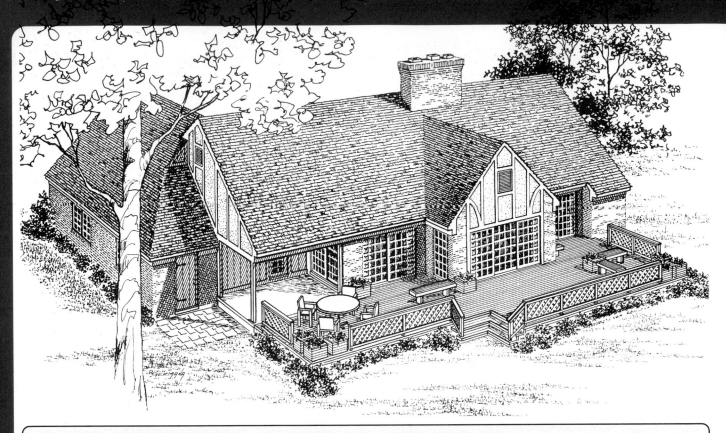

This rectangular-shaped deck is long and spacious (over 800 square feet)—perfect for entertaining. In this instance, it adjoins a covered porch—a real advantage in certain regions when the weather does not cooperate. Multiple access—from the master bedroom, gathering room and dining room—helps ensure this deck's utility. A table-and-chairs setting is positioned near the dining room to make it convenient to serve outdoor meals.

The stairway is built wide in a striking V design. Additional custom features include built-in benches and planters. Railings, too, surround the perimeter of the decking for safety. In this example, latticework has been added to the railing for the enhanced feeling of privacy and enclosure. Though it is adaptable to any size or style of house, this deck was created to complement Home Planners Design HPB802. For more information about ordering blueprints for this home, call 1-800-521-6797.

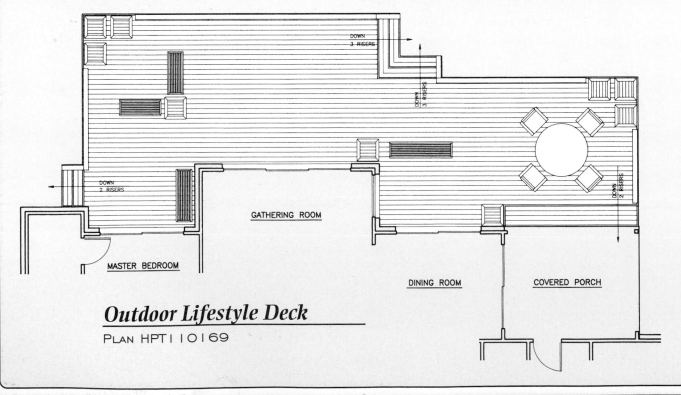

Outdoor Lifestyle Deck

PLAN HPT110169

With three levels totaling over 650 square feet and an elongated shape, this deck is well-suited for simultaneous activities without disturbing the participating parties. Because the deck areas are linked and easy to reach, it is also excellent for large gatherings. Stairways are not required to go from one level to the next—the deck is thoughtfully designed so that each level has a change in elevation equal to a step. The result is a deck composed of three separate areas, made even more distinctive by contrasting surface patterns for each area. The geometric angles of the deck's perimeter add interest and provide the opportunity for some unique features, such as the large, three-sided bench that wraps around one extended deck section. With the garage access next to the covered porch, transportation of furniture to and from the deck is made simple.

In addition to the expansive bench seating, a moveable grill is installed near the kitchen door for barbecues. The grill can also be built as a wet bar. Planters add a finishing touch. Access to the ground level is via two exits: one near the kitchen, the other outside the covered porch. Though it is adaptable to any size or style of house, this deck was created to complement Home Planners Design HPB356. For information about ordering blueprints for this home, call 1-800-521-6797.

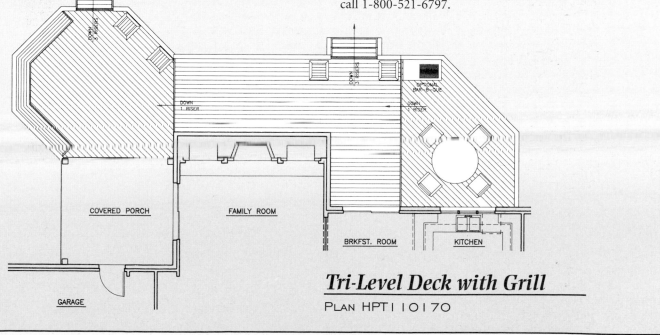

Tri-Level Deck with Grill
PLAN HPT110170

A contemporary design is just one attribute of this diminutive yet appealing deck. An overall feeling of spaciousness is achieved in a small area (550 square feet) due to the creative changes in angle and space. This design would work extremely well on an odd-shaped lot, or where existing trees or other landscape features require some ingenuity and imagination to achieve a good "fit." Benches are built between matching planters in an area outside of the living room for an intimate seating arrangement.

The deck extends outward dramatically to create a large area outside of the family room, with plenty of space for a table and chairs. Railings surround the deck for a finishing touch, as well as for safety. A simple single step down provides access to ground level in three different corners of the deck. Though it is adaptable to any size or style of house, this deck was created to complement Home Planners Design HPB379. For information about ordering blueprints for this home, call 1-800-521-6797.

Contemporary Leisure Deck

PLAN HPT110171

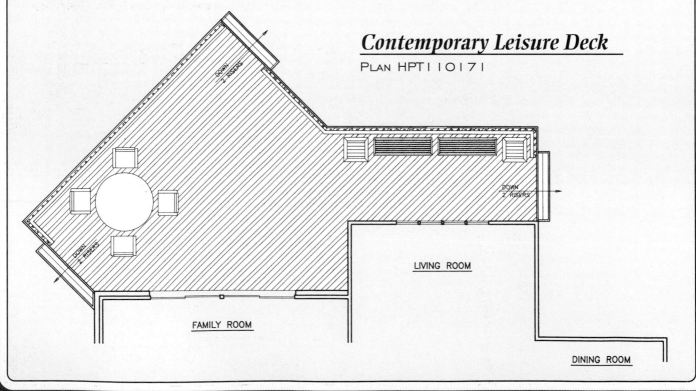

This is an exciting, symmetrical deck of over 1,500 square feet that invites exploration. It is a perfect deck for a site blessed with a view—the deck angles command the eye outside and away toward the horizon. Three levels and three accesses—from the study, gathering room and master bedroom—make this a highly versatile and usable deck. It can be utilized as three private decks, or one extremely spacious deck. The centered V-shaped section, reached by twin sliding doors from the gathering room, is on a level two steps down from smaller matching decks on opposite sides.

The deck surface pattern is laid in a V pointing outward, reinforcing the engaging geometric design. The deck can be built in stages, beginning with the center section and later adding the wings. Three exits to the ground level make it easy to move about the backyard. Built-in benches flank each exit; planters at selected corners add the finishing touches to a truly fine deck design. Though it is adaptable to any size or style of house, this deck was created to complement Home Planners Design HPB781. For more information about ordering blueprints for this home, call 1-800-521-6797.

Angular Winged Deck

PLAN HPT110172

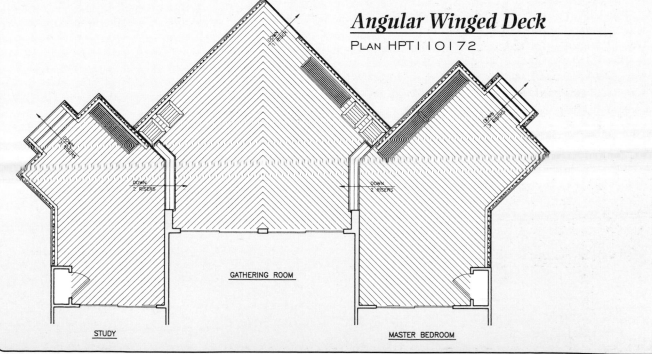

Deck for a Split-Level Home

PLAN HPT110173

The split-level design of this deck is the perfect complement to the split-level house plan and even enhances its dramatic style. With a square footage of over 1,100, it allows two activities to go on simultaneously in almost complete privacy because the deck areas are that separate and distinct. The main deck level can be reached by twin sliding doors from the family room or from an additional set of sliding doors in the breakfast room. The spacious, rectangular shape of this level provides ample room for activities. A table and chairs fit nicely into a corner directly across from the breakfast room entrance. Nearby, a stairway leads to the ground. An extensive L-shaped built-in bench provides lots of seating. A low dividing screen repeats the L-shape of the bench to separate the two deck areas.

A railed stairway with seven steps takes you to the second deck, which can also be reached from the teenage activities room. Here the kids can enjoy get-togethers, homework or plain old relaxing without bothering the neighboring deck upstairs. In some house plans, this deck area could serve a lower-level bedroom wing. Built-in planters and a pair of benches help make this deck cozy. Access to ground level is simple with two exits—one near the stairway to the main deck; the second heading toward a side yard. Though it is adaptable to any size or style of house, this deck was created to complement Home Planners Design HPB850. For information about ordering blueprints for this home, call 1-800-521-6797.

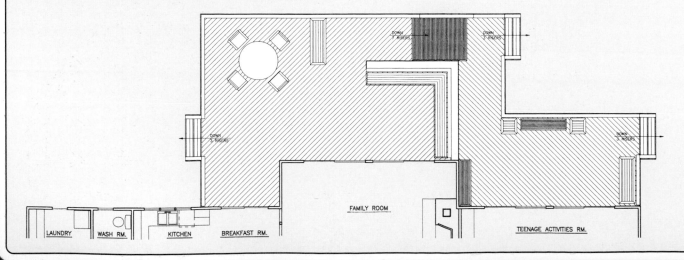

This spacious, terraced deck encompasses over 1,600 square feet and features three levels flowing quite naturally from one to another. The shapes and levels have a dual purpose: Each level could easily accommodate a small get-together. Or, when entertaining, large groups of people can overflow to the different levels, creating a variety of outdoor spaces for separate conversations.

Entrance to the deck can be made from the breakfast room, dining room, a family bedroom and the master bedroom. A matching pair of built-in benches flank the deck at opposite sides near the breakfast-room and master-bed-room entrances. Gathering-room windows on opposite sides of the fireplace provide dramatic views of the deck where the steps link one level to another. Table and chairs are set into a V-shaped nook directly in front of the dining room and near the stairs that take you to the lower-level deck. Stairs on the lowest level provide a central exit to the backyard. Though it is adaptable to any size or style of house, this deck was created to complement Home Planners Design HPB913. For more information about ordering blueprints for this home, call 1-800-521-6797.

Terraced Deck for Entertaining

PLAN HPT110174

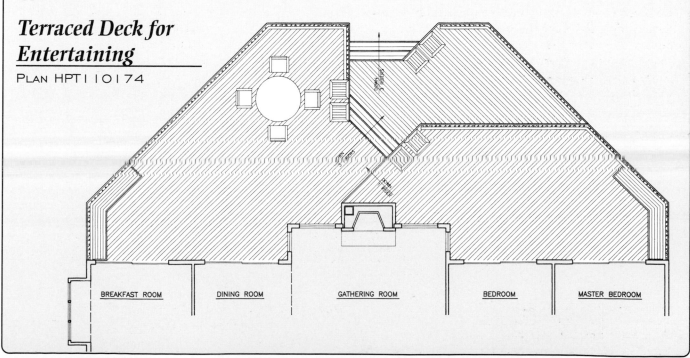

BREAKFAST ROOM   DINING ROOM   GATHERING ROOM   BEDROOM   MASTER BEDROOM

Plan HPT110192; see page 290 for more information

Studios and Storage Spaces:

47 spacious garage & guest house designs

A garage is the perfect complement to a comfortable home, serving as a shelter for precious vehicles, a storage space for tools and lawn equipment, and often as a work space for the home mechanic. But sometimes you need more—more work space, more storage, or even more amenities. The following pages feature a wide variety of garage designs that range from the simplest utilitarian garages to larger facilities that accommodate three cars and include areas for office space, guest apartments or even swimming pools. Best of all, many of the garage designs come with several different elevations, so you can choose the exterior style that best complements your home.

Browse through our gallery of garage designs to find the one that's right for you, whether you're looking for extra work space, a home office or a cozy guest house.

Sweet Simplicity

PLAN HPT110175
SQUARE FOOTAGE: 528
WIDTH: 22'-0"
DEPTH: 24'-0"

The high-pitched roof of this free-standing, 528-square-foot garage shelters two cars, plus room enough for a workbench and welcome extra storage. Slotted shutters on the opposing double-hung windows are repeated in miniature to flank the louvered vent at the peak of the roofline. Wide wood trim around the recessed-pattern garage door creates a clean, uncluttered line.

WORK BENCH - STOR. AREA

TWO CAR
GARAGE
21^5 x 23^3

One Car, Plus

PLAN HPT110176
SQUARE FOOTAGE: 385
WIDTH: 18'-0"
DEPTH: 24'-0"

Store your car and your bike or motorcycle, plus have room left over for a workbench and generous storage areas. The 385-square-foot floor plan has a curbed work area at the back with fourteen feet of garage storage. Additional storage is provided in a second area—4' x 11' -5"—adjacent to the garage door. Both storage areas are easy to reach through an exterior side door. Natural light enters through a double-hung window in the twenty-four-foot side wall.

WORK BENCH - STOR. AREA

CURB

1½ CAR GARAGE
$13^5 \times 23^5$

STOR. AREA
$4^0 \times 11^5$

CURB

The Compact

Plan HPT110177
Square Footage: 484
Width: 22'-0"
Depth: 22'-0"

A wide-gable roofline provides a generous overhang on all sides of this compact garage with a single 16' x 7' garage door flanked by exterior lights. The 484-square-foot floor plan allows space for a work-bench and storage area along the back wall. A double-hung window along the side wall provides natural light, while an exterior door in the back wall gives easy access to the work and storage area.

WORK BENCH – STOR. AREA

TWO CAR
GARAGE
21^5 x 21^5

WORK BENCH - STOR. AREA

TWO CAR
GARAGE
$21^5 \times 23^3$

Versatile Design

PLAN HPT110178
SQUARE FOOTAGE: 528
WIDTH: 22'-0"
DEPTH: 24'-0"

This simple design will suit the garage needs of any family. It will blend nicely with a wide variety of home styles as well—the steeply pitched roof, wood siding, and wrought-iron exterior lights on each side of the door are attractive exterior features. There's room for two cars, along with a workbench and a storage area—the workbench is perfect for do-it-yourself projects, and the storage area offers room for yard and garden tools and more.

Adaptable Design

PLAN HPT110179
SQUARE FOOTAGE: 384
WIDTH: 16'-0"
DEPTH: 24'-0"

Let the size of your lot dictate how large you decide to make this functional single-car garage. This plan allows for an additional four feet to be added to the depth for 384 square feet of area. Choose a garage door style with clear panels to provide natural light. Optional electric service in the center of the parking bay adds versatility to the many uses of this sturdy structure. A wide gable roofline and vertical siding allow this design to blend easily with many traditional and contemporary house styles. Access the storage in the back through a pre-hung exterior door in the side wall.

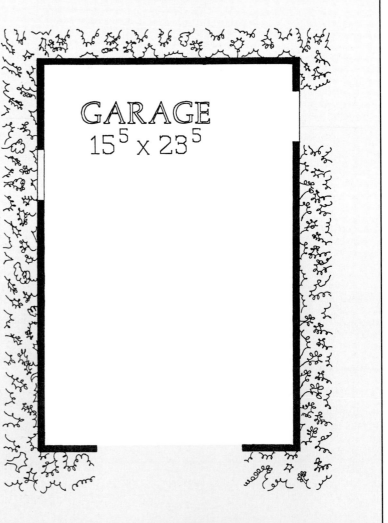

GARAGE
15⁵ x 23⁵

GARAGE
23⁵ x 31⁵

Secure Shelter

PLAN HPT110180
SQUARE FOOTAGE: 768
WIDTH: 24'-0"
DEPTH: 32'-0"

Ready to suit your needs, this garage has 768 square feet of usable space. Intended to provide shelter and security for two cars, this garage also offers four conveniently placed electric outlets to expand your options. A large work area at the rear of this structure is accessed through a pre-hung steel door at the rear of the side wall.

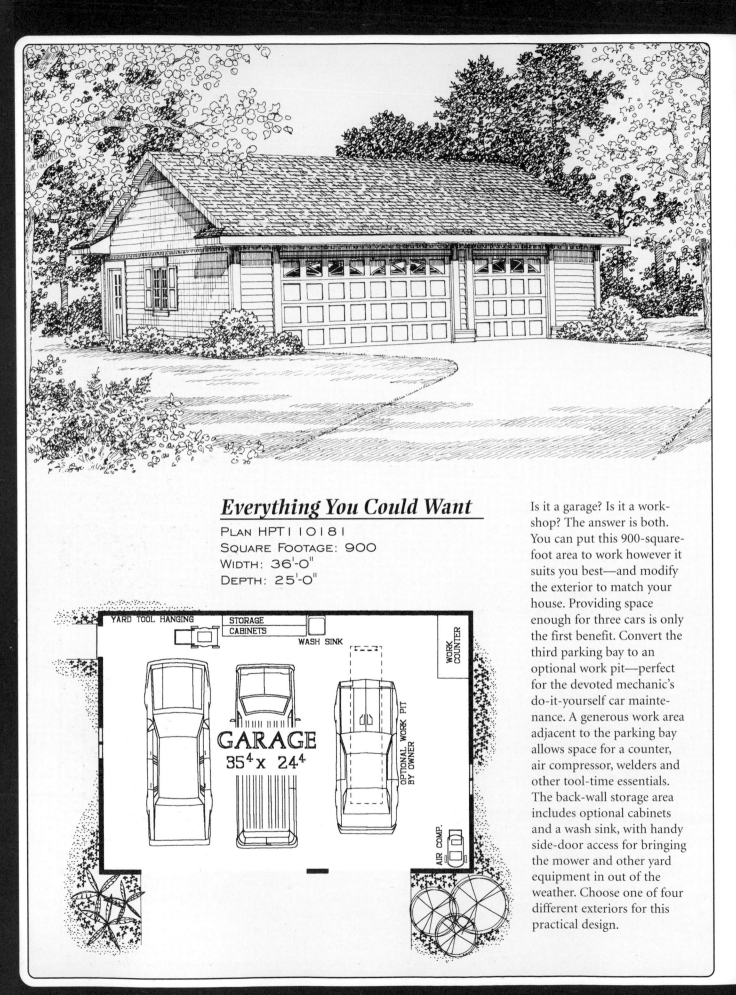

Everything You Could Want

PLAN HPT110181
SQUARE FOOTAGE: 900
WIDTH: 36'-0"
DEPTH: 25'-0"

YARD TOOL HANGING

STORAGE
CABINETS

WASH SINK

WORK COUNTER

GARAGE
35⁴ x 24⁴

OPTIONAL WORK PIT
BY OWNER

AIR COMP.

Is it a garage? Is it a work-shop? The answer is both. You can put this 900-square-foot area to work however it suits you best—and modify the exterior to match your house. Providing space enough for three cars is only the first benefit. Convert the third parking bay to an optional work pit—perfect for the devoted mechanic's do-it-yourself car mainte-nance. A generous work area adjacent to the parking bay allows space for a counter, air compressor, welders and other tool-time essentials. The back-wall storage area includes optional cabinets and a wash sink, with handy side-door access for bringing the mower and other yard equipment in out of the weather. Choose one of four different exteriors for this practical design.

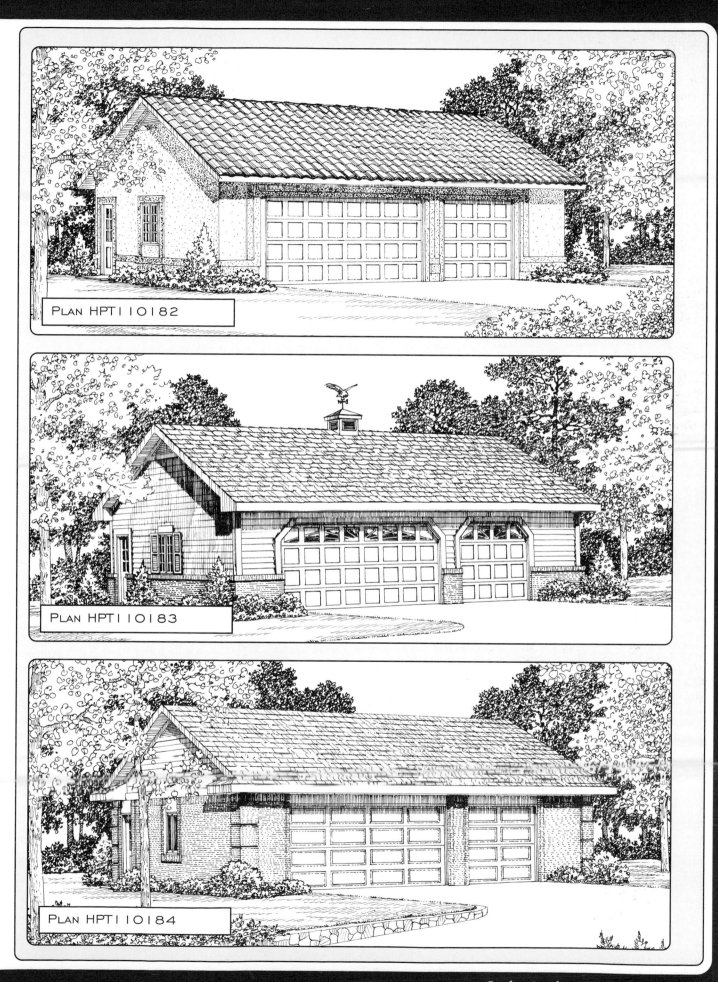

PLAN HPT110182

PLAN HPT110183

PLAN HPT110184

Double Duty

PLAN HPT110185
SQUARE FOOTAGE: 431
WIDTH: 24'-0"
DEPTH: 26'-0"

The engaging country charm of this two-car garage, plus the functionality of the 431-square-foot, room-to-grow second floor, provides the added space you need. The horizontal clapboard siding of the structure is accented by the vertical panels of the twin garage doors. The modified gambrel-style roof shelters a 16' x 16'-6" living area to use as a future apartment, study or playroom. It is accessed by interior stairs in the back of the garage.

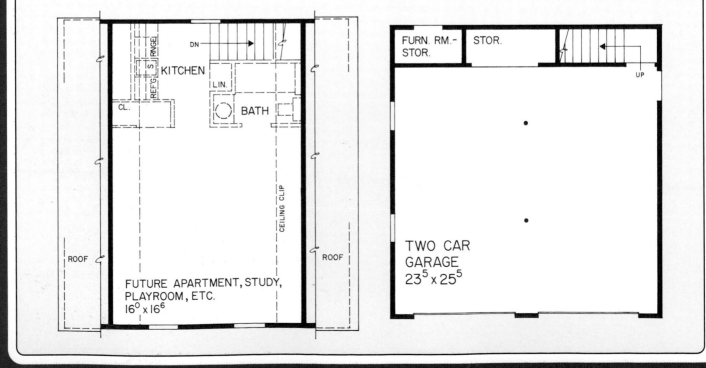

KITCHEN

REF'G | S | RNGE

DN

CL.

LIN.

BATH

CEILING CLIP

ROOF

ROOF

FUTURE APARTMENT, STUDY, PLAYROOM, ETC.
16⁰ x 16⁶

FURN. RM.- STOR.

STOR.

UP

TWO CAR GARAGE
23⁵ x 25⁵

Generous Work Space

PLAN HPT110187
SQUARE FOOTAGE: 784
WIDTH: 24'-0"
DEPTH: 24'-0"

Intended to be versatile, this 784-square-foot two-car garage with deep eaves and wide-panel siding offers a generous work area. Enter by either of the 9' x 7' garage doors, or by the pre-hung steel door in the back side wall. Natural light is provided through translucent panels in the garage doors. Conveniently placed electric outlets in each parking bay and two in the back wall increase the practicality of this multi-use structure. Choose from two facades.

GARAGE
23^5 x 23^5

PLAN HPT110186

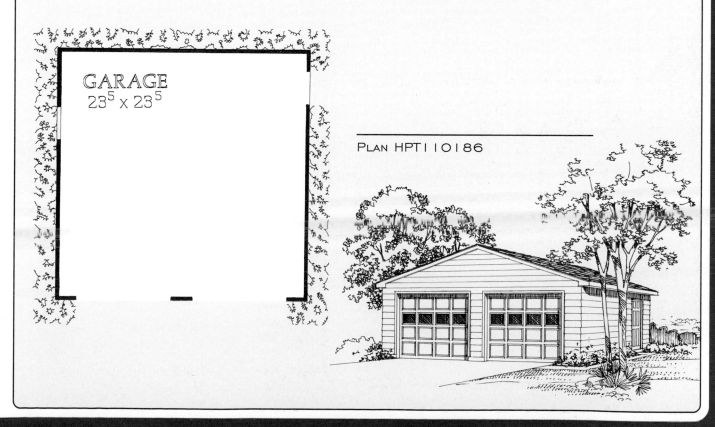

My Workshop

PLAN HPT110188
SQUARE FOOTAGE: 306
WIDTH: 36'-0"
DEPTH: 25'-0"

Behind what looks like just another garage door is just what you've always wanted—a fully equipped workshop. Accessed through an 8' x 7' garage door, or from an interior door within the garage itself, is 300 square feet of workshop area. The workshop contains plenty of room for your favorite power tools, a work table, storage cabinets, counter space and overhead racks for lumber. On the garage side of this multi-use structure is a two-car garage with a 16' x 7' door. The garage allows space for yard and garden equipment, plus a convenient area for recycling bins and garbage cans. Choose one of four attractive elevations.

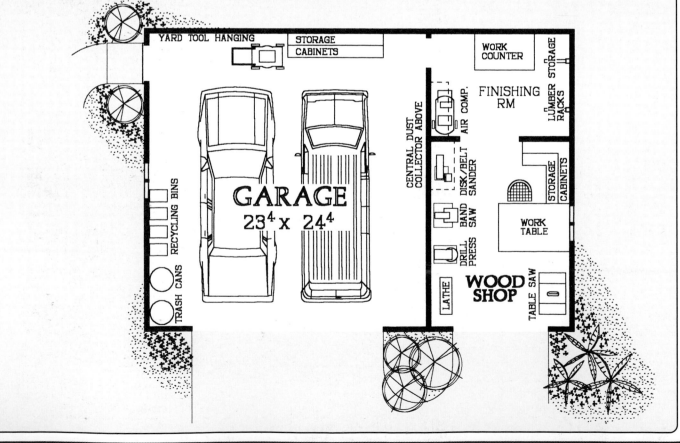

PLAN HPT110189

PLAN HPT110190

PLAN HPT110191

Grand View

PLAN HPT110192
FIRST FLOOR: 1,167 SQ. FT.
SECOND FLOOR: 640 SQ. FT.
TOTAL: 1,807 SQ. FT.
WIDTH: 44'-0"
DEPTH: 33'-0"

LIVING RM.
10'-8"x13'

KIT.
9'x7'

STUDY
7'-10"x8'

BATH

BEDRM.
15'x9'

GARAGE
· 42'-8"x22'-8" ·

Almost too grand to be a mere garage, this design provides enough space for three vehicles, plus a handy work area at the garage level. The second-floor apartment weighs in at a sizable 640 square feet and allows for a large living room, a serviceable kitchen, a bedroom with a full bath and even a study. Use it for frequent guests, a mother-in-law, college student or even as a home office. The exterior of this garage fits nicely with almost any style of home, but will work especially well with European, South-western or Mediterranean designs.

The Convertible

PLAN HPT110193
SQUARE FOOTAGE: 768
WIDTH: 32'-0"
DEPTH: 24'-0"

Three 9' x 7' garage doors convert this 768-square-foot area equally well to private or commercial use. Vary the selection of siding and door jambs on this wide-gable roof structure to blend with the style of your home. For use on a commercial site, choose the options for electric outlets in each bay area. Plenty of room is provided along the thirty-two-foot back wall for a workbench and a storage area. A pre-hung steel door at the back side wall allows convenient entry and exit.

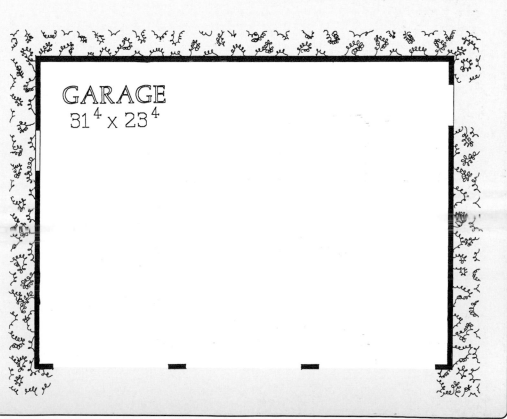

GARAGE
31^4 x 23^4

Sunrise, Sunset

PLAN HPT110194
SQUARE FOOTAGE: 600
WIDTH: 24'-0"
DEPTH: 25'-0"

This two-car garage also accommodates adequate storage areas for tools, yard and gardening equipment, and recycling and trash bins. A 16' x 7' garage door provides safe passage for vehicles, and an exterior door at the back of the side wall offers easy access to the storage areas. Four different exterior elevations are available, ensuring a perfect blend of style with the main house structure.

YARD TOOL HANGING STORAGE
CABINETS

GARAGE
23⁴ x 24⁴

RECYCLING BINS

TRASH CANS

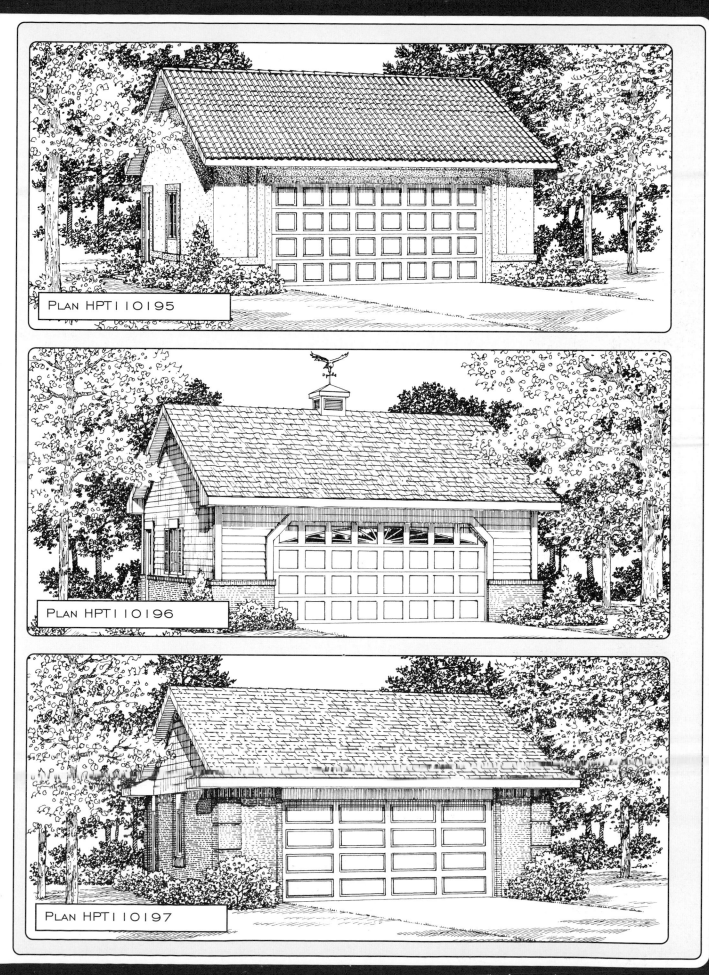

Plan HPT110195

Plan HPT110196

Plan HPT110197

Attractive and functional, this impressive structure has room for three cars in the garage section and 670 square feet of living area—complete with a kitchen, a bathroom, bookshelves and a closet—to use as a studio or a hideaway loft for guests. The treatment of the steeply pitched gable roof is repeated in three gabled dormers, each with tall narrow windows framed with shutters. Access the second-floor loft area via a railed exterior stairway which leads to a small landing with its own covered roof supported by wooden columns. The clipped corners of the trim around each of the three car bays lend country charm. Four wrought-iron coach lights complete the effect.

REFG RANGE | KITCHEN | DW | SHWR | BATH

BOOKSHELVES

CLOSET

STUDIO/LOFT
$33^8 \times 14^2$

DN

CEILING CLIP

RAILING

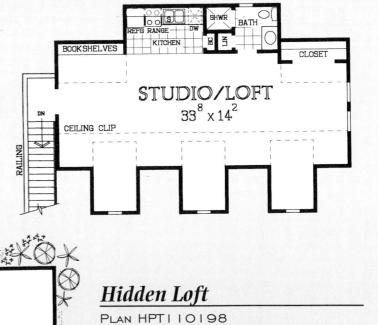

3-CAR GARAGE

$33^8 \times 23^4$

RAILING

UP

Hidden Loft

PLAN HPT110198
SQUARE FOOTAGE: 1,494
WIDTH: 34'-4"
DEPTH: 24'-0"

The Studio

PLAN HPT110199
SQUARE FOOTAGE: 428
WIDTH: 24'-0"
DEPTH: 24'-0"

Winner of the Best Use of Space Award! This design provides protection for two cars, plus a 23'-4" x 13'-2" second-floor studio with a shower bath and storage in just 428 square feet. Entry to the second floor is via an exterior railed stairway with roofed landing. Two gable-roofed dormers and two windows in the side wall provide plenty of light for arts and crafts and space for the college set to toss sleeping bags for a weekend visit. Access the garage through two wide doors, or through a standard entry door with a porch at the back wall.

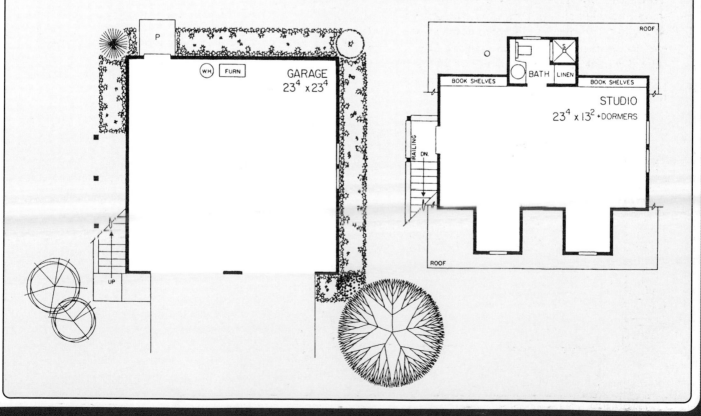

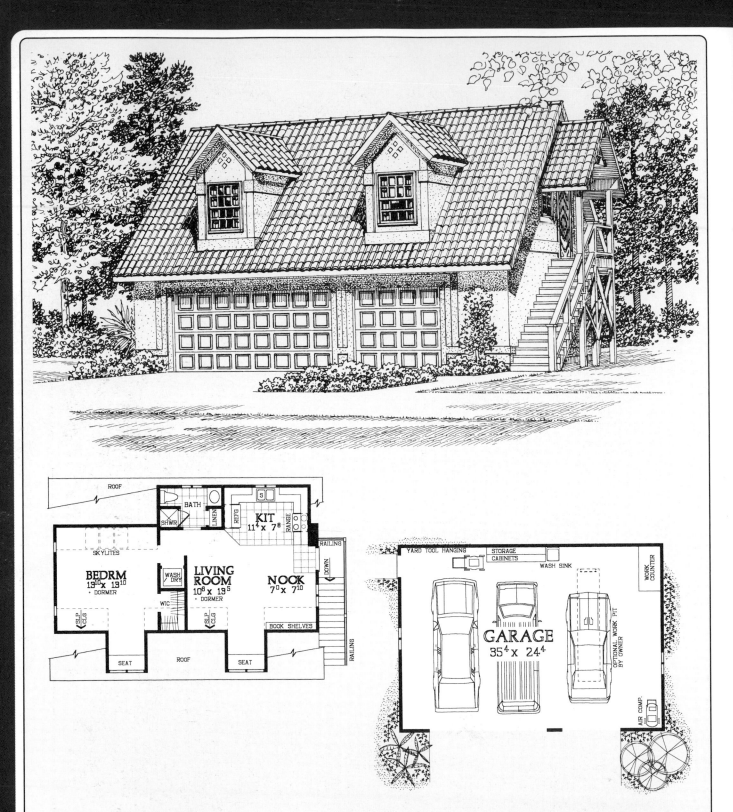

The floor plan labels include:

ROOF
BATH
LINEN
SHWR
REFG
KIT
11⁴ x 7⁸
RANGE
S
SKYLITES
BEDRM
13¹⁰ x 13¹⁰
+ DORMER
WASH DRY
LIVING ROOM
10⁶ x 19⁵
+ DORMER
NOOK
7⁰ x 7¹⁰
RAILING
DOWN
WIC
SLP CLG
SLP CLG
BOOK SHELVES
SEAT
ROOF
SEAT
RAILING

YARD TOOL HANGING
STORAGE CABINETS
WASH SINK
WORK COUNTER
GARAGE
35⁴ x 24⁴
OPTIONAL WORK PIT BY OWNER
AIR COMP.

Decorative Details

PLAN HPT110200
SQUARE FOOTAGE: 690
WIDTH: 36'-0"
DEPTH: 25'-0"

Decorative touches grace the exterior of this garage and guest cottage. The first-floor space holds room for a work pit or for three parking bays. The second floor has a complete guest apartment. A fully equipped kitchen is on the right and ahead is a generous living room with built-in bookshelves and a tempting window seat in the dormer window. A full bath with a shower, linen closet and laundry facilities adds to the functional floor plan. A large bedroom features sloping ceilings and a welcome walk-in closet. For a different exterior look, choose one of the other three elevations shown.

Plan HPT110201

Plan HPT110202

Plan HPT110203

Gardener's Delight

PLAN HPT110204
SQUARE FOOTAGE: 294
WIDTH: 36'-8"
DEPTH: 24'-8"

Nestled at the back of your property or located adjacent to the main house, this spacious 294-square-foot hip-roof garage provides shelter and security for one, two or three vehicles. A raised curb, stretching the entire 36'-8" width, can be used to accommodate a workbench for small projects. Or, because of proximity and access to the backyard through an exterior door, the curb area is a natural for a potting bench. The addition of brick and masonry planters at each outside corner of the garage adds architectural interest and softens the lines of this straightforward design.

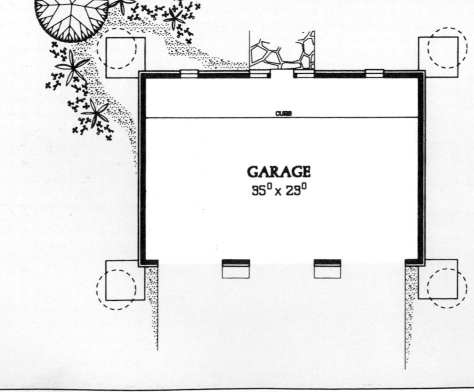

CURB

GARAGE
35⁰ x 23⁰

Apartment Addition

PLAN HPT110205
SQUARE FOOTAGE: 904
WIDTH: 61'-10"
DEPTH: 49'-8"

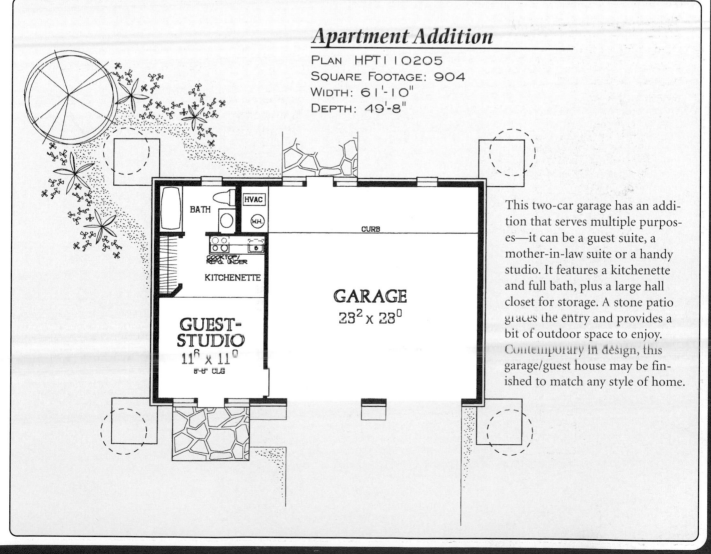

BATH

HVAC

W.H.

COOKTOP/
REFG. UNDER

KITCHENETTE

CURB

GARAGE
23² x 23⁰

GUEST-
STUDIO
11⁶ x 11⁰
8'-0" CLG

This two-car garage has an addition that serves multiple purposes—it can be a guest suite, a mother-in-law suite or a handy studio. It features a kitchenette and full bath, plus a large hall closet for storage. A stone patio graces the entry and provides a bit of outdoor space to enjoy. Contemporary in design, this garage/guest house may be finished to match any style of home.

Hobbies and More

PLAN HPT110206
SQUARE FOOTAGE: 306
WIDTH: 36'-0"
DEPTH: 25'-0"

The two-car garage area of this plan provides the basics, but the more than 300 square feet of optional-use area can be transformed into a game room, an exercise room or a separate space for sewing or other hobbies. Extra convenience is provided by a full bath with a shower and both linen and storage closets. Let your imagination take over when deciding which amenities you need to create a special work space for your projects. In the garage, you'll find more than enough room for two cars, plus plenty of storage for yard and garden equipment, garbage cans and recycling bins. Choose the one of the four elevations that best suits your style.

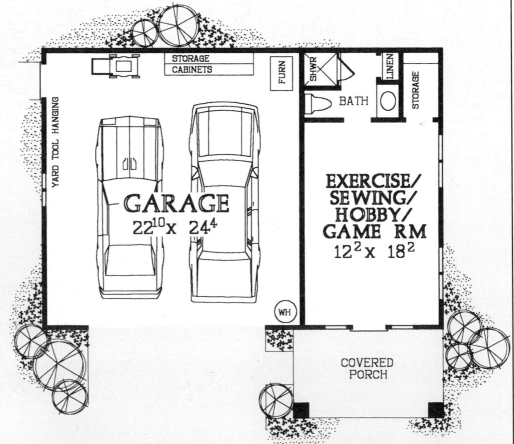

STORAGE
CABINETS

FURN

SHWR

LINEN

STORAGE

BATH

YARD TOOL HANGING

GARAGE
22^{10}x 24^{4}

EXERCISE/
SEWING/
HOBBY/
GAME RM
12^{2}x 18^{2}

WH

COVERED
PORCH

Plan HPT110207

Plan HPT110208

Plan HPT110209

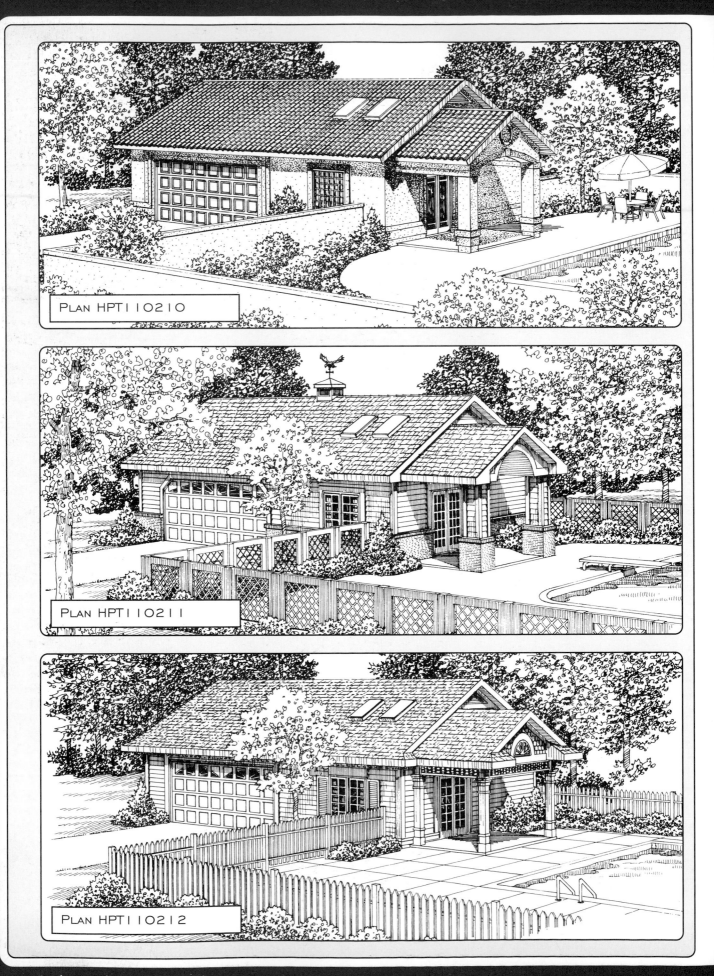

PLAN HPT110210

PLAN HPT110211

PLAN HPT110212

Poolside

PLAN HPT110213
SQUARE FOOTAGE: 321
WIDTH: 36'-0"
DEPTH: 25'-0"

Locate this roomy structure near the pool and provide security for two cars, plus a spacious bathhouse with a changing room and an outdoor patio/lounge area shaded by a generous roof extension. The garage area provides plenty of space to store yard and garden equipment and other necessities like garbage cans and recycling bins. Natural light enters the interior of the changing area through two skylights over the bath and shower area. Built-in benches and countertops, plus storage and linen closets, offer lots of convenience. The kitchenette is cooled by a ceiling fan and French doors leading to the patio. Four different elevations are available for this plan.

YARD TOOL HANGING
STORAGE CABINETS
WH
BATH
SHOWER
LINEN
STOR
SAUNA/ CHANGING
CLG
AUDIO
SPACE COUNTER
CLG FAN
LOUNGE AREA
SINK REF
STOR
OUTDOOR GRILL
KIT
TRASH CANS RECYCLING BINS

GARAGE
22¹⁰x24⁴

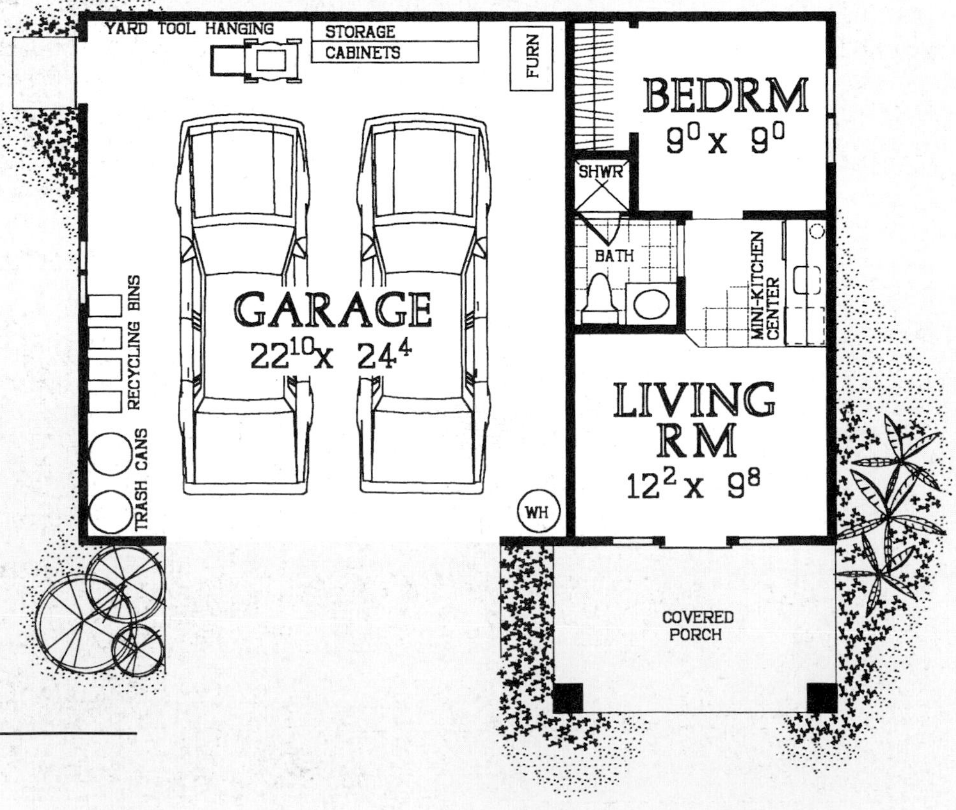

This well-thought-out floor plan is the perfect solution for a home office addition. A single 16' x 7' garage door provides shelter for two cars, plus storage areas for yard and garden equipment, garbage cans and recycling bins. A columned porch provides entry to the compact apartment or office area. A mini-kitchen (or make this extra work area) and a bath with a shower provide added convenience. The bedroom at the back could also be used for additional storage. Four different exterior elevations are available.

Consultant's Choice

PLAN HPT110214
SQUARE FOOTAGE: 321
WIDTH: 36'-0"
DEPTH: 25'-0"

Floor Plan Labels

YARD TOOL HANGING

STORAGE
CABINETS

FURN

RECYCLING BINS

TRASH CANS

BEDRM
9^0 x 9^0

SHWR

BATH

MINI-KITCHEN CENTER

GARAGE
22^{10} x 24^4

WH

LIVING RM
12^2 x 9^8

COVERED PORCH

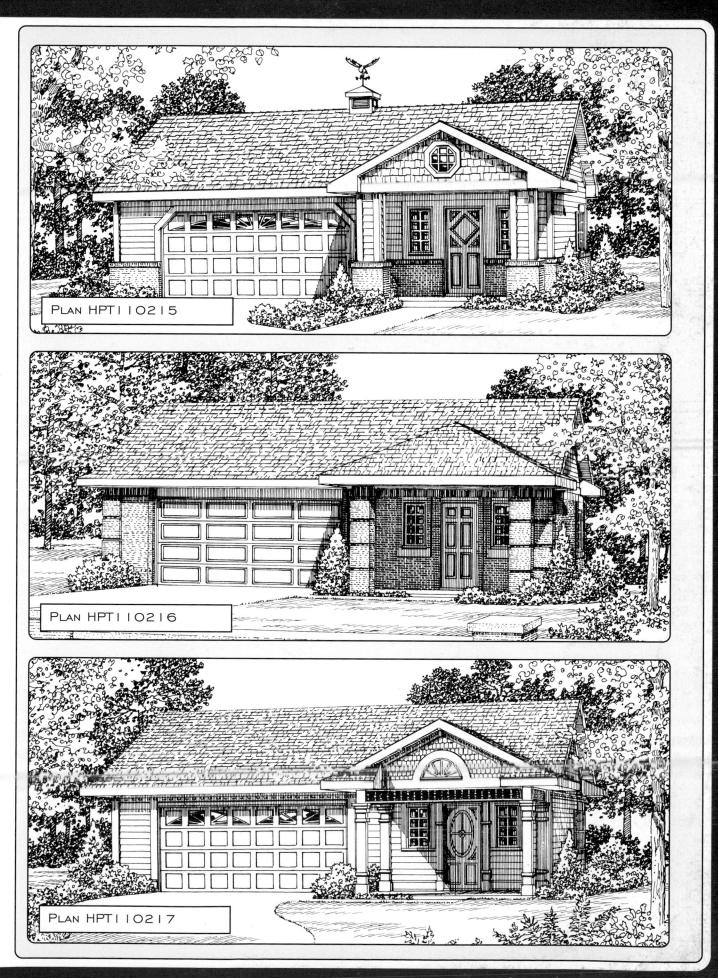

PLAN HPT110215

PLAN HPT110216

PLAN HPT110217

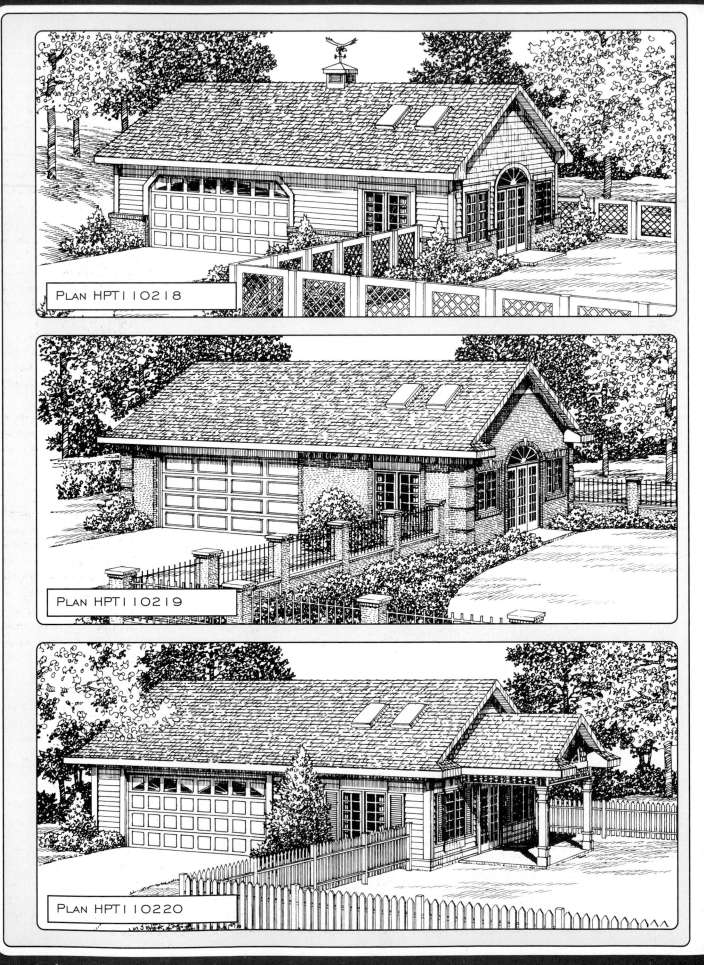

PLAN HPT110218

PLAN HPT110219

PLAN HPT110220

COPYRIGHT DOS & DON'TS

Blueprints for residential construction (or working drawings, as they are often called in the industry) are copyrighted intellectual property, protected under the terms of United States Copyright Law and, therefore, cannot be copied legally for use in building. However, we've made it easy for you to get what you need to build your home, without violating copyright law. Following are some guidelines to help you obtain the right number of copies for your chosen blueprint design.

COPYRIGHT DO

■ Do purchase enough copies of the blueprints to satisfy building requirements. As a rule for a home or project plan, you will need a set for yourself, two or three for your builder and subcontractors, two for the local building department, and one to three for your mortgage lender. You may want to check with your local building department or your builder to see how many they need before you purchase. You may need to buy eight to 10 sets; note that some areas of the country require purchase of vellums (also called reproducibles) instead of blueprints. Vellums can be written on and changed more easily than blueprints. Also, remember, plans are only good for one-time construction.

■ Do consider reverse blueprints if you want to flop the plan. Lettering and numbering will appear backward, but the reversed sets will help you and your builder better visualize the design.

■ Do take advantage of multiple-set discounts at the time you place your order. Usually, purchasing additional sets after you receive your initial order is not as cost-effective.

■ Do take advantage of vellums. Though they are a little more expensive, they can be changed, copied, and used for one-time construction of a home. You will receive a copyright release letter with your vellums that will allow you to have them copied.

■ Do talk with one of our professional service representatives before placing your order. They can give you great advice about what packages are available for your chosen design and what will work best for your particular situation.

COPYRIGHT DON'T

■ Don't think you should purchase only one set of blueprints for a building project. One is fine if you want to study the plan closely, but will not be enough for actual building.

■ Don't expect your builder or a copy center to make copies of standard blueprints. They cannot legally—most copy centers are aware of this.

■ Don't purchase standard blueprints if you know you'll want to make changes to the plans; vellums are a better value.

■ Don't use blueprints or vellums more than one time. Additional fees apply if you want to build more than one time from a set of drawings. ■

LET US SHOW YOU
OUR HOME BLUEPRINT PACKAGE

BUILDING A HOME? PLANNING A HOME?

Our Blueprint Package has nearly everything you need to get the job done right,
whether you're working on your own or with help from an architect, designer, builder or subcontractors. Each
Blueprint Package is the result of many hours of work by licensed architects or professional designers.

QUALITY

Hundreds of hours of painstaking effort have gone into the development of your blueprint set. Each home has been quality-checked by professionals to insure accuracy and buildability.

VALUE

Because we sell in volume, you can buy professional quality blueprints at a fraction of their development cost. With our plans, your dream home design costs substantially less than the fees charged by architects.

SERVICE

Once you've chosen your favorite home plan, you'll receive fast, efficient service whether you choose to mail or fax your order to us or call us toll free at 1-800-521-6797. For customer service, call toll free 1-888-690-1116.

SATISFACTION

Over 50 years of service to satisfied home plan buyers provide us unparalleled experience and knowledge in producing quality blueprints.

ORDER TOLL FREE 1-800-521-6797

After you've looked over our Blueprint Package and Important Extras, call toll free on our Blueprint Hotline: 1-800-521-6797, for current pricing and availability prior to mailing the order form on page 317. We're ready and eager to serve you. For customer service, call toll free 1-888-690-1116.

Each set of blueprints is an interrelated collection of detail sheets which includes components such as floor plans, interior and exterior elevations, dimensions, cross-sections, diagrams and notations. These sheets show exactly how your house is to be built.

SETS MAY INCLUDE:

FRONTAL SHEET

This artist's sketch of the exterior of the house gives you an idea of how the house will look when built and landscaped. Large floor plans show all levels of the house and provide an overview of your new home's livability, as well as a handy reference for deciding on furniture placement.

FOUNDATION PLANS

This sheet shows the foundation layout including support walls, excavated and unexcavated areas, if any, and foundation notes. If slab construction rather than basement, the plan shows footings and details for a monolithic slab. This page, or another in the set, may include a sample plot plan for locating your house on a building site.

DETAILED FLOOR PLANS

These plans show the layout of each floor of the house. Rooms and interior spaces are carefully dimensioned and keys are given for cross-section details provided later in the plans. The positions of electrical outlets and switches are shown.

HOUSE CROSS-SECTIONS

Large-scale views show sections or cut-aways of the foundation, interior walls, exterior walls, floors, stairways and roof details. Additional cross-sections may show important changes in floor, ceiling or roof heights or the relationship of one level to another. Extremely valuable for construction, these sections show exactly how the various parts of the house fit together.

INTERIOR ELEVATIONS

Many of our drawings show the design and placement of kitchen and bathroom cabinets, laundry areas, fireplaces, bookcases and other built-ins. Little "extras," such as mantelpiece and wainscoting drawings, plus molding sections, provide details that give your home that custom touch.

EXTERIOR ELEVATIONS

These drawings show the front, rear and sides of your house and give necessary notes on exterior materials and finishes. Particular attention is given to cornice detail, brick and stone accents or other finish items that make your home unique.

THE LANDSCAPE BLUEPRINT PACKAGE

THE LANDSCAPE BLUEPRINT PACKAGE AVAILABLE FROM HOME PLANNERS includes all the necessary information you need to lay out and install the landscape design of your choice. Professionally designed and prepared with attention to detail, these clear, easy-to-follow plans offer everything from a precise plot plan and regionalized plant and materials list to helpful sheets on installing your landscape and determining the mature size of your plants. These plans will help you achieve professional-looking results, adding value and enjoyment to your property for years to come. Each set of blueprints is a full 18"x24" in size with clear, complete instructions and easy-to-read type. Consisting of six detailed sheets, these plans show how all plants and materials are put together to form an exciting landscape for your home.

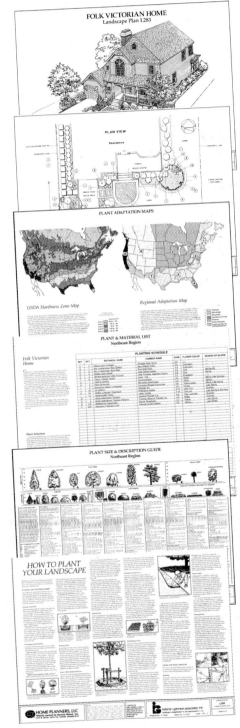

FRONTAL SHEET

This artist's line sketch shows a typical house (if applicable) and all the elements of the finished landscape when plants are at or near maturity. This will give you a visual image or "picture" of the design and what you might expect your property to look like when fully landscaped.

PLAN VIEW

This is an aerial view of the property showing the exact placement of all landscape elements, including symbols and call-outs for flowers, shrubs, groundcovers, walkways, walls, gates and other garden amenities. This sheet is the key to the design and shows you the contour, spacing, flow and balance of all the elements in the design, as well as providing an exact "map" for laying out your property.

ZONE MAPS

These two informative maps offer detailed information to help you better select and judge the performance of your plants. Map One is a United States Department of Agriculture Hardiness Zone Map that shows the average low temperatures by zones in various parts of the United States and Canada. The "Zone" listing for plants on Sheet 3 of your Plant and Materials List is keyed to this map. Map Two is a Regional Adaptation Map, which takes into account other factors beyond low temperatures, such as rainfall, humidity, extremes of temperature, and soil acidity or alkalinity. Both maps are key to plant adaptability and are used for the selection of landscape plants for your plans.

REGIONALIZED PLANT & MATERIALS LIST

Keyed to the Plan View sheet, this page lists all of the plants and materials necessary to execute the design. It gives the quantity, botanical name, common name, flower color, season of bloom and hardiness zones for each plant specified. This becomes your "shopping list" for dealing with contractors or buying the plants and materials yourself. Most importantly, the plants shown on this page have been chosen by a team of professional horticulturalists for their adaptability, availability and performance in your specific part of the country.

PLANT SIZE & DESCRIPTION GUIDE

Because you may have trouble visualizing certain plants, this handy regionalized guide provides a scale and silhouettes to help you determine the final height and shape of various trees and shrubs in your landscape plan. It also provides a quick means of choosing alternate plants appropriate to your region in case you do not wish to install a certain tree or shrub, or if you cannot find the plant at local nurseries.

PLANTING & MAINTAINING YOUR LANDSCAPE

This valuable sheet gives handy information and illustrations on purchasing plant materials, preparing your site and caring for your landscape after installation. Includes quick, helpful advice on planting trees, shrubs and groundcovers, staking trees, establishing a lawn, watering, weed control and pruning.

OUR PLANS AND DETAILS ARE CAREFULLY PREPARED

in an easy-to-understand format that will guide you through every stage of your deck-building project. The Deck Blueprint Package contains four sheets outlining information pertinent to the specific Deck Plan you have chosen. A separate package—Deck Construction Details—provides the how-to data for building any deck, including instructions for adaptations and conversions.

DECK CONSTRUCTION DETAILS

In five information-packed sheets, these standard details provide all the general data necessary for building, adapting and converting any deck. Included are layout examples, framing patterns and foundation variation; details for ledgers, columns and beams; schedules and charts; handrail, stair and ramp details; and special options like spa platforms, planters, bars, benches and overhead trellises. This is a must-have package for the first-time deck builder and a useful addition to the custom deck plans in this book.

Or buy the Complete Construction Set that includes plans for the Deck of your choice plus the Deck Construction Details—see page 313 for price information.

CUSTOM DECK PLANS

Each deck plan in this book has been custom-designed by a professional architect.
With each Custom Deck Plan you receive the following:

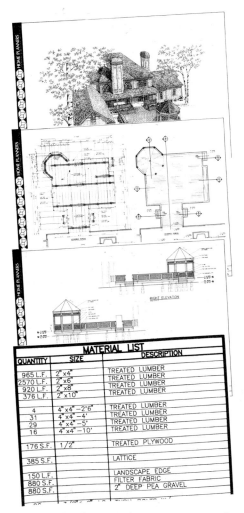

DECK PLAN FRONTAL SHEET

An artist's line drawing shows the deck as it connects to its matching or corresponding house. This drawing provides a visual image of what the deck will look like when completed, highlighting the livability factors.

DECK FRAMING AND FLOOR PLANS

In clear, easy-to-read drawings, this sheet shows all component parts of the deck from an aerial viewpoint with dimensions, notes and references. Drawn at 1/4"=1'-0", the floor plan provides a finished overhead view of the deck including rails, stairs, benches and ramps. The framing plan gives complete details on how the deck is to be built, including the position and spacing of footings, joists, beams, posts and decking materials. Where necessary, the sheet also includes sections and close-ups to further explain structural details.

DECK ELEVATIONS

Large-scale front and side elevations of the deck complete the visual picture of the deck. Drawn at 3/8"=1'-0", the elevations show the height of rails, balusters, stair risers, benches and other deck accessories.

DECK MATERIALS LIST

This is a complete shopping list of all the materials needed (including sizes and amounts) to build your deck. The Materials List is complemented by section drawings showing placement of hardware such as thru-bolts, screws, nuts, washers and nails and how these items are used to secure deck flooring, rails, posts and joists.

THE BLUEPRINT PACKAGE FOR THESE INSPIRING YARD AND GARDEN

structures contains everything you need to plan and build the outdoor amenity of your choice. Some of the more complicated gazebos and lawn-shed packages will have several sheets to thoroughly explain how the structure will go together. The simpler structures such as bridges and arbors have fewer sheets. To help you further understand the process of constructing an outdoor structure, we also offer a separate package—Gazebo Construction Details—that outlines general information for construction of gazebos and similar outdoor amenities. Included are numerous illustrations, an explanation of building terms and general tips and hints to make your building project progress smoothly.

GAZEBO CONSTRUCTION DETAILS

This set of 24"x18" sheets contains a wealth of valuable information for gazebos and other outdoor building projects. Included are the steps of the building process; an explanation of terms; details for locating footings, piers and foundations; information about attaching posts to piers or footings; creating free-standing benches; and much, much more. These sheets will facilitate many different outdoor construction projects for the do-it-yourselfer and will make working with contractors and subcontractors more comfortable.

Or buy the Complete Construction Set that includes plans for the Yard or Garden Structure of your choice plus the Gazebo Construction Details—see page 313 for price information.

PROJECT STRUCTURE PLANS

The plans for our Yard and Garden Structures have been custom-created by a professional designer. Among the helpful sheets for building your structure may be such information as:

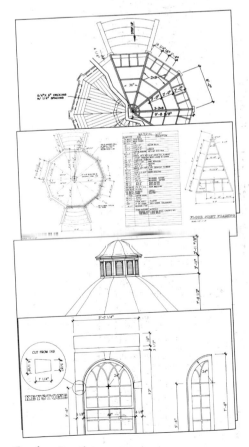

FLOOR PLAN
Done in 1/2"=1'-0" scale, this sheet shows the exact floor plan of the structure with dimensions, flooring patterns and window and door call-outs. Details found on other sheets may also be referenced on this sheet.

FOUNDATION AND JOIST DETAILS/MATERIALS LIST
This schematic of the foundation and floor and rafter joists, done in 1/4"=1'-0" or 1/2"=1'-0" scale, gives dimensions and shows how to pour or construct the foundation and flooring components. The materials list is invaluable for estimating and planning work and acts as an accurate "shopping list" for the do-it-yourselfer.

ELEVATIONS AND FRAMING PLANS/WALL SECTIONS
Shown in 1/4"=1'-0" or 1/2"=1'-0" scale, these helpful drawings show various views of the structure plus a complete framing plan for the flooring. Wall sections provide stud sizes, connector types, and rafter and roofing materials. They may also show mouldings or other trim pieces.

DETAILS
Cut-out details, shown in 1/4"=1'-0" or 1"=1'-0" scale, are given for items such as pilaster framing, doors, side panels and rafter profiles. These details provide additional information and enhance your understanding of other aspects of the plans.

TO ORDER YOUR PLANS...

simply find the Plan Number of the design of your choice in the Plans Index on pages 314-315. Consult the Price Schedule to determine the price of your plans, choosing the 1-set package for Landscape Plans and any additional or reverse sets you desire. If ordering Landscape Plans, make sure your Plant and Materials List contains the best selection for your area by referring to the Regional Order Map below and specifying the region in which you will be building. Fill out the Order Coupon on page 317 and mail it to us for prompt fulfillment or call our Toll-Free Order Hotline for even faster service.

REGIONAL ORDER MAP

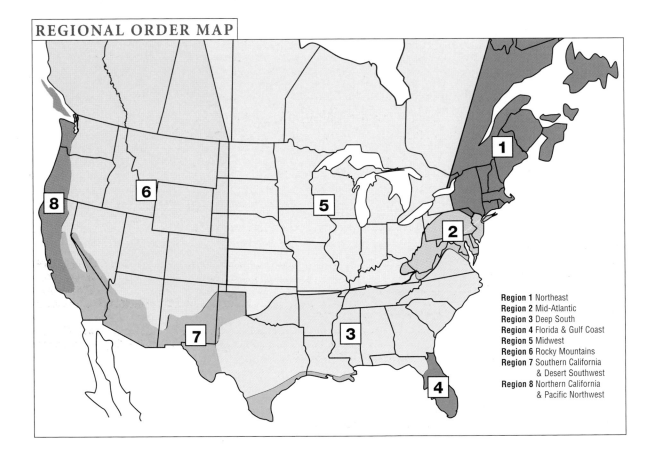

Region 1 Northeast
Region 2 Mid-Atlantic
Region 3 Deep South
Region 4 Florida & Gulf Coast
Region 5 Midwest
Region 6 Rocky Mountains
Region 7 Southern California
& Desert Southwest
Region 8 Northern California
& Pacific Northwest

BLUEPRINT PRICE SCHEDULE

Prices guaranteed through December 31, 2003

TIERS	1-SET CUSTOM PLANS	4-SET CUSTOM PLANS	8-SET CUSTOM PLANS	1-SET REPRODUCIBLE*
P1	$20	$50	$90	$140
P2	$40	$70	$110	$160
P3	$70	$100	$140	$190
P4	$100	$130	$170	$220
P5	$140	$170	$210	$270
P6	$180	$210	$250	$310

* Requires a fax number

COMPLETE CONSTRUCTION PACKAGE

1 set Custom Plans, plus 1 set Standard Gazebo or Deck Details:

PRICE GROUP	P1	P2	P3	P4	P5	P6
	$30	$50	$80	$110	$150	$190

AVAILABLE OPTIONS

Additional Identical Blueprints in same order for price plans..**$10 per set**
Reverse Blueprints (mirror image) for price plans ....**$10 fee per order**
1 Set of Deck Construction Details...**$14.95 each**
Deck Construction Package ....**add $10 to Building Package price**
(includes 1 set of plans, plus 1 set Standard Deck Construction Details)
1 Set of Gazebo Construction Details ....**$14.95 each**
Gazebo Construction Package ....**add $10 to Building Package price**
(includes 1 set of plans, plus 1 set Standard Gazebo Construction Details)

IMPORTANT NOTES
• The 1-set study package is marked "not for construction."
• Prices for 4- or 8-set Building Packages honored only at time of original order.
• Right-reading reverse blueprints, if available, will incur a $165 surcharge.
• Additional identical blueprints may be purchased within 60 days of original order.

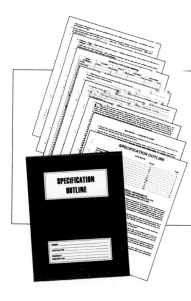

ALSO AVAILABLE:

SPECIFICATION OUTLINE

This valuable 16-page document is critical to building your house correctly. Designed to be filled in by you or your builder, this book lists 166 stages or items crucial to the building process. It provides a comprehensive review of the construction process and helps in choosing materials. When combined with the blueprints, a signed contract, and a schedule, it becomes a legal document and record for the building of your home.

PLAN INDEX

TO USE THE INDEX, refer to the design number listed in numerical order (a helpful page reference is also given). Note the price tier and refer to the Blueprint Price Schedule above for the cost of one, four or eight sets of blueprints or the cost of a reproducible drawing. Additional prices are shown for identical and reverse blueprint sets, as well as a very useful Materials List for some of the plans. **TO ORDER,** Call toll free 1-800-521-6797 or 520-544-8200 for current pricing and availability prior to mailing the order form on page 317. FAX: 1-800-224-6699 or 520-544-3086.

DESIGN	PRICE	PAGE	REGIONS
HPT110001	P4	12	12345678
HPT110002	P4	14	12345678
HPT110003	P3	16	12345678
HPT110004	P4	18	12345678
HPT110005	P3	20	1235678
HPT110006	P3	22	12345678
HPT110007	P3	24	12345678
HPT110008	P3	26	12345678
HPT110009	P3	28	12345678
HPT110010	P3	30	1235678
HPT110011	P3	32	12345678
HPT110012	P3	34	123568
HPT110013	P3	36	1234568
HPT110014	P3	38	123568
HPT110015	P4	40	12345678
HPT110016	P3	42	12345678
HPT110017	P4	44	1235678
HPT110018	P4	46	12345678
HPT110019	P3	48	12345678
HPT110020	P3	50	12345678
HPT110021	P3	52	12345678
HPT110022	P3	54	12345678
HPT110023	P3	56	12345678
HPT110024	P3	58	12345678
HPT110025	P3	60	12345678
HPT110026	P3	62	12345678
HPT110027	P3	64	12345678
HPT110028	P4	66	12345678
HPT110029	P3	68	12345678
HPT110030	P4	70	12345678
HPT110031	P3	72	12345678
HPT110032	P4	74	12345678
HPT110033	P4	76	12345678
HPT110034	P3	78	12345678
HPT110035	P3	80	12345678
HPT110036	P2	82	12345678
HPT110037	P3	84	12345678
HPT110038	P2	86	12345678
HPT110039	P3	88	12345678
HPT110040	P2	90	12345678
HPT110041	P2	92	12345678
HPT110042	P2	94	1235678
HPT110043	P3	96	1235678
HPT110044	P3	98	1235678
HPT110045	P3	100	12345678
HPT110046	P3	102	12345678
HPT110047	P2	104	12345678
HPT110048	P3	108	12345678
HPT110049	P3	110	12345678
HPT110050	P3	112	12345678
HPT110051	P3	114	123568
HPT110052	P3	116	123568
HPT110053	P3	118	123568
HPT110054	P3	120	123568
HPT110055	P3	122	123568
HPT110056	P3	124	123568

DESIGN	PRICE	PAGE	REGIONS
HPT110057	P3	126	123568
HPT110058	P4	128	1234568
HPT110059	P3	130	123568
HPT110060	P3	132	1234568
HPT110061	P4	134	12345678
HPT110062	P4	136	347
HPT110063	P3	138	123568
HPT110064	P4	140	123568
HPT110065	P4	142	12345678
HPT110066	P3	144	12345678
HPT110067	P4	146	1234568
HPT110068	P4	148	1234568
HPT110069	P4	150	123568
HPT110070	P3	152	123568
HPT110071	P4	154	123568
HPT110072	P3	156	12345678
HPT110073	P3	158	12345678
HPT110074	P3	160	12345678
HPT110075	P4	162	12345678
HPT110076	P3	164	1234568
HPT110077	P4	166	123568
HPT110078	P4	168	123568
HPT110079	P4	170	12345678
HPT110080	P3	172	12345678
HPT110081	P4	174	12345678
HPT110082	P4	176	12345678
HPT110083	P3	178	12345678
HPT110084	P3	180	12345678
HPT110085	P3	182	12345678
HPT110086	P2	184	12345678
HPT110087	P3	186	12345678
HPT110088	P3	188	12345678
HPT110089	P3	190	12345678
HPT110090	P3	192	12345678
HPT110091	P4	194	12345678
HPT110092	P3	196	12345678
HPT110093	P2	198	12345678
HPT110094	P2	200	12345678
HPT110095	P2	206	
HPT110096	P2	207	
HPT110097	P3	208	
HPT110098	P2	209	
HPT110099	P2	210	
HPT110100	P2	211	
HPT110101	P2	212	
HPT110102	P1	213	
HPT110103	P2	213	
HPT110104	P1	214	
HPT110105	P2	215	
HPT110106	P1	216	
HPT110107	P2	217	
HPT110108	P1	218	
HPT110109	P1	218	
HPT110110	P1	219	
HPT110111	P2	220	
HPT110112	P1	221	

PLAN INDEX

DESIGN	PRICE	PAGE	REGIONS
HPT110113	P4	222	
HPT110114	P3	222	
HPT110115	P1	223	
HPT110116	P2	223	
HPT110117	P3	224	
HPT110118	P4	224	
HPT110119	P2	225	
HPT110120	P3	225	
HPT110121	P2	226	
HPT110122	P2	226	
HPT110123	P1	227	
HPT110124	P1	227	
HPT110125	P2	228	
HPT110126	P3	229	
HPT110127	P2	230	
HPT110128	P3	231	
HPT110129	P2	232	
HPT110130	P2	233	
HPT110131	P2	233	
HPT110132	P1	234	
HPT110133	P2	235	
HPT110134	P3	236	
HPT110135	P3	236	
HPT110136	P3	237	
HPT110137	P2	238	
HPT110138	P2	239	
HPT110139	P3	239	
HPT110140	P2	240	
HPT110141	P4	241	
HPT110142	P2	242	
HPT110143	P4	243	
HPT110144	P2	244	
HPT110145	P4	244	
HPT110146	P1	245	
HPT110147	P1	246	
HPT110148	P3	247	
HPT110149	P1	248	
HPT110150	P6	249	
HPT110151	P2	252	
HPT110152	P2	253	
HPT110153	P4	254	
HPT110154	P2	255	
HPT110155	P3	256	
HPT110156	P2	257	
HPT110157	P3	258	
HPT110158	P3	259	
HPT110159	P2	260	
HPT110160	P3	261	
HPT110161	P2	262	
HPT110162	P3	263	
HPT110163	P2	264	
HPT110164	P2	265	
HPT110165	P2	266	
HPT110166	P2	267	
HPT110167	P2	268	
HPT110168	P3	269	

DESIGN	PRICE	PAGE	REGIONS
HPT110169	P2	270	
HPT110170	P3	271	
HPT110171	P2	272	
HPT110172	P3	273	
HPT110173	P3	274	
HPT110174	P3	275	
HPT110175	P3	278	
HPT110176	P2	279	
HPT110177	P3	280	
HPT110178	P3	281	
HPT110179	P2	282	
HPT110180	P3	283	
HPT110181	P3	284	
HPT110182	P3	285	
HPT110183	P3	285	
HPT110184	P3	285	
HPT110185	P4	286	
HPT110186	P3	287	
HPT110187	P3	287	
HPT110188	P4	288	
HPT110189	P4	289	
HPT110190	P1	289	
HPT110191	P4	289	
HPT110192	P6	290	
HPT110193	P3	291	
HPT110194	P3	292	
HPT110195	P3	293	
HPT110196	P3	293	
HPT110197	P3	293	
HPT110198	P6	294	
HPT110199	P5	295	
HPT110200	P5	296	
HPT110201	P5	297	
HPT110202	P5	297	
HPT110203	P5	297	
HPT110204	P6	298	
HPT110205	P6	299	
HPT110206	P4	300	
HPT110207	P4	301	
HPT110208	P4	301	
HPT110209	P1	301	
HPT110210	P4	302	
HPT110211	P4	302	
HPT110212	P4	302	
HPT110213	P4	303	
HPT110214	P4	304	
HPT110215	P4	305	
HPT110216	P4	305	
HPT110217	P4	305	
HPT110218	P4	306	
HPT110219	P4	306	
HPT110220	P4	306	
HPT110222	P2	232	
HPT112001	P3	202	12345678

OUR EXCHANGE POLICY

With the exception of reproducible plan orders, we will exchange your entire first order for an equal or greater number of blueprints within our plan collection within 90 days of the original order. The entire content of your original order must be returned before an exchange will be processed. Please call our customer service department for your return authorization number and shipping instructions. If the returned blueprints look used, redlined or copied, we will not honor your exchange. Fees for exchanging your blueprints are as follows: 20% of the amount of the original order...plus the difference in cost if exchanging for a design in a higher price bracket or less the difference in cost if exchanging for a design in a lower price bracket. **(Reproducible blueprints are not exchangeable or refundable.)** Please call for current postage and handling prices. Shipping and handling charges are not refundable. Please call our customer service department for your return authorization number and shipping instructions.

ABOUT REPRODUCIBLES

When purchasing a reproducible you may be required to furnish a fax number. The designer will fax documents that you must sign and return to them before shipping will take place.

ABOUT REVERSE BLUEPRINTS

Although lettering and dimensions will appear backward, reverses will be a useful aid if you decide to flop the plan. See Price Schedule and Plans Index for pricing.

REVISING, MODIFYING AND CUSTOMIZING PLANS

Like many homeowners who buy these plans, you and your builder, architect or engineer may want to make changes to them. We recommend purchase of a reproducible plan for any changes made by your builder,

licensed architect or engineer. As set forth below, we cannot assume any responsibility for blueprints which have been changed, whether by you, your builder or by professionals selected by you or referred to you by us, because such individuals are outside our supervision and control.

ARCHITECTURAL AND ENGINEERING SEALS

Some cities and states are now requiring that a licensed architect or engineer review and "seal" a blueprint, or officially approve it, prior to construction due to concerns over energy costs, safety and other factors. Prior to application for a building permit or the start of actual construction, we strongly advise that you consult your local building official who can tell you if such a review is required.

ABOUT THE DESIGNS

The architects and designers whose work appears in this publication are among America's leading residential designers. Each plan was designed to meet the requirements of a nationally recognized model building code in effect at the time and place the plan was drawn. Because national building codes change from time to time, plans may not comply with any such code at the time they are sold to a customer. In addition, building officials may not accept these plans as final construction documents of record as the plans may need to be modified and additional drawings and details added to suit local conditions and require-

ments. We strongly advise that purchasers consult a licensed architect or engineer, and their local building official, before starting any construction related to these plans.

LOCAL BUILDING CODES AND ZONING REQUIREMENTS

At the time of creation, our plans are drawn to specifications published by the Building Officials and Code Administrators (BOCA) International, Inc.; the Southern Building Code Congress (SBCCI) International, Inc.; the International Conference of Building Officials (ICBO); or the Council of American Building Officials (CABO). Our plans are designed to meet or exceed national building standards. Because of the great differences in geography and climate throughout the United States and Canada, each state, county and municipality has its own building codes, zone requirements, ordinances and building regulations. Your plan may need to be modified to comply with local requirements regarding snow loads, energy codes, soil and seismic conditions and a wide range of other matters. In addition, you may need to obtain permits or inspections from local governments before and in the course of construction. Prior to using blueprints ordered from us, we strongly advise that you consult a licensed architect or engineer—and speak with your local building official—before applying for any permit or beginning construction. We authorize the use of our blueprints on the express condition that you strictly comply with all local building codes, zoning requirements and other applicable laws, regulations, ordinances and requirements. Notice: Plans for homes to be built in Nevada must be re-drawn by a Nevada-registered professional. Consult your building official for more information on this subject.

Before filling out the order form, please call us on our Toll-Free Blueprint Hotline. You may want to learn more about our services and products. Here's some information you will find helpful.

DISCLAIMER

The designers we work with have put substantial care and effort into the creation of their blueprints. However, because they cannot provide on-site consultation, supervision and control over actual construction, and because of the great variance in local building requirements, building practices and soil, seismic, weather and other conditions, WE CANNOT MAKE ANY WARRANTY, EXPRESS OR IMPLIED, WITH RESPECT TO THE CONTENT OR USE OF THE BLUEPRINTS, INCLUDING BUT NOT LIMITED TO ANY WARRANTY OF MERCHANTABILITY OR OF FITNESS FOR A PARTICULAR PURPOSE. **ITEMS, PRICES, TERMS AND CONDITIONS ARE SUBJECT TO CHANGE WITHOUT NOTICE. REPRODUCIBLE PLAN ORDERS MAY REQUIRE A CUSTOMER'S SIGNED RELEASE BEFORE SHIPPING.**

TERMS AND CONDITIONS

These designs are protected under the terms of United States Copyright Law and may not be copied or reproduced in any way, by any means, unless you have purchased Reproducibles which clearly indicate your right to copy or reproduce. We authorize the use of your chosen design as an aid in the construction of one single family home only. You may not use this design to build a second or multiple dwellings without purchasing another blueprint or blueprints or paying additional design fees.

HOW MANY BLUEPRINTS DO YOU NEED?

Although a standard building package may satisfy many states, cities and counties, some plans may require certain changes. For your convenience, we have developed a Reproducible plan which allows a local professional to modify and make up to 10 copies of your revised plan. As our plans are all copyright protected, with your purchase of the Reproducible, we will supply you with a Copyright release letter. The number of copies you may need: 1 for owner; 3 for builder; 2 for local building department and 1-3 sets for your mortgage lender.

BLUEPRINTS ARE NOT REFUNDABLE EXCHANGES ONLY

FOR CUSTOMER SERVICE,
CALL TOLL FREE 1-888-690-1116.

ORDER TOLL FREE!
FOR INFORMATION ABOUT ANY OF OUR SERVICES OR TO ORDER CALL

1-800-521-6797
OR 520-544-8200
Browse our website:
www.eplans.com

ORDER FORM

HOME PLANNERS, LLC
Wholly owned by Hanley-Wood, LLC
3275 WEST INA ROAD, SUITE 220
TUCSON, ARIZONA 85741

Please rush me the following:

_____	Set(s) of reproducibles*, Plan _____	$_____
_____	Set(s) of Landscape Plan _____	$_____
_____	Set(s) of Deck Plan _____	$_____
_____	Set(s) of Project Plan _____	$_____
	(see Index and Price Schedule)	
_____	Additional identical blueprints (standard or reverse) in same order at $10 per set	$_____
_____	Reverse blueprints at $10 per set	$_____
_____	Sets of Deck Construction Details @ $14.95 per set.	$_____
_____	Sets of Gazebo Construction Details @ $14.95 per set.	$_____
_____	Sets of Complete Construction Package (Best Buy!)	
	Includes Custom Plan _____	
	Plus Deck or Gazebo Construction Details	$_____

Please indicate the appropriate region of the country for Plant and Materials List (see map on page 312):

❑ Region 1 Northeast
❑ Region 2 Mid-Atlantic
❑ Region 3 Deep South
❑ Region 4 Florida & Gulf Coast (Zone 9 only)
❑ Region 5 Midwest
❑ Region 6 Rocky Mountains
❑ Region 7 Southern California & Desert Southwest
❑ Region 8 Northern California & Pacific Northwest

IMPORTANT EXTRA
Rush me the following:
Specification Outlines @ $10 each $_____

POSTAGE AND HANDLING (signature is required for all deliveries)		
CARRIER DELIVERY		
No CODs (Requires street address—No P.O.Boxes)		
• **Regular Service** (Allow 7–10 business days for delivery)	$8.00	$_____
• **Priority** (Allow 4–5 business days for delivery)	$12.00	$_____
• **Express** (Allow 3 business days for delivery)	$22.00	$_____
Overseas Delivery	Phone, FAX or Mail for Quote	

NOTE: All delivery times are from date blueprint package is shipped.

POSTAGE (from box above) $_____

SUBTOTAL $_____

SALES TAX (AZ & MI residents, please add appropriate state & local sales tax.) $_____

TOTAL (Subtotal and Tax) $_____

YOUR ADDRESS (please print legibly)

Name _____

Street _____

City _____ State _____ ZIP _____

Daytime telephone number (required) _____

" Fax number (required for reproducible orders) _____

TeleCheck® Checks By Phone℠ available

FOR CREDIT CARD ORDERS ONLY Please fill in the information below:

Credit card number_____ Exp: Month/Year _____

Check One: ❑ Visa ❑ MasterCard ❑ American Express

Signature (required) _____

Please check appropriate box: ❑ Licensed Builder-Contractor ❑ Homeowner

ORDER TOLL FREE
1-800-521-6797 OR 520-544-8200
BY FAX:
Copy the order form above and send it on our FAXLINE: 1-800-224-6699 or 1-520-544-3086

Order Form Key
HPT113

1 BIGGEST & BEST

1001 of our best-selling plans in one volume. 1,074 to 7,275 square feet. 704 pgs $12.95 1K1

2 ONE-STORY

450 designs for all lifestyles. 800 to 4,900 square feet. 384 pgs $9.95 OS

3 MORE ONE-STORY

475 superb one-level plans from 800 to 5,000 square feet. 448 pgs $9.95 MO2

4 TWO-STORY

443 designs for one-and-a-half and two stories. 1,500 to 6,000 square feet. 448 pgs $9.95 TS

5 VACATION

430 designs for recreation, retirement and leisure. 448 pgs $9.95 VS3

6 HILLSIDE

208 designs for split-levels, bi-levels, multi-levels and walkouts. 224 pgs $9.95 HH

7 FARMHOUSE

300 Fresh Designs from Classic to Modern. 320 pgs. $10.95 FCP

8 COUNTRY HOUSES

208 unique home plans that combine traditional style and modern livability. 224 pgs $9.95 CN

9 BUDGET-SMART

200 efficient plans from 7 top designers, that you can really afford to build! 224 pgs $8.95 BS

10 BARRIER-FREE

Over 1,700 products and 51 plans for accessible living. 128 pgs $15.95 UH

11 ENCYCLOPEDIA

500 exceptional plans for all styles and budgets—the best book of its kind! 528 pgs $9.95 ENC

12 ENCYCLOPEDIA II

500 completely new plans. Spacious and stylish designs for every budget and taste. 352 pgs $9.95 E2

13 AFFORDABLE

300 Modest plans for savvy homebuyers.256 pgs. $9.95 AH2

14 VICTORIAN

210 striking Victorian and Farmhouse designs from today's top designers. 224 pgs $15.95 VDH2

15 ESTATE

Dream big! Eighteen designers showcase their biggest and best plans. 224 pgs $16.95 EDH3

16 LUXURY

170 lavish designs, over 50% brand-new plans added to a most elegant collection. 192 pgs $12.95 LD3

17 EUROPEAN STYLES

200 homes with a unique flair of the Old World. 224 pgs $15.95 EURO

18 COUNTRY CLASSICS

Donald Gardner's 101 best Country and Traditional home plans. 192 pgs $17.95 DAG

19 COUNTRY

85 Charming Designs from American Home Gallery. 160 pgs. $17.95 CTY

20 TRADITIONAL

85 timeless designs from the Design Traditions Library. 160 pgs. $17.95 TRA

21 COTTAGES

245 Delightful retreats from 825 to 3,500 square feet. 256 pgs. $10.95 COOL

22 CABINS TO VILLAS

Enchanting Homes for Mountain Sea or Sun, from the Sater collection. 144 pgs $19.95 CCV

23 CONTEMPORARY

The most complete and imaginative collection of contemporary designs available anywhere. 256 pgs. $10.95 CM2

24 FRENCH COUNTRY

Live every day in the French countryside using these plans, landscapes and interiors. 192 pgs $14.95 PN

25 SOUTHERN

207 homes rich in Southern styling and comfort. 240 pgs $8.95 SH

26 SOUTHWESTERN

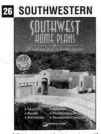

138 designs that capture the spirit of the Southwest. 144 pgs $10.95 SW

27 SHINGLE-STYLE

155 Home plans from Classic Colonials to Breezy Bungalows. 192 pgs. $12.95 SNG

28 NEIGHBORHOOD

170 designs with the feel of main street America. 192 pgs $12.95 TND

29 CRAFTSMAN

170 Home plans in the Craftsman and Bungalow style. 192 pgs $12.95 CC

30 GRAND VISTAS

200 Homes with a View. 224 pgs. $10.95 GV

HOME PLANNING RESOURCES